PLATO'S *REPUBLIC*

Plato's *Republic*

An Introduction

Sean McAleer

OpenBook
Publishers

https://www.openbookpublishers.com

© 2020 Sean McAleer

ISBN Paperback: 9781800640535
ISBN Hardback: 9781800640542
ISBN Digital (PDF): 9781800640559
ISBN Digital ebook (epub): 9781800640566
ISBN Digital ebook (mobi): 9781800640573
ISBN XML: 9781800640580
DOI: 10.11647/OBP.0229

Cover image: Anselm Feuerbach, The Symposium (1873). Berlin State Museum, Wikimedia, https://commons.wikimedia.org/wiki/File:Anselm_Feuerbach_-_Das_Gastmahl._Nach_Platon_(zweite_Fassung)_-_Google_Art_Project.jpg. Public domain.

Cover design by Anna Gatti.

Table of Contents

Acknowledgments

This book springs from the happy confluence of two sources: my teaching the *Republic* every semester in PHIL 101 at the University of Wisconsin–Eau Claire and my offering a three-session class on the *Republic* to Chippewa Valley Learning in Retirement in the fall of 2013. Dr Mike O'Halloran, the indefatigably cheerful and intellectually curious retiree who thought the group would enjoy a presentation on philosophy turned out to be correct: the sessions were well attended and well received — if subsequent requests for more philosophy sessions are any indication. Although some philosophical friends were skeptical at my plan to devote an entire 'intro' course to the *Republic,* many students seem to have found the experience worthwhile, so I have continued with this somewhat old-fashioned way of introducing students to philosophy. This book has been shaped by my experience with both kinds of audiences. I thank the students it has been my privilege to teach over the years and the CVLR audiences for their questions, feedback, criticisms, and their laughing at some of my jokes.

Many friends have helped in a variety of ways. Erica Benson, the life partner than which none greater could be conceived, provided insightful feedback on the entire manuscript, created the figures for the Divided Line, and talked me off the ledge more than once. Geoff Gorham has used parts of the manuscript in some of his courses and has given feedback and encouragement, as has his wife, the philosopher Amy Ihlan. Rod Cooke unwittingly served as a 'responsibility buddy' during a sabbatical, regularly asking me how it was going and when it might it be finished. My colleagues at UW–Eau Claire — Kristin Schaupp, Matt Meyer, and Steve Fink — models of collegiality all, have been sources of intellectual stimulation and delight during trying times in higher education. I gratefully acknowledge the support of the University of Wisconsin–Eau Claire Faculty Sabbatical Leave Program, which supported me during the 2017–2018 academic year, during which time the bulk of this book was written. I conceived the book as a philosophical instance of The Wisconsin Idea, a guiding principle of the University of Wisconsin system, which bids faculty and staff to 'extend knowledge and its application beyond the boundaries of its campus'. I have tried to do that here, to help general readers with little to no background in philosophy to understand this philosophical masterpiece. Thus I am most grateful to Open Book Publishers for publishing it, since I too believe that 'knowledge is for sharing'. I thank Alessandra Tosi for her wisdom, guidance, and patience; the two readers for their helpful suggestions, Anna Gatti for designing the cover; and Melissa Purkiss for her careful proofreading and her excellent editorial judgment.

I have benefitted from some wonderful teachers over the years, starting in high school with Frank Townsend, who gave me my first glimpse of the life of the mind, continuing through my undergraduate education at Shimer College with Eileen Buchanan and Harold Stone, who provided such fine, living models of inquiry and engaged classrooms, and lastly in graduate school at Syracuse, where Michael Stocker and Jonathan Bennett showed me what doing excellent philosophy looks like. I am grateful to them all, and to all the other fine teachers I haven't space to name individually.

I thank Hackett Publishing for their kind permission to quote so frequently from the Grube-Reeve translation of the *Republic*. Lastly, I thank the Office of Research and Sponsored Programs at UW-Eau Claire for financial assistance with the publication of this book.

It is a good light, then, for those
That know the ultimate Plato,
Tranquillizing with this jewel
The torments of confusion.

— Wallace Stevens, 'Homunculus et La Belle Étoile'

For Erica, my SLPF

Attic Greek Black-figure Neck Amphora attributed to the Princeton
Painter, ca. 550–540 BCE depicting an elderly king or man seated
between two men and two women. Photograph by Aisha Abdel (2018),
Wikimedia, Pulic Domain, https://commons.wikimedia.org/wiki/
File:Terracotta_neck-amphora_of_Panathenaic_shape_(jar)_MET_
DP161828_white_balanced_white_bg.png

Introduction

Plato's *Republic* is one of those books that most people have probably heard of, even if they have not actually read it. Even Bubbles, the good-hearted, bespectacled doofus of the long-running Canadian comedy *Trailer Park Boys* knows enough of the *Republic* to appeal to the famous Noble Lie in a conversation with another resident of Sunnyvale Trailer Park.

I first encountered the *Republic* like so many others have: in my first semester of college. This was many years ago, but my memory of the experience was one of feeling lost much of the time. I had a fine high school education, but philosophy was new to me, with its focus on big, abstract questions and especially on rigorous, rational arguments as the means to answering them. I did reasonably well in the course, but the *Republic* was tricky terrain, and I did not really know my way about. My aim in this book is to help readers traverse Plato's philosophical masterpiece with fewer falls and less befuddled wandering than I experienced. I try to do this by pointing out important landmarks and interesting bits of topography, helping readers not to miss the forest for the trees, as the saying goes, but also to appreciate the importance of particular trees, hills, and streams. I consider objections to the views and arguments Plato has Socrates express and make. Thinking philosophically requires, among other things, stating arguments clearly and carefully, articulating assumptions that lurk in the background, and making judgments—hopefully, good judgments—about whether the reasons offered in support of a claim are good reasons.

    https://doi.org/10.11647/OBP.0229.16

The *Republic*'s Two Main Questions

The *Republic* addresses two overarching questions, *What is justice?* and *Is a just life happier—more profitable or personally advantageous— than an unjust life?* Plato addresses these questions in what is for modern readers an unexpected way: in dialogue form. Instead of writing an essay or a treatise directly arguing for his view, he gives us a philosophical drama, so to speak, a conversation between Socrates and several others in which answers are offered, discussed, and typically rejected. Plato wrote almost all of his philosophy as dialogues, most of them featuring Socrates talking with someone he would encounter in Athens (though Plato's later dialogues no longer feature Socrates). Plato was not Socrates' student in a formal sense, since Socrates himself wrote nothing and started no school—unlike Plato, who founded the Academy, where Aristotle studied before founding his own school, the Lyceum. But like many young men of his day, Plato was taken with Socrates, struck by his sharp and open mind and his fearless but often failed pursuit of knowledge. Whether the views the character Socrates expresses in the *Republic* are his own or whether Plato uses him to express his own views is an interesting issue, but it is not one that we need worry over to come to terms with the *Republic*. I will usually make no distinction between Plato and Socrates in this book, except when doing so helps our understanding, as when, for example, Socrates seems to make an error in reasoning or allows a crucial assumption to pass unquestioned. Is the mistake one that Plato himself does not recognize? Or does he intentionally have Socrates stumble or 'pull a fast one' because this is what actually happened in the conversation, of which the dialogue is a faithful but stylized representation? Or—more likely, I think—because he wants us, his readers, to engage in imaginary dialogue with Socrates, to raise objections and questions where the other characters are silent or too agreeable? That Plato writes philosophy in dialogue-form complicates the life of the reader, but it is a complication that is rich and rewarding, and also enables Plato to manifest respect for his readers. His aim is not the transmission of truth or doctrine from the knowing sage to a passive but receptive learner—indeed, in presenting the famous Allegory of the Cave he explicitly rejects the idea that education is 'putting knowledge into souls that lack it, like putting sight into blind eyes' (7.518b).[1] Instead, we are expected to be active, engaged readers who wrestle with the questions and arguments for ourselves. Writing dialogues suggests that philosophy—which I take to be clear, rigorous thinking about those important questions that are outside the ambit of the natural or social sciences—is best done in conversation with others rather than alone in one's study.

Readers with some familiarity with philosophy will not be surprised that one of our first tasks in trying to understand how Plato has Socrates answer the *Republic*'s two main questions is to question the questions themselves. What exactly does Plato mean when he asks about the nature of justice and whether it is 'more profitable' than injustice? An important point straightaway is that δικαιοσύνη (*dikaiosunê*), which is translated as 'justice', can have broader meaning than the English word 'justice' has, which typically involves fair distributions or the idea of rights. *Dikaiosunê* certainly has this narrower sense too; in Book V of his *Nicomachean Ethics*, Plato's student Aristotle distinguishes between specific and general senses of justice, where specific justice concerns what today we would call distributive justice (which asks whether a particular distribution of goods is fair) and retributive justice (which asks if and how wrongdoers should be punished). The broader sense that Plato has in mind connotes moral goodness more generally, a virtue of 'doing the right thing' (though we will ultimately see that for Plato justice is primarily about being a certain sort of person rather than doing certain kinds of things). Justice in this broad sense might be rendered by 'righteousness', but that seems rather archaic and can have misleading religious connotations. Aristotle suggests that justice in this general sense is 'complete virtue', the whole of virtue, of which the narrower kind of justice is a part.[2] When Socrates asks what justice is, he is asking

---

1   I will cite the *Republic* in this way. '7.518b' means that the passage quoted is in Book VII of the *Republic* at page 518 in the standard Greek text of Plato's work, section b (about one-fifth of the way down that page). Thus, regardless of which translation readers have before them, we can all quite literally 'be on the same page', so long as the translation provides the 'Stephanus numbers'—named after a sixteenth-century editor of Plato's works—in the margins. I will quote from G.M.A. Grube's translation, as revised by C.D.C. Reeve (Indianapolis: Hackett Publishing, 1992), which is excellent and inexpensive.

2   *Nicomachean Ethics*, trans. by W. D. Ross and rev. by J. O. Urmson, in *The Complete Works of Aristotle* (*Revised Oxford Translation*), ed. by Jonathan Barnes (Princeton: Princeton University Press, 1984), p. 1783 [Book V, Chapter 1, Bekker page 1129b25].

about the nature of moral goodness generally, asking what is it to be a good person.

The *Republic*'s second question asks whether being a good person makes one personally better off—whether it 'would make living most worthwhile for each of us' (1.344e). There is no question of whether a just life is a *morally* better than an unjust life; the issue the second question raises, by contrast, is whether a just life is *prudentially* better, as philosophers often put it—whether it is in one's interest to be just and act justly. This question has great practical importance, given the overwhelmingly plausible assumption that each of us wants to be happy. As Socrates puts it, 'the argument concerns no ordinary topic but the way we ought to live' (1.352d). In ordinary English there is a subtle distinction between *leading* a good life and *having* a good life. At the funeral of a friend who was devoted to the wellbeing of others we expect the eulogy to focus on the former: they led a good life, helping others without thought of self and often to their own detriment. At the funeral of a friend devoted to the pleasures of the table and the bedroom we are likelier to hear that they *had* a good life. So the *Republic*'s second question inquires about the connection between *leading* a good life and *having* a good life. It is a comparative question, asking if the just person is happier than the unjust person. Socrates is not arguing that justice is *sufficient* for happiness, that being just alone makes for a happy life. Instead, he will argue that justice is *necessary* for happiness, that we cannot be happy without being just. Socrates thinks that justice alone will not guarantee happiness, since there may be external circumstances that make happiness impossible, even for the just person. But the just or morally good person will be as happy as it is possible to be in those circumstances and always be happier than the unjust person, since justice always makes one better off than injustice, he thinks. As we follow along, it will be helpful to bear in mind ways in which 'happiness' can be a misleading translation for the Greek word εὐδαιμονία (*eudaimonia*), which connotes flourishing or thriving, something deeper and longer lasting than the perhaps fleeting psychological state of enjoyment that we might associate with our word 'happiness'. A flourishing person

---

All translations of Aristotle will be drawn from *The Complete Works* and will be cited by title, book and chapter, and Bekker page (the Aristotelian analog of the Platonic 'Stephanus' numbers), thus: Aristotle, *Nicomachean Ethics*, V.1 1129b25.

will typically enjoy their life, but the enjoyment is best thought of as a by-product of happiness rather than its essence.

The Structure of the *Republic*

The *Republic*'s two main questions give it its structure, which I sketch here:

Book I introduces but ultimately fails to answer the *Republic*'s two main questions. Socrates discusses the nature and value of justice first with Cephalus and Polemarchus and then with Thrasymachus, a more sophisticated and less friendly interlocutor. Socrates initially thinks that he has refuted Thrasymachus' view that the unjust life is happier than the just life, but he soon realizes that he has left the *Republic*'s first question unanswered and thus that he has not really answered the second question; how could he know which life is happier if he does not yet know what justice is?

Books II–IV answer the *Republic*'s first question, 'What is justice?'. Socrates' young friends Glaucon and Adeimantus (who in real life are Plato's brothers) challenge Socrates to continue after the failure of Book I. They agree with him that the just life is happier than the unjust life, but they recognize that they cannot justify their view and thus do not really *know* that the just life is more profitable. They press Socrates to forgo the rapid-fire argumentation of Book I and to offer a more intuitive, accessible way of answering the *Republic*'s questions. Although these questions concern justice as a virtue of persons (which we'll call personal justice), Socrates suggests that, since a *polis* (a Greek city-state) is just like a person, only bigger, the best way to figure out the nature of personal justice is to investigate justice in the *polis* (political justice) since it will be easier to find justice in the larger thing. Thus they set out to theoretically construct an ideal *polis*, which is completed by the end of Book III. And by the end of Book IV, Socrates thinks he has answered the first question and starts on the second.

In Books V–VII, Socrates answers questions about and objections to his answer to the *Republic*'s first question. These are dubbed 'the Three Waves', since they threaten to destroy the ideal city. The First Wave concerns whether women can be rulers in the ideal *polis*. Socrates' view on this might surprise you. The second addresses the ideal city's communal life, especially how children are to be raised—which seems to do away with the traditional family. The third and most threatening concerns the ideal *polis* itself: is their ideal city merely theoretical, or could it be realized in the actual world? Socrates thinks such a city can be realized only if it is ruled by philosophers, which leads to an investigation of what a philosopher is. This investigation will last through Book VII. In addressing the Third Wave, Plato has Socrates introduce the famous theory of the Forms and offer one of the *Republic's* central arguments, the Powers Argument, in defense of this view; he presents the analogies of the Sun and the Divided Line in Book VI, and the famous Allegory of the Cave in Book VII, among other things.

Having addressed the Three Waves to the company's satisfaction, in Books VIII-IX Socrates turns to the *Republic's* second question, 'Is the just life happier than the unjust life?'. Expanding on the psychology and political philosophy developed earlier, he distinguishes between five possible kinds of souls and city-states and argues that the just life is happier than the unjust life.

Having answered the *Republic's* two questions, in Book X Socrates returns to the status of poetry, which featured prominently in the educational program sketched in Books II and III. Despite his love for poetry, especially the works of Homer, he argues that most poetry should not be allowed in the ideal city because of its power to corrupt us. He concludes with the intriguing Myth of Er, about the importance of choice in a happy, well-lived life.

Readers will often find it helpful to keep the *Republic's* overall structure in mind while making their way through the text, since *what* a character is talking about often makes more sense when we understand *why* they are talking about it. So it can be helpful, when feeling a little lost, to orient oneself by asking which question of the *Republic's* two main questions is being addressed—although it might take a bit of intellectual sleuthing to determine that. For example, the details of the educational program Socrates develops in Books II and III are interesting in their own right, but it is easy to lose sight of why he devotes so much time and intellectual energy to this topic. If we keep the *Republic's* overall structure in mind, we can see that Socrates discusses education and culture because he is exploring what an ideal *polis* is like, which requires an understanding of how the *polis's* rulers will be educated. And of course, he wants to create this ideal *polis* because the plan is to define political justice in order to define personal justice. And while the *Republic's* first question about the nature of personal justice is interesting in its own right, Socrates wants to answer it because, as he realizes at the end of Book I, we cannot satisfactorily answer the *Republic's* second question about whether the just life is happier until we know what justice is.

As orienting oneself by overall structure is an aid to understanding, I will try to offer signposts and reminders as we proceed through the *Republic*. Shortly I will offer more detail about what individual chapters of this book will contain, but before doing that I want to draw the reader's attention to one more big-picture topic.

Arguing about Justice

Thrasymachus, Socrates' main antagonist in the second half of Book I, thinks that justice and happiness are at odds with each other, that being just and acting justly leave one worse off. Socrates disagrees, and it is instructive to see what he does and does not do in the face of this disagreement. First, what he does not do: he does not insult Thrasymachus or impugn his intelligence or his motives. Sadly, the same cannot be said for Thrasymachus, who responds to Socrates' arguments in a rather nasty way. Nor does Socrates shrug and say things like, 'Everyone's got a right to their opinion, I guess' or 'Who's to say?' or 'That's just your opinion, man', like a Lebowski of classical antiquity who has traded his bathrobe for a chiton (the ancient Greeks did not wear togas; that was a Roman thing). Socrates does not think that reason merely sheds light on the *Republic's* main questions, he thinks it can answer them. Some readers will be less confident in the power of rational argument and conceptual clarity; they may be more comfortable than Socrates and Plato are with there being more than one correct answer to these questions—or with there being none. But even though Socrates himself is not a moral pluralist, it is important to see that the method he employs in arguing against Thrasymachus is consistent with there being a plurality of answers to moral questions of the sort that the *Republic* devotes itself to. For while Socrates' method of question-and-answer—formally called *elenchus*, a kind of cross-examination—is impersonal in the sense of focusing on principles rather than personalities, it is in another sense profoundly personal, for its focus is what the person he is engaging with thinks. The best way to investigate the nature of justice, he thinks, is to critically examine the views of someone who claims to know what justice is, to see if such a view can survive rigorous cross-examination and coherently hang together. So he proceeds from premises that his interlocutors endorse. Although Socrates thinks that there is an Archimedean point from which one can definitively settle moral questions, the Socratic method of question-and-answer does not presuppose this exalted view of reason. Its aim is more modest: to discover whether one's philosophical and moral beliefs are internally consistent. While this method is no respecter of persons in that it does not defer to someone based upon their social class, etc., it is, I think, profoundly respectful of persons, since it takes seriously a person's moral and philosophical views. Even though these views are usually found wanting, a willingness to examine a person's views about the nature of justice or courage or knowledge or whatever is certainly a way of taking those views, and that person, seriously.

What to Expect in this Book

This book is not a line-by-line commentary of the *Republic,* but it hews closely to the main contours of the *Republic.* I intend it as an aid to reading the *Republic* rather than as a substitute for doing so. In the chapters to come I try to guide readers, especially those new to the *Republic* or returning to it after a long absence, to a clear understanding of the *Republic*'s main themes and distinctive arguments. But we will also pause to linger over details that are interesting in themselves and which contribute to a nuanced understanding of Plato's philosophical thought and literary artistry. I will try to clearly and accurately spell out the arguments Plato has Socrates offer and then critically reflect on them, asking questions such as 'Does the conclusion logically follow from the premises?' and 'Do we have good reasons to think the premises are true?' and 'What assumptions are driving the argument?', etc. We will see that Socrates' interlocutors often accept arguments that they have good reason to doubt. This is something most of us do, especially when we think the conclusion is true, but setting aside one's belief in a conclusion and querying the quality of the reasons offered in support of it is the hallmark of good critical thinking. I will try to model that in the pages to come and hopefully help readers sharpen their own philosophical skills. Since one of Plato's aims is for us, his readers, to think philosophically for ourselves, nothing would delight me more than readers disagreeing with and arguing against claims, interpretations, and assessments I make. Needless to say, there is a lot I will leave out as we proceed through the *Republic,* but by the end readers should have a good sense of the main themes and arguments of the *Republic* and of some of the philosophical problems with them. Here is a chapter-by-chapter rundown of the main issues to be discussed.

Chapter One, 'Fathers and Sons', covers the first half of Book I of the *Republic,* where Socrates raises the *Republic's* first question about the nature of justice at the home of Cephalus, a wealthy merchant who lives in a suburb of Athens. Cephalus suggests that justice is paying one's debts and telling the truth, but Socrates thinks this cannot be the essence of justice, since there are times when one should not return what one has borrowed. This alerts us to an important fact about what Socrates is looking for in an account of justice: the account should be unconditionally correct, with no ifs, ands, or buts. Cephalus' son Polemarchus jumps into the conversation and offers a revision of his father's definition, suggesting that justice—right conduct, generally—is benefiting one's friends and harming one's enemies. Socrates finds this account has implications that Polemarchus himself cannot accept, so the chapter explores Socrates' reasoning, especially the assumption that justice, a virtue of character, is a craft or skill. We then discuss Socrates' more direct argument against Polemarchus' account, that the just person would not harm anyone.

Chapter Two, 'Taming the Beast: Socrates versus Thrasymachus', is devoted to Socrates' encounter with the sophist Thrasymachus in the second half of Book I. Thrasymachus' answers to the *Republic's* main questions are a provocative challenge to the reverential attitude Socrates has toward justice in particular and virtue in general. Thrasymachus defines justice as whatever benefits the politically powerful and argues that a conventionally just person lives less happily than their unjust counterpart. Socrates offers five different arguments against Thrasymachus' views, which are spelled out clearly and evaluated carefully, with attention paid to the connections between them and to the crucial concepts around which they orbit (e.g., the notion of a virtue). Socrates' arguments fall short of the mark, and we will examine why this is the case, exploring avenues of response that Thrasymachus could but does not take. By the close of Book I, Socrates realizes that he has not answered the *Republic's* second question because he has not yet answered the first: we cannot know whether the just life is happier until we first know what justice is.

Chapter Three, 'A Fresh Start', explores the way in which Socrates tries to address the *Republic's* two questions, 'What is justice?' and 'Is the just life happier than the unjust life?'. Rather than offering a battery of arguments as he did in Book I, Socrates offers an analogy between the *polis* (the Greek city-state) and the *psychê* (individual soul) that will structure the rest of the *Republic*. The plan is to first discover the nature of justice as a political virtue—as a virtue of the *polis*—and then apply this to the individual soul in order to discover the nature of personal justice.

Chapter Four, 'Blueprints for a Platonic Utopia: Education and Culture', examines Socrates' account of education in the ideal polis, focusing especially on informal, cultural education in music and poetry. We will explore the fascinating connections Socrates draws between aesthetic and moral development, especially the role that poetic and musical style play over and above content. We then discuss Socrates' rather disturbing attitude toward disabled citizens before focusing on the famous Noble Falsehood, which concludes Book III, discussing the role that myth, especially myths of origin, play in civic self-understanding.

Chapter Five, 'Starting to Answer the First Question: The Political Virtues', focuses on the first third of Book IV. The ideal *polis* complete, Socrates and company investigate the political virtues of wisdom, courage, moderation, and justice, defining each and discussing their location in the *polis*. We will explore these accounts and the issues they raise, for example how the kind of agreement that constitutes political moderation differs from the idea of consent in modern liberal political thought, and the question of whether there are other virtues in addition to the four cardinal virtues.

We continue discussing Book IV of the *Republic* in Chapter Six, 'The Republic's First Question Answered at Last: Personal Justice'. We first attend to Plato's foray into psychology (literally, his account (*logos*) of the soul (*psuchê*)) in which he tries to justify the analogy between city and soul that has shaped the *Republic*. By appealing to the idea that the same thing cannot simultaneously undergo or perform opposite states or activities (dubbed the Opposition Principle), Socrates argues that the soul has a three-part structure, just as the city does: a rational part, which corresponds to the guardian-rulers in the *polis*; a spirited part (the seat of anger and pride), which corresponds to the soldierly auxiliaries of the *polis*; and an appetitive part, which corresponds to the craftspeople. Socrates then derives the personal virtues by applying the political virtues to the soul. The most important personal virtue, of course, is justice, which he conceives of as each part of the soul doing its own work: reason, not appetite or spirit, governs the just soul. We will pay attention to important features of this account, for example how it differs from Cephalus' and Polemarchus', for whom justice is a matter of interpersonal, external doing (of how one treats one's fellows), while for Socrates and Plato is it a matter of intrapersonal, internal being, of what one's soul is like.

In Chapter Seven, 'Questions about the Ideal Polis: The Three Waves', we see Polemarchus and Adeimantus begin Book V by putting the brakes on Socrates' attempt to immediately begin answering the *Republic*'s second question, whether living a morally good life is good for the person living it. They raise questions about and objections to the ideal *polis*, known as 'the Three Waves', which is an apt metaphor for a sea-faring culture. The First Wave concerns the question of whether women can be guardian-rulers in the ideal city. Socrates' affirmative answer—surprising to his companions and to many readers alike (though for different reasons)—raises the question of whether Plato is a feminist. The Second Wave concerns the ideal city's communal living arrangements, especially child-rearing. Socrates argues that not only is the abolition of the traditional family possible, it is beneficial. The Third Wave is the subject of the next chapter.

Chapter Eight, 'Surfing the Third Wave: Plato's Metaphysical Elevator, the Powers Argument, and the Infallibility of Knowledge', focuses on the Third Wave, which concerns the very possibility of the ideal city. Socrates famously claims that the ideal city can be made real only if philosophers rule. This leads him to explore how philosophers differ from non-philosophers, which will guide the last part of Book V as well as Books VI and VII. A crucial point of difference is that philosophers have knowledge while non-philosophers merely have belief, a distinction which is explored in some depth and detail. We devote special attention to one of the *Republic's* most crucial arguments, the Powers Argument, in which Socrates argues for the existence of the Forms, the mind-independently real, timeless essences of the many particular things that populate the everyday world of our senses. The reality of the Forms is perhaps Plato's most distinctive metaphysical view, so we devote quite a bit of attention to stating, explaining, and evaluating the Powers Argument, and to discussing the implications of its being seriously flawed.

Chapter Nine, 'The Philosopher's Virtues', continues to explore the distinction between philosophers and non-philosophers, focusing on their different characters. Central to the discussion is the distinction between virtues of character (for example, justice), intellectual virtues (for example, a good memory), and virtues of personal style (for example, grace and elegance), attending to the light this last category sheds on Plato's moral vision. As a prelude to the key analogies of Book VI, the rest of this chapter is devoted to the interesting analogies Socrates appeals to in addressing features of the Third Wave.

Chapter Ten, 'Metaphors to Think By: The Sun and Divided Line Analogies', is devoted to the marquee analogies of Book VI, both of which address the Third Wave by developing the distinction between the sensible world of concrete particular things and the intelligible world of the Forms. Having suggested that the Form of the good is even more important than justice, Socrates cannot or will not say what the good is, but he does say what he thinks it is like: the good plays the same role in the intelligible world as the sun plays in the visible world. In the Analogy of the Divided Line, Socrates further develops the distinction between belief, which is appropriate to the sensible, visible world, and knowledge, which is appropriate to the intelligible world of the Forms. By exploring the role that hypotheses play in reasoning, he distinguishes philosophical knowledge from mathematical knowledge, somewhat surprisingly taking the former to be more rigorous.

True to its name, Chapter Eleven, 'Shedding Light on the Allegory of the Cave', devotes itself to exploring the famous Allegory of the

Cave from Book VII of the *Republic,* carefully considering its various stages and themes before examining the issue posed by the enlightened philosopher's return to the Cave. As Socrates describes it, the enlightened philosopher descends back into the Cave not because they want to, but because they recognize that justice requires them to do so. This raises an issue for discussion that Socrates does not seem to notice: the enlightened philosopher would be happier if they ignored the demands of justice and remained in the intelligible world of the Forms, which suggests that, contrary to Socrates' view, the just life is not happier than the unjust life.

In Chapter Twelve, 'The Decline and Fall of the Ideal City-Soul', we begin exploring Socrates' answer to the *Republic*'s second question. In Books VIII and IX, Socrates sketches five kinds of cities and souls, noting what each takes as its primary end or goal and which part or class governs the soul and city, respectively. We trace the decay from the best city-soul to the worst, attending to the role that changes to education play and to interesting features of each stage, and discuss at some length Plato's distinction between necessary and unnecessary desires.

Chapter Thirteen, 'The Republic's Second Question Answered: Three and a Half Arguments that the Just Life is Happier', explores the arguments Socrates gives in Book IX that the just life is happier—indeed, 729 times happier—than the unjust life. There are fascinating features of the first two arguments, for example that the tyrannical person is incapable of friendship and that each part of the soul has a distinctive kind of pleasure. The third argument, the Metaphysics of Pleasure Argument, argues that since what is more filling is more pleasant and what is more real is more filling, the Forms, being the most real things, ground the most pleasant pleasures. We discuss this argument at some length, noting its dependence on the Powers Argument but also exploring ways in which Socrates seems to anticipate and preemptively respond to objections. In the last argument, which Socrates does not identify as such (hence the 'half'), is a metaphorical argument which, despite its being less philosophically rigorous than the Metaphysics of Pleasure Argument, is more intuitively persuasive and in no way relies on the problematic Powers Argument. This chapter concludes with a discussion of Plato's paternalism: his view that most of us, being incapable of the philosophical wisdom that consists of knowledge of the good, are incapable of good self-governance, so we are all better off being governed by someone else's (i.e., a philosopher-king's or -queen's) reason.

Chapter Fourteen, 'Are We There Yet? Tying up Loose Ends in Book X', explores the three topics of the *Republic*'s final book, Book X. The first is the status of poetry, which Socrates wants to revisit since he now has a psychology (the three-part soul) that he lacked when poetry was first discussed. He concludes, quite reluctantly, that very little poetry will be allowed in the ideal city, mainly because of its power to corrupt us: we give ourselves over to emotion and thus dethrone reason from its rightful place. After exploring his arguments for this view, we turn to his argument for the immortality of the soul, which Socrates offers in the context of showing the external advantages of living a just life (namely, having a reputation for justice), which were set aside to answer Glaucon's and Adeimantus' challenge of showing that justice was intrinsically good—that all by itself it made its possessor better off. Lastly, we attend to the Myth of Er, with which the *Republic* ends. Er's story is an allegory about the importance of careful choice in living justly and thus happily. It is a fascinating way to end the *Republic*, in terms of both content and style; we briefly explore what philosophical points Plato might be making by ending a work of philosophy this way.

Needless to say, I have not mentioned everything we will discuss, but this should give readers a good sense of the main contours of the *Republic* and a decent idea of what is to come. Now, on to the *Republic!*

Theodoor van Thulden, *Telemachus and Ulysses Meet in Eumaeus' Hut*
(1632–1633). Photograph by Mr. Nostalgic (2019), Wikimedia, Public
Domain, https://commons.wikimedia.org/wiki/File:Odysseus_en_
Telemachus_in_de_hut_van_Eumaeus_De_werken_van_Odysseus_
(serietitel),_RP-P-OB-66.764.jpg

1. Fathers and Sons

Book I

Plato packs a lot into the *Republic's* first book, so we will have an easier time of it if we break the discussion into two chapters. In this chapter we will examine Socrates' conversations with Cephalus and then with Cephalus' son, Polemarchus. In the next chapter we will explore Socrates' encounter with Thrasymachus.

The ever-curious Socrates wants to know what justice is not simply for its own sake but to determine whether a just life—a morally good life—is happier than an unjust one. As mentioned in the Introduction, the Greek word δικαιοσύνη (*dikaiosunê*) is broader in meaning than the English word 'justice', which often suggests fair distributions or the idea of rights. I will continue to use it, but I will often also use synonyms such as 'right' and 'moral goodness' and their ilk. 'Righteousness' seems a bit archaic and can have religious connotations that can be misleading. It is often thought that Book I of the *Republic* was initially a stand-alone dialogue as it ends, like so many of Plato's other dialogues do, without an answer to its central question. Most of these dialogues have Socrates asking, 'What is ____?' where an important notion like justice, knowledge, or courage fills in the blank. Socrates examines the answers his companions propose but typically finds them wanting, usually because they conflict with other beliefs held by the interlocutor. While not knowing what something is can be frustrating, knowing what it is not is often a helpful kind of knowledge, as it narrows the field and leaves us a bit closer to knowing what the thing—here, justice—is. Though Book I ends without a satisfactory answer to its central question, rather

https://doi.org/10.11647/OBP.0229.01

than the discussants going their separate ways, as usually happens in Plato's dialogues, two of the participants, Glaucon and Adeimantus (Plato's real-life brothers) insist that Socrates continues, that he shares his beliefs about the nature and value of justice, even if he cannot in good conscience claim to *know* its nature and value.

Polemarchus Wants You to Wait (1.327a–328c)

One of the many rewards of reading Plato is the literary quality of the dialogues, which are extraordinarily well crafted. That Plato writes dialogues rather than straightforward essays suggests that he regards philosophy as essentially conversational, that it involves back-and-forth, give-and-take, that two (or three) heads are better than one when addressing philosophical topics like the nature of justice. The dialogue form also invites us to be active rather than passive readers, to engage in the dialogue by thinking of responses and questions that the people on the page do not make. In addition to Plato's making a philosophical point by writing in dialogue form, his writing this way allows him to raise themes and issues that are at work in the background, where the conversation he is depicting is in the foreground. The opening lines of the *Republic* are an excellent example of this.

The *Republic* is Socrates' first-person account of a long conversation about the nature and value of justice that he has at the house of Cephalus, a wealthy merchant who lives in the Piraeus, the port of Athens. Plato's situating the conversation outside of Athens might be his way of suggesting that the ideal city Socrates and his friends will imaginatively construct is an alternative to Athens; he is not offering suggestions for ways in which Athens might change for the better but instead offers a different political arrangement entirely.

It is worth noting that the *Republic* is written around 380 BCE, in the shadow of Athens' defeat in the Peloponnesian War about twenty years previously. The conversation depicted takes place well before that, though scholars disagree about the dialogue's dramatic date. One likely candidate is 421 BCE, during 'the optimistic springtime Peace of Nicias', the truce marking the end of the first phase of the War; another is 411 BCE, after the War has resumed and is going quite badly for Athens, 'a gloomy, violence-torn, pessimistic time'.[1] Plato's contemporaries would know—and many contemporary readers will know—that Socrates was tried, convicted, and executed in 399 BCE for corrupting the youth and introducing false gods. Few contemporary readers, by contrast, will know that Polemarchus, who features prominently in Book I, was executed by the so-called Thirty Tyrants, who, installed by Sparta at the War's end, ruled briefly and bloodily in 404 BCE.

Socrates' reason for venturing out of Athens—to attend a religious festival and 'offer up my prayers to the goddess' (1.327a)—is a good example of Plato's subtle authorial artistry. As we noted above, the historical Socrates was tried, convicted, and put to death by the citizens of Athens for impiety and corrupting the youth. Plato memorably recounts Socrates' defense speech in the *Apology* (a title that will seem odd, given how unapologetic Socrates is in it, until we realize that *apologia* is Greek for defense). So Plato's depiction of Socrates' conventional piety at the very outset of the *Republic* provides an ironic take on then-recent Athenian history that would not be lost on any of Plato's contemporaries.

Socrates' opening words, 'I went down', which translate the Greek κατέβην (*katabên*), seem an unremarkable way to begin a remarkable book. But we will appreciate their significance and Plato's subtle authorial artistry later in the *Republic*, when, in the famous Allegory of the Cave, Socrates insists that the enlightened philosophers 'go down again' into the cave to govern its benighted prisoners and free those who are capable of making it out. It is the same verb in both cases, and in subtly drawing this parallel Plato seems to be telling us that Socrates' interlocutors—and by extension, us, his readers, whatever our accomplishments and pretension—do indeed live in the darkness of the Cave. 'It's a strange image you are describing', says Glaucon, 'and strange prisoners'. 'They are like us', Socrates replies. (7.515a)

Socrates tells his unnamed audience that Polemarchus' slave tugged on his cloak and asked him to wait. The casual invocation of slavery may bring many contemporary readers up short. Slavery was a fact of life in the Greek world, and lovers of Plato and other great classical authors such as Aeschylus, Aristophanes, and Aristotle, to name just three near the beginning of the alphabet, should at the very least pause

---

1   Debra Nails, 'The Dramatic Date of Plato's *Republic*', *The Classical Journal*, 93.4 (1998), 383–96 (p. 385).

at the possibility that the cultural achievement of classical Athens was possible only because it was a slave society. Although the claim is not uncontroversial, the consensus of contemporary scholars is that there *is* slavery in Plato's ideal *polis*. We may have occasion to investigate this later, but for now we might just note the fact that Polemarchus' slave is the first person Socrates quotes in the *Republic*. Although Athenian slavery might partially frame the *Republic* for modern readers, Plato does not seem to raise it as a background issue worthy of philosophical attention and there is no explicit discussion of its nature or moral status. Plato seems to accept it as something natural (later, he suggests that an individual might be 'by nature suited to be a slave' (4.444b), an idea Aristotle develops in the first book of his *Politics*) but subject to moral constraint—for example, we are told that Greeks should not enslave other Greeks (5.469c) and that rather than being harsh with his slaves, a good and properly educated person will merely look down on them (8.549a).

When Polemarchus finally catches up to Socrates he tells him, 'You must either prove stronger than we are or you will have to stay here' (1.327c). This sounds ominous, but it is just an innocent pun on Socrates' name, the central element of which is κράτος (*cratos*), meaning 'strength' or 'power'. One suspects this is not the first time Socrates has endured this rather lame pun, but he replies graciously and without groaning, asking if there is not another alternative, 'that we persuade you to let us go' (1.327c). This little exchange is Plato's way of raising an important theme of the *Republic:* the opposition between force and persuasion, between the irrational and the rational. The conflict sometimes comes to the surface, for example, in the Cave Allegory mentioned above. Education, as Plato conceives of it, involves quite a bit of force: the freed prisoner is 'compelled to stand up, turn his head [...] and look up toward the light' (7.515c) and is 'dragged [...] from there by force, up the rough, steep path' and then 'dragged [...] into the sunlight' (7.515e). Though the enlightened philosophers would rather remain above, they return to the cave—not because they are physically or psychologically compelled to do so, but because they are persuaded to.

In response to Socrates' appeal to persuasion, Polemarchus jokingly plays a trump card: 'But could you persuade us, if we won't listen?' (1.327e). Here Plato is recognizing a practical limit to the power of rational persuasion: people who refuse to listen cannot be persuaded. Most of us have probably encountered people who seem impervious to evidence and argument. More chillingly, the psychologists Brendan Nyhan and Jason Reifler have identified what they call the backfire effect: some of us are psychologically constituted so as to not merely remain unpersuaded by evidence and reasons that should lead us to give up certain beliefs, but actually tend to hold such beliefs even more strongly in the face of such evidence—so attempts to persuade the other by appeals to good evidence are likely to backfire.[2] Plato is reminding us that genuine discussion and dialogue, as opposed to dueling monologues, cannot occur when we refuse to entertain reasons and evidence that go against our views. He is raising an important theme that will be at work in the background of the *Republic,* and raising it in the subtle way skilled literary artists do.

There is more we could say about the subtleties of the *Republic's* opening, however the goal was not an exhaustive—and exhausting— catalog and discussion of them but rather to help the reader begin to appreciate the literary quality of the *Republic* and how inseparable its literary and philosophical aspects are for Plato.

Cephalus: Justice is Paying Your Debts and Telling the Truth (1.328c–331d)

The entire conversation that *is* the *Republic* takes place at the suburban home of Cephalus, a wealthy merchant, whose son, Polemarchus, has a keen interest in philosophy. Cephalus likes Socrates, and Socrates clearly likes him. Nowadays telling someone that you enjoy talking to them because you 'enjoy talking with the very old' (1.328d) is unlikely to be well received, but Cephalus does not mind, in part because of the association of age and wisdom: since Cephalus is farther along the road of life, he might have some insight about whether that road is 'rough and difficult or smooth and easy' (1.328e). The metaphor of the road or path is one we will see elsewhere in the *Republic.*

---

2   Brendan Nyhan and Jason Reifler, 'When Corrections Fail: The Persistence of Political Misperceptions', *Political Behavior,* 32 (2010), 303–30, https://doi. org/10.1007/s11109–010–9112–2

Cephalus is a fine spokesperson for moral common sense; his idea of a good life is not a life of 'sex, drinking parties, [and] feasts' (1.329a) but rather one of moderation. Being wealthy does not hurt, he admits, but all by itself material comfort is not sufficient for living well. 'A good person would not easily bear old age if he were poor', he remarks, 'but a bad one would not be at peace with himself, even if he were wealthy' (1.330a). Despite his conventional decency, Cephalus is not especially reflective and when the discussion turns philosophical, he congenially excuses himself to take care of a religious sacrifice. Cephalus exhibits an attractive kind of humility, as he is sufficiently self-aware to recognize that external factors play an important role in his being morally decent and thus that he himself is not the sole cause of his goodness. Plato is deftly setting up a contrast between character and circumstance, between the inner and the outer, that will come into play later in the *Republic* as he addresses the question of whether one can cultivate one's soul in such a way that one is more or less impervious to external forces that can lead one to act unjustly.

Before Cephalus leaves, Socrates pursues this question of wealth a bit further, asking Cephalus what the greatest good that his wealth has brought him is. Cephalus' answer is a bit surprising (and is no doubt part of why Socrates likes him). It is not that it enables a life of self-indulgence, cushy comfort, and lots of toys. Rather, it is that wealth is a kind of buffer against moral temptation: 'Wealth can do a lot to save us from having to cheat and deceive' (1.331b), Cephalus says, and thus it allows a person to face the afterlife without trepidation, since it enables one to live 'a just and pious life' (1.331a).

Most of us will agree that wealth is merely instrumentally and not intrinsically valuable—that it is not good in itself, but rather it is good as a means to something else. Cephalus is making a related but subtly different point about the sort of value wealth possesses, that wealth is conditionally good: its goodness depends not just upon the use to which it is put, but on who is doing the putting—on whose wealth it is. If my wealth enables my pursuing pleasures that are ultimately self-destructive, then my being wealthy is bad for me. A 'decent and orderly' (1.331a) person will benefit from their wealth, since they will use it well.

This distinction between conditional and unconditional value provides a nice segue to a distinctively philosophical turn in the conversation.

Though Cephalus has not himself offered a definition of justice, Socrates hears one lurking beneath the surface and asks, 'But speaking of this very thing itself, namely, justice, are we to say unconditionally that it is speaking the truth and paying whatever debts one has incurred? Or is doing these things sometimes just, sometimes unjust?' (1.331c) It is important to understand that Socrates is not looking for a *verbal* definition of 'justice' here, the sort of thing that one can look up in a dictionary or use to explain its meaning to someone learning one's language. He is looking for the *real* definition of justice, for an account of the thing itself. (Here 'real' does not contrast with 'fake' or 'imaginary' but with 'verbal'; etymologically 'real' derives from the Latin word *'res'*, which means 'thing' or 'matter'.) There is no question about the verbal definition of *dikaiosunê,* the word we are translating 'justice': it means morally right conduct generally. But exactly what morally right conduct *is* is what Socrates wants to know. Trying to get clear about everyday concepts like justice, courage, knowledge, etc., by making explicit what is usually left implicit is one of philosophy's main tasks, for Plato. Plato's dialogues typically consist of Socrates encountering someone who claims to know the real definition of a virtue like justice or courage or temperance. But after some Socratic question and answer, it becomes clear that the proposed definition will not work, usually because it is inconsistent with other things his interlocutor believes, and that is what happens here. Most of the dialogues end without a definition being arrived at—they end in what scholars call ἀπορία (*aporia*) difficulty, perplexity.

On Cephalus' definition of justice (more accurately, the definition Socrates attributes to him) justice is telling the truth and paying one's debts. It is instructive to note what Socrates does *not* do here. He does not shrug and offer a relativistic platitude such as, 'well, everyone's got a right to their opinion'. Socrates does not think that questions like the one he is asking are mere matters of taste, and there would be little point in discussing them if they were. If you think broccoli is delicious and I cannot stand it, an argument about who is right is pointless, since there is no fact of the matter about whether broccoli is delicious—hence the maxim *de gustibus non est disputandem:* there is no disputing about matters of taste. If, by contrast, we disagree about the cube root of 729, at least one of us is wrong. Philosophical questions about the nature of justice (and knowledge, courage, temperance, love, etc.) will seem to many thoughtful people to fall somewhere in between these extremes, not mere matters of taste but not as certain as truths of mathematics.

Socrates thinks that there *is* a correct answer to his question about the nature of justice (and about knowledge, courage, temperance, etc.), so in one sense of the term, he is a realist: he thinks there really is a fact of the matter of what justice is, a way things are that is independent of what we might think, which is the very thing the relativist denies. When Hamlet, by contrast, says that 'there is nothing either good or bad, but thinking makes it so' (*Hamlet*, II.2.244–45), he is expressing an antirealist view about the nature of goodness: things are not mind-independently good or bad; their being good or bad is determined by our attitudes toward them. Realism is not an all-or-nothing affair: one can be a realist about morality, thinking that there really are moral facts such as 'murder is wrong' and 'kindness is good', but an anti-realist about aesthetics, thinking that beauty really is just in the eye of the beholder. While many readers will be leery about Socrates' moral realism, an attractive feature of his method of rigorous cross-examination is that it does not depend on his realism, for it aims to discover whether someone's view is consistent with other things they believe. So the *elenchus* aims to lead the cross-examined party not to the unvarnished moral truth but rather to intellectual self-awareness—and, hopefully, to intellectual humility if, as is often the case, one recognizes that one's beliefs do not hang together consistently.

Having noted what Socrates does not do in his conversation with Cephalus, let us look at what he does do. He argues that if Cephalus' definition of justice is correct, then it would be just to return a borrowed weapon when its now-deranged owner asks for it back. But Cephalus himself does not think this. Since his definition implies something that he thinks is false, Cephalus should think that his definition is false. This form of argument is as common in everyday life as it is in philosophy. If A implies B and B is false, A must be false too. Any argument that fits this pattern is valid: *if* its premises are true then its conclusion must be true. If it is true that the sidewalk gets wet if it rains and it is true that the sidewalk is not getting wet, then it must also be true that it is not raining—for if it *were* raining, the sidewalk would be getting wet, and it is not; thus, it cannot be raining. If my aggrieved friend says, 'if (A) you were a good friend, then (B) you would have helped me move', I know how the rest of the argument goes even if they do not spell it out: (not-B) you did not help me move; therefore (not-A) you are not a good friend. I might reply by hanging my head in shame and conceding that I am not a good friend. That is, I take the argument to be not only logically valid (in other words, its conclusion must be true *if* its premises are true) but sound as well: it is valid *and* its premises are in fact true. But I might also reply by insisting that while the argument is logically valid, it is not sound, since its first premise is false. While it is *generally* true that a good friend will help one move, it is not true without exception. If I was in the hospital donating a kidney to another friend and was unable to help you move, my not helping does not imply that I am not a good friend. A more plausible version of the first premise would be 'if (A) you were a good friend *and* (C) were able to help me move, then (B) you would have done so.' On this more nuanced version of the argument, the conclusion to draw from the fact that I did not help is that *either* (not-A) I am not a good friend *or* (not-C) I was not able to help. I do not want us to get too bogged down in detail, but attention to the logic of the arguments offered is crucial to doing philosophy in general and to understanding the *Republic* in particular, especially Book I.

Now, just as I had some options in responding to my friend's argument, so too does Cephalus have options in responding to Socrates. Perhaps he should concede that his definition is false. But he could also change his mind about whether it would be wrong to return the weapon. This seems less plausible; most of us are surer of particular moral judgments we make than we are about more general moral principles. But if Cephalus is very confident in the truth of his definition, we might be willing to 'bite the bullet', as philosophers say, and accept an initially unpalatable claim. Another option would be to argue that the definition does not actually imply the problematic judgment, much as I did with my friend in the example above. Or he can challenge Socrates' unstated assumption that the definition of justice must be unconditional, never allowing any exceptions. Note that this is not a challenge to Socrates' definitional realism; Cephalus can still think that there is a uniquely correct definition while at the same time thinking that the correct definition is the sort of thing that holds only for the most part. In his imposingly titled *Groundwork of the Metaphysics of Morals,* the great modern philosopher Immanuel Kant insisted that moral principles must hold universally and not merely generally,[3] while Plato's student Aristotle, by contrast, thought that moral truths hold only for the most part, and that we must not demand more rigor than a subject affords.[4] Plato is closer to Kant on this score than he is to Aristotle. We will not settle this dispute here (or anywhere in this book); I raise it not only to show that Cephalus has philosophical options he does not seem to be aware of, but also to show that an important task of philosophy is making the implicit explicit: Socrates assumes that real definitions must hold without exception. While he may be correct about this, he may not be: moral definitions and principles might lack the universality and precision we expect of their mathematical cousins.

A related assumption Socrates makes is that there really is one feature that all just things have in common, something in virtue of which they are all just. In other words, there must be an essence of justice—and similarly an essence of courage, wisdom, tree, table, etc. Plato has a surprising view about the nature of these essences, which he calls the Forms: he not only thinks that the Forms are mind-independently real, he thinks that they are *more real* than the particular things that are instances of them. We will get to that in Chapter Eight, when we will also query the assumption that there is an essence—a real definition—of justice and that the task of philosophy is to figure out what that essence is.

Polemarchus: Justice is Benefiting Friends and Harming Enemies (1.331d–336a)

Socrates thinks that the proposed definition of justice has been decisively refuted, but Polemarchus, Cephalus' son, disagrees, and for support he appeals to the poet Simonides. This appeal to poetic authority raises an important theme that will be explored later in the *Republic*: do poets— especially great poets such as Homer—have *knowledge* of things such as the nature of justice? Does the fact that Homer or Pindar or Simonides says something give us a good reason to think that it is true? Anyone who

---

3   Immanuel Kant, *Kant: Groundwork of the Metaphysics of Morals,* trans. and ed. by Mary K. Gregor (New York: Cambridge University Press, 1998), p. 34 [*Ak.* 4:424].
4   Aristotle, *Nicomachean Ethics,* I.3 1294b12–15.

has spent much time on Facebook and who has a philosophical bent has probably asked similar questions. Does the fact that George Clooney, for example, thinks drastic action needs to be taken to deal with climate change give me good reason to think so, too? It seems not, but many of us find the deliverances of celebrities persuasive nonetheless. Socrates plainly loves Homer; he quotes him and other poets throughout the *Republic.* He will reluctantly conclude in Book X that poets and artists generally do not possess the moral authority that the Polemarchuses of the world attribute to them. But for now, he sets this issue aside and queries the definition of justice Polemarchus appeals to.

Polemarchus first suggests that justice is giving to each what they are owed. While his father's definition was too specific, Polemarchus' is perhaps too general: what exactly are people owed? Polemarchus answers that we owe good to our friends and bad to our enemies. This is not an outlandish view; indeed, it is commonsense to Polemarchus and his contemporaries. The countervailing Christian idea that we should love our enemies would find few adherents in classical Athens.

Socrates makes two arguments against Polemarchus' definition of justice as benefiting one's friends and harming one's enemies, but before looking at them, we should attend to a problematic feature of his definition: it divides the moral world into *friends* and *enemies*—but surely that does not exhaust the possibilities. It is likely that most of the people one encounters on any given day do not fall into either category. And though I am lucky enough to have some people I consider genuine friends, my life is not interesting enough for me to have any enemies, alas. A central moral question most thoughtful people ask is what if any moral duties they have toward strangers, especially strangers halfway around the world, who do not fit into either camp. Polemarchus' definition of justice gives us no help in answering that question.

As with his argument against Cephalus, Socrates' argument against Polemarchus' account of justice is an indirect argument, aiming to show that the definition implies things that Polemarchus himself thinks are false. Socrates argues that Polemarchus' account of justice implies that justice is not especially valuable and moreover that it is a craft of stealing. Since Polemarchus does not think either of those implications is true, Socrates argues, his definition must be false. The pattern is the same one we saw above: A implies B, B is not true, so A must not be true. Here, B has two parts, the sub-claims that justice is not valuable and that justice is a craft of stealing, so the argument is a slightly more complex variation on the argument Socrates made against Polemarchus, but they exhibit essentially the same pattern.

P1   If Polemarchus' definition of justice is correct, then justice is not valuable and it is a craft of stealing.

P2   But it is false that justice is not valuable and that it is a craft of stealing.

C   Therefore, Polemarchus' definition of justice is not correct.

As with the argument above, this one is valid: if its premises are true, its conclusion—that Polemarchus' definition is mistaken—must be true. Since the argument is valid, the only way to avoid the truth of the conclusion is to find at least one of the premises to be false. Polemarchus feels himself in a bind because he thinks that his definition is true (and thus that the conclusion of Socrates' argument is false), and also that both premises seem true. He does not seem to know how to respond: 'I do not know any more what I did mean, but I still believe that to benefit friends and harm one's enemies is justice' (1.334b).

Polemarchus' plight is not uncommon among Plato's characters: they recognize that Socrates has them intellectually cornered but they do not seem to know what to do. Adeimantus describes the experience of many of Socrates' interlocutors a bit later in the *Republic:* 'Just as inexperienced checkers players are trapped by the experts in the end and cannot make a move, so [your interlocutors] too are trapped in the end and have nothing to say in this different kind of checkers, which is played not with discs but with words' (6.487b).

I think that Plato puts Polemarchus in this predicament because he wants us, his readers, to engage philosophically in the discussion by doing for ourselves what Polemarchus is not able to do: to carefully scrutinize Socrates' reasoning and to think through his assumptions. Perhaps we can help Polemarchus out. Since Socrates' argument is valid, the main issue is whether it is sound. Why should we think that its first premise is true?

Is Justice a Craft? (1.332c–334b)

Socrates' argument that P1 is true (and notice that he offers an argument for a premise that itself is part of a larger argument) turns on the idea of a craft—τέχνη (*technê*), in Greek, from which words like 'technique' and 'technology' derive. A doctor is a person skilled in the craft of medicine; they know how to use their skill to benefit their friends by healing them and harm their enemies by poisoning them. Similarly, the person skilled in the craft of cooking can use that skill to benefit their friends and harm their enemies via the food they cook. (Readers who have seen the film *The Help* might think of Minny's special chocolate pie as an example.)

The crucial move takes place when Socrates says, 'Now, what does the craft we call justice give, and to whom or what does it give it?' (1.332d) If justice is a craft in the same way that medicine, cooking, navigation, and the like are crafts, then like them it will have its own special sphere in which it operates to benefit friends and harm enemies. Medicine's sphere or domain is health; it is there that its skilled practitioner can benefit friends and harm enemies. Medicine is not useful outside its sphere—for example, the person skilled in navigation can benefit friends and harm enemies at sea, not the person skilled in medicine. This is not to say that these spheres do not overlap: there is a sense in which a doctor can benefit and harm passengers on a ship, but their being at sea is irrelevant to the doctor benefiting and harming them.

Polemarchus does not challenge the assumption that justice is a craft; indeed, he agrees that partnerships are the sphere of the craft of justice. But, Socrates argues, when choosing a partner for checkers we want a skillful checkers player, not someone skilled in the craft of justice. The same can be said for other crafts such as house-building and horse-breeding. When we form a partnership to build a house or buy a horse, we want someone skilled in those crafts, and being just does not make anyone a better builder or breeder. It is when we are not using something and want to safeguard it, Socrates argues, that we choose the person skilled in justice, who will not steal our money or our horse or our prized violin. So, Socrates concludes, 'justice is not worth very much, since it is only useful for useless things' (1.333e).

This conclusion is an embarrassing one for Polemarchus' view, but it is not fatal to it. The fatal blow comes next. The person most skilled at protecting a computer network, to use an anachronistic example, is the person most skilled at hacking into networks; since they know where the weak spots are, they will know how to patch them. At the end of the film *Catch Me If You Can*,[5] master forger Frank Abagnale goes to work for the FBI, teaching agents how to spot forgeries. Socrates' general point is this: 'Whenever someone is a clever guardian, then, he is also a clever thief' (1.334a). But since the person skilled in the craft of justice is the best guardian of an item, they will also be best able to steal it and presumably avoid detection. Thus the just person is a kind of thief, and justice, by being a craft of guarding what is valuable, turns out to be a craft of stealing. Polemarchus is flummoxed. He does not think that justice is useless or a craft of stealing, but he has been led to the view that justice is useless and a craft of stealing by a series of steps that he agreed to.

I think that Polemarchus should, but does not, question the assumption driving the argument: that justice is a craft. Certainly, character virtues like justice are similar to crafts in interesting and important ways. For example, both are practical, involving know-how. Both are acquired by practice, by doing. Both are desirable to possess and objects of praise. But the (or at least a) crucial difference between them is that crafts are morally neutral, while character virtues—moral virtues—are not. As Socrates points out, the doctor, who possesses the craft of medicine, can use their craft for good or ill, to benefit and harm. If Polemarchus' definition of justice is correct, the doctor uses their craft to benefit their friends and harm their enemies and thereby exhibits justice. But a doctor who uses the craft of medicine to harm their friends is acting unjustly, on Polemarchus' view. Whether the doctor acts justly depends upon how they use their craft. Crafts are good—but they are *conditionally* good, good only if used appropriately; their moral goodness is not intrinsic. Virtues, by contrast, seem to be unconditionally, intrinsically good. Possessing them makes their possessor morally better off, even if it makes them, say, financially worse off. (Courage might seem to pose a problem for this claim, but

---

5   *Catch Me If You Can*, dir. by Stephen Spielberg (DreamWorks Pictures, 2002).

we can set that worry aside for now.) When Socrates asks, 'Is someone a good and useful partner in a game of checkers because he is just or because he is a checkers player?' (1.333a), he is treating the craft and the virtue as the same kind of thing. Instead of agreeing, Polemarchus should say, 'That is a false dilemma, Socrates. You are assuming that someone cannot be both just and a good checkers player—because you are assuming that justice is a craft, and it is not. I want to play against someone who is good at checkers—the challenge makes the game more fun—*and* someone who is not going to cheat.' Being just does not make anyone a better builder or breeder or checkers player, but it *does* make someone a better partner to engage in those crafts with, since it makes her less likely to take unfair advantage or cheat. Perhaps Polemarchus has some implicit grasp of this point, which may be one reason why he remains unconvinced by Socrates' argument against his definition.

It turns out that the first premise of Socrates' argument against Polemarchus' definition is more complex than it initially seemed. It is not

P1   If (A) Polemarchus' definition of justice is correct, then (C) justice is not valuable and (D) justice is a craft of stealing

but rather

P1*   If (A) Polemarchus' definition of justice is correct *and* (B) justice is a craft, then (C) justice is not valuable and (D) justice is a craft of stealing.

With the structure of P1 thus clarified, Polemarchus has a good response to Socrates. His conceding that C and D are both false no longer entails that A is false (i.e., that his definition of justice is not correct). Instead, the falsity of C and D entail that *either* A is false *or* B is false (and maybe both). And we have independent reasons for thinking B is false: character virtues such as justice are like crafts in many ways, but they are not crafts, since crafts are morally neutral while character virtues (and vices) are morally loaded.

Speaking of Friends... (1.334c–335a)

The next argument has the same structure as the first: the definition implies something that is false, so it must be false—or at least Polemarchus ought to think it is false. In fact, Socrates seems to show that Polemarchus' definition implies that it is just to harm people who have done us no injustice—i.e., who are not our enemies: 'Then, according to your account, it is just to do bad things to those who do no injustice' (1.334d). Here the culprit is Polemarchus' mistaken account of who a friend is. Socrates distinguishes between subjective and objective accounts of friendship. On a subjective view, you are my friend if I think you are good and useful; what matters are my beliefs about you. On the objective view, you are my friend if in fact you are good and useful, regardless of whether I think so. Polemarchus opts for the first, subjective option, but Socrates points out that we are often mistaken about this sort of thing, which can lead to harming our friends and benefitting our enemies.

Notice that here Polemarchus recognizes that his view is defective, since it implies something he knows to be false. 'My account (λόγος [*logos*]) must be a bad one' (1.334d), he says, proposing that they modify the subjective account of friendship, opting for a hybrid account that combines the objective and subjective accounts: 'Someone who is both believed to be useful and is useful is a friend; someone who is believed to be useful but is not, is believed to be a friend but is not' (1.334e).

This exchange shows Polemarchus in a better light than the first. He is much more active than in the first argument, where for the most part he limited himself to one-word replies to Socrates' somewhat leading questions. At the conclusion of the first argument he seemed helplessly befuddled, vaguely recognizing that there was some problem with his view but sticking to it nonetheless: 'I do not know any more what I did mean, but I still believe that to benefit one's friends and harm one's enemies is justice' (1.334b). In this exchange he not only clearly recognizes the problem (his subjective account of friendship) but articulates the solution: 'let us change our definition' (1.334e) of friendship. He is more rationally engaged in this exchange and provides a pretty good model for thinking philosophically—which, in the end, really just comes down to thinking clearly. It may be that his rational vision is sharper in this exchange, however I suspect it is not that his vision has improved, but rather that the problem is more visible in this exchange than in the first.

But Does the Just Person Harm Anyone? (1.335b–336a)

Where Socrates' first criticisms of Polemarchus' definition are indirect, aiming to show that it implies things that Polemarchus himself rejects, the last criticism is more direct, challenging the definition itself—and, indeed, is a direct challenge to an element of Greek commonsense morality that would seem to most Athenians to be unassailable. The proposed definition cannot be right, Socrates argues, because 'it is never just to harm anyone' (1.335e). It is an argument that is important both to the scheme of Book I of the *Republic* and to moral philosophy generally.

One of the argument's key elements is the concept of a virtue, which we employed without exploring whether a virtue such as justice is a craft. While we are perhaps likelier to think of virtue in the singular, referring to someone's character in general (or, anachronistically, to sexual chastity), it is usually plural in the *Republic*. Indeed, in Book IV we will find Socrates giving accounts of the four cardinal virtues: justice, moderation, courage, and wisdom. The Greek word is ἀρετή (*aretê*), which does not have the necessarily moral connotation that the English word 'virtue' possesses. The word 'virtuoso' retains this non-moral sense; it is still an evaluative term, but not a *morally* evaluative one. The word 'good' often functions this way. When you call someone a good person, you are morally evaluating and praising them; when you call them a good dancer or a good mechanic or a good thief, you are evaluating them, but you are not evaluating them morally; you are saying that they are good at a particular craft or activity. Some translators try to remind their readers of this non-moral aspect by opting for 'excellence' instead of 'virtue' in translating *aretê*. This makes sense, since if things like dogs and knives have virtues—which they do, as Plato understands the concept—it must have a non-moral dimension. But our translator opts for 'virtue', so to avoid confusion we will follow his lead.

The concept of a virtue is best understood in terms of the concept of a function. A thing's function is the work it does, its goal-directed purpose. The Greek word for function is ἔργον (*ergon*), which is the root of the

English word 'ergonomic'. Some readers have 'ergonomic' computer keyboards that are wedge-shaped or chairs that are 'ergonomically designed', which means that they are designed to enable their users to work more efficiently as they carry out the object's function. More technically, the function is the goal-directed activity characteristic of the kind of thing in question. Artifacts like knives and cars have functions, but so too do natural objects. The function of a knife is to cut; the function of a heart is to pump blood. In one sense, a thing's function is what makes it what it is. Understood in terms of function, a plastic knife and a metal knife have more in common with each other than a plastic knife and a plastic fork do. Understood materially rather than functionally—that is, understood in terms of the matter they are composed of rather than their tasks—the plastic knife and plastic fork are more similar to each other than either is to the metal knife. A hallmark of modern science since Galileo and Newton is jettisoning functional or teleological (that is, goal-directed) explanations of natural phenomena in favor of material and mechanistic explanations. Rain does not have a purpose in the modern worldview; that rain waters crops and thus enables life is a welcome side-effect of rain. A scientific account of why it rained this morning will appeal to various meteorological facts, not to the function or purpose of rain. But these functional or teleological explanations, while out of place in physics and chemistry, still find a home in biology and psychology, for example, and in ordinary life. When in *The Silence of the Lambs* Clarice seeks Hannibal's help in catching Buffalo Bill, he encourages her to think teleologically: 'What does he do, this man you seek?' When she answers, 'He kills women', Hannibal replies in his eerie, sing-song voice, 'No! That is incidental'. He is telling her that until she understands the goal around which he organizes his murderous activity—i.e., until she understands Bill's function—she will not be able to understand him, much less to catch him.[6] A virtue, then, is the state that enables the thing to perform its function well, and a vice, by contrast, is the state that prevents the thing from performing its function well. Sharpness is the virtue of a knife, since sharpness is what enables the knife to cut well, and dullness is a knife's vice, since it prevents the knife from cutting well. A dull knife still might cut, but it will not cut

---

6   *The Silence of the Lambs,* dir. by Jonathan Demme (Orion Pictures, 1991).

well. So a virtue is a good-making feature of thing: sharpness makes for a good knife, since a sharp knife cuts well. If it sounds odd to talk of a knife's virtue, keep in mind that 'excellence' is another way to translate *aretê*. The virtue of a heart is a bit more complicated, which makes sense, given how complicated hearts are, but the basic idea is the same: the heart's virtue is the condition that enables it to pump blood well.

Now that we have explored the concept of a virtue, let us see how Socrates puts it to work in his third, direct argument against Polemarchus' definition of justice. Since possessing the relevant virtue makes something good, you make something worse by depriving it of its virtue. Thus, making a knife duller makes it worse. Now of course there may be times when a dull knife is preferable to a sharp one: one does not use a sharp knife as a prop in a movie or play, because it is too dangerous. But notice how the knife's function has quietly changed: as a prop, its function is not to cut but to *appear to* do so. You do not give scalpel-sharp scissors to a kindergartener but instead scissors that do not cut as well, since we will sacrifice cutting capacity in favor of safety. The upshot of all this is that to harm something is to make it worse off with respect to the relevant virtue.

The key move in the argument occurs when Polemarchus agrees with Socrates' suggestion that justice is the human virtue (1.335c). There is no mention of the human function here—something that Plato's student Aristotle will make the centerpiece of his ethics—but we can reason backwards to it, if we are so inclined. Perhaps our function is, at least in part, to live peacefully in communities; if so, then justice will be the trait, or surely among the traits, that will enable us to do so. When speaking of making objects worse, we tend to reserve 'harm' for animate objects and employ 'damage' for inanimate ones. It sounds odd to say that I harmed the lawnmower by not putting oil in the engine. But harm and damage are both ways to make something worse, and in both cases I make the thing worse by depriving it of the relevant virtue. So, just as I would damage the knife by depriving it of its characteristic virtue, sharpness, I would harm a person by depriving them of the characteristic human virtue, justice: 'people who are harmed must become more unjust' (1.335c).

But, Socrates asks, how could a just person, acting justly, make someone else less just? A musician cannot by exhibiting musical excellence make others less musical, he thinks, any more than an excellent parent or teacher can make someone else a worse parent or teacher through the very exercise of their excellence. The very idea is incoherent, Socrates thinks. Thus the proposed definition is intrinsically, rather than extrinsically, flawed: the problem is not that the definition has false or undesirable implications; the problem is that its core idea, that justice involves harming those who deserve it, makes no sense.

This conclusion has fascinating implications for theories of punishment—though this is not something that Socrates pursues here. If Socrates is correct, then retributivist accounts of punishment are deeply morally mistaken. Only punishment aiming at the wrongdoer's moral improvement would be justified; retributive punishments, which seek to inflict harm because the wrongdoer deserves to suffer, would not be justifiable. Here it is important to remember that not all pain is harmful; we often inflict pain on ourselves and others for our and their own good—and it is especially heart-rending when that other is a small child or companion animal with whom we cannot communicate our reasons for inflicting pain.

We will see in the next chapter that Thrasymachus, who bursts on the scene at this argument's conclusion, has a lot to say in opposition to this argument's key premise, that justice is the human virtue, so we will not explore the argument in great detail here. One might wonder, though, about Socrates' point that a person or thing possessing virtue V cannot, by exercising V, make other things un-V or less V. Sharp knives become dull by their repeated use, after all—though the great Daoist Zhuangzi (aka Chuang Tzu) might attribute this to a lack of excellence in the person wielding the knife, since Cook Ding's knife finds the empty spaces between the joints and thus 'is still as sharp as if it had just come off the whetstone, even after nineteen years'.[7] But let us set this aside and attend to how differently Polemarchus reacts to this Socratic refutation. After the first argument, he still stuck to his definition, insisting that justice was benefiting friends and harming enemies, even though he sensed something was amiss. Here, by contrast, he is completely convinced that his definition is mistaken, and profoundly so.

---

7   *Zhuangzi: The Complete Writings*, trans. by Brook Ziporyn (Indianapolis: Hackett Publishing, 2020), p. 30.

Moreover, he agrees to be Socrates' 'partner in battle' (1.335e) against those who advocate it.

It is worth noting, as we wind down this chapter, how Socrates seeks to preserve the moral authority of the poet Simonides, to whose definition Polemarchus appealed when entering the conversation. When Polemarchus first jumps into the argument, Socrates describes Simonides as 'a wise and godlike man' (1.333e)—though perhaps a bit ironically. A few pages later, having, he thinks, decisively refuted the definition, he suggests that the definition could not be Simonides' after all, since no wise and godlike person could be so mistaken about the nature of justice. Instead, it must be the definition of a wealthy and powerful person seeking to cloak their bad conduct in the mantle of justice. This is yet another of the subtle ways in which Plato works important themes into the argument. As noted above, whether poets have the moral authority customarily ascribed to them will be explored later in the *Republic*.

We have covered a lot of ground in this chapter. Hopefully readers have a good grasp of some of the key concepts that will be explored in the remainder of the *Republic* and especially of the give-and-take that characterizes philosophical conversation.

Some Suggestions for Further Reading

Kenneth Dover, *Greek Popular Morality in the Time of Plato and Aristotle* (Indianapolis: Hackett Publishing, 1994), is a rich source for the shared morality of the day.

Gregory Vlastos, 'Socrates' Rejection of Retaliation', in *Socrates: Ironist and Moral Philosopher* (Ithaca: Cornell University Press, 1991), pp. 179–99, investigates the radical nature of Socrates' separating justice and retaliation. Vlastos was one of the preeminent Plato scholars of the twentieth century.

Interested readers with a fondness for Greek tragedy will want to see Mary Blundell, *Helping Friends and Harming Enemies: A Study in Sophocles and Greek Ethics* (New York: Cambridge University Press, 1991).

M.I. Finley, *Ancient Slavery, Modern Ideology* (New York: Penguin Books, 1983) is a classic historical study of slavery both ancient and modern. A revised version, edited by Brent Shaw, which includes a long essay by Shaw on the responses to Finley's arguments, was published by Markus Weiner Publishers in 2017.

Zhuangzi: The Essential Writings, trans. by Brook Ziporyn (Indianapolis: Hackett Publishing, 2009), will interest readers intrigued by the story of Cook Ding. It and the *Dao De Jing,* which appears in several translations, are foundational texts of philosophical Daoism and present a stark contrast with Plato's intellectualism and rationalism.

Readers interested in the historical persons depicted in the *Republic* and the other dialogues will find Debra Nails, *The People of Plato* (Indianapolis: Hackett Publishing, 2002) a fascinating and valuable resource.

Greek vase, ca. 550 BCE. Photograph by Materia Viva (2010),
Wikimedia, CC BY-SA 4.0, https://commons.wikimedia.org/wiki/
Category:Mus%C3%A9e_Saint-Raymond,_26172#/media/File:MSR-
26172-MV-R-b.jpg

2. Taming the Beast
Socrates versus Thrasymachus
Book I

The last half of Book I (336a–354c) depicts Socrates' encounter with Thrasymachus. Like most characters in the *Republic*, Thrasymachus is a real person, and the views Plato attributes to him square with what is known of the historical Thrasymachus. Thrasymachus is a sophist—a professional, itinerant teacher of rhetoric, or the art of persuasion. Plato's worry about sophists is that their teaching is neither grounded in nor aimed at the truth; its only concern is persuasion.

Enter Thrasymachus: Justice Is Whatever Benefits the Powerful (1.336a–39b)

Thrasymachus bursts into the conversation like a wild beast, and Socrates twice remarks how frightening it was. His entrance might be merely an overly aggressive case of 'calling bullshit' were it not for the antipathy he clearly has for Socrates. Socrates asks questions but never answers them, Thrasymachus complains—and not, Thrasymachus thinks, because of any 'Socratic wisdom' of knowing that he does not know the answers, but because of his 'love of honor' (1.336c): Thrasymachus thinks that Socrates just wants to win arguments. He responds to Socrates' assertions of the value of justice as 'a thing more valuable than even a large quantity of gold' (1.336e) and of intellectual humility ('we are incapable of finding it' (1.336e)) with 'a loud,

   https://doi.org/10.11647/OBP.0229.02

sarcastic laugh', dismissing them as 'just Socrates' usual irony' (1.337a). This last charge might sound strange to modern ears; irony is often prized for its elegance. But here, irony (εἰρωνεία [*eirôneia*]) is seen as false modesty and thus a vice. In his *Nicomachean Ethics* Aristotle rates irony—which he calls 'mock modesty'—as one of the vices flanking the virtue of truthfulness (roughly: being a straight shooter), the other being boastfulness,[1] and in his *Rhetoric* he notes that people often respond to irony with anger, since it can seem to show contempt.[2] Perhaps that is what earns Thrasymachus' ire.

In any case, Thrasymachus has an answer to Socrates' question about the nature of justice, one he is very proud of: 'justice is nothing other than the advantage of the stronger' (1.338c). Two things to notice straightaway about Thrasymachus' account are its political nature and its reductive, deflationary tone. By 'the stronger' he means the politically powerful, who make laws to benefit themselves; good people follow those rules, thinking it just to do so, which benefits the rule-makers. The definition's deflationary, reductive aspect is brought out in the 'nothing other than' locution. Claims that love *is nothing but* a biochemical phenomenon or a fairy tale or a social construction are meant to deflate the kinds of lofty claims one encounters at wedding receptions and on Valentine's Day cards. Thrasymachus offers his definition of justice in a similar vein.

Though Socrates and Thrasymachus agree that justice is beneficial, they disagree about whom it benefits. Socrates thinks that justice, like any character virtue, benefits its possessor: my being just makes my life better. Thrasymachus, who will soon deny that justice is a virtue at all, claims that my being just benefits someone else—namely, the politically powerful rule-makers, who benefit from my following the rules which they have crafted for their own benefit. A just person, Thrasymachus argues, always gets less than an unjust one (1.343d): they do not cheat their business partners or customers, they do not cheat on their taxes, and when they govern they make laws that benefit others rather than themselves.

We will see soon enough that Socrates rejects Thrasymachus' picture of what a happy or flourishing human life looks like. Thrasymachus is a materialist—not in the philosophical sense of thinking that there are no

---

1   Aristotle, *Nicomachean Ethics*, IV.7 1127b22–31.
2   Aristotle, *Rhetoric*, II.2 1379b30–31.

immaterial objects, but in the everyday sense of thinking that material success is the main goal of life and measure of success. Thrasymachus is also an egoist: one's own interests are the ultimate standard for how one should act. Note that the egoist does not counsel doing whatever one feels like doing at any moment, for that may not be in one's interest. Acting impulsively is often at odds with enlightened self-interest, so it is not something Thrasymachus endorses. And there may be times when following the rules will be to one's advantage, especially if one is likely to be caught and punished for breaking the rules. While it is almost always in one's interest to *appear* to be just—a point that Glaucon and Adeimantus will focus on in Book II—it is rarely in one's interest to actually *be* just, Thrasymachus thinks. On his view, people who wish to be just are either naïve simpletons who cluelessly enable their own exploitation, or they are savvy enough to recognize their own inability to act unjustly with impunity and so agree to the rules in order to protect themselves against those strong enough to do so. Justice is for the weak, he thinks: 'Those who reproach injustice do so because they are afraid not of doing it but of suffering it' (1.344c).

Five Arguments Against Thrasymachus' Definition of Justice

There is more to say about Thrasymachus' definition of justice, but the best way to do that is to turn to the arguments Socrates gives against it. As with the conversations with Cephalus and Polemarchus, Socrates will argue from premises that Thrasymachus accepts to conclusions that are at odds with those premises. That is, he will try to show that Thrasymachus' view is at odds with itself, and thus that Thrasymachus himself has reason to discard or at least revise his view. Socrates makes five such arguments. The first two target Thrasymachus' answer to the *Republic*'s first question about the nature of justice—that is, his claim that justice is whatever benefits the stronger. The last three target his answer to the *Republic*'s second question about whether a just life is happier than an unjust one. We will take them each in turn.

The Error Argument (1.338c–343a)

I have dubbed the first argument 'the error argument' because it turns on the possibility that rulers, being fallible, are prone to error in crafting laws. The argument is straightforward. Thrasymachus agrees that justice is or at least requires following laws laid down by the rulers. But rulers, being fallible, sometimes make mistakes and thus enact laws that are *not* in their own interests. So—sometimes, at least—justice *is not* what benefits the stronger. Since on Socrates' view an adequate definition of a thing's essence must not allow for exceptions, Thrasymachus' definition must be rejected or revised, since there are times when justice does not benefit the stronger. Reconstructed in premise-conclusion form, Socrates' Error Argument against Thrasymachus goes like this:

P1   In a political system, the rulers are stronger than the ruled. (1.339a)

P2   Justice is (obedience to) whatever the rulers command. (1.339c)

P3   Rulers sometimes err and do not command what is to their advantage. (1.339d)

C   So, justice is not (always) the advantage of the stronger. (1.339d)

The argument seems deductively valid; that is, its conclusion must be true if its premises are true. Since Thrasymachus rejects the conclusion, rational consistency requires him to reject at least one of the premises. Hopefully this requirement makes sense. Since the argument is valid, if all its premises are true, its conclusion would have to be true. So if I think the conclusion of a valid argument is false, I cannot think that all the premises are in fact true, because if the premises were in fact true, the conclusion would be true, too. It is irrational to think that all the premises of a valid argument are in fact true and to think that the conclusion that follows from them is false. If I think the conclusion of a valid argument is false, I must also think at least one of the premises is false.

Someone who does not value consistency will be unmoved by all of this. We have probably all encountered a kind of skepticism—and perhaps embodied it with youthful exuberance—that is skeptical about consistency itself. 'What is so great about consistency?', such a skeptic asks. 'Who cares if I am being inconsistent'? If the skeptic is bookish, they might even quote from Ralph Waldo Emerson's well-known essay, 'Self-Reliance': 'A foolish consistency is the hobgoblin of little minds, adored by little statesmen and philosophers and divines'.[3] Or they might appeal to F. Scott Fitzgerald's assertion in *The Crack-Up* that 'the test of a first-rate intelligence is the ability to hold two opposed ideas in the mind at the same time, and still retain the ability to function'.[4] One way to respond to our skeptic is to point out that for Emerson the bogeyman wasn't consistency but rather *foolish* consistency: 'With consistency a great soul has simply nothing to do [...] Speak what you think now in hard words, and to-morrow speak what to-morrow thinks in hard words again, though it contradict every thing you said to-day'.[5] It is refusing to change one's mind that Emerson is attacking here. And Fitzgerald is not questioning the value of consistency or celebrating inconsistency; he is concerned less with belief than he is with action: 'One should, for example, be able to see that things are hopeless and yet be determined to make them otherwise'.[6] There is nobility in fighting the good fight, he suggests, even when we do not believe we will succeed.

Ultimately, though, if the skeptic continues to deny the value of consistency, there is little one can say to convince them otherwise, since rational argument depends upon consistency. Such a person is in effect demanding a sound argument for why they should find sound arguments persuasive. It they stick to their guns, there is no point in arguing with them. To do falls afoul of the folksy wisdom of a needlepoint pillow I happened upon years ago: 'Never try to teach a pig to sing; it wastes your time and annoys the pig.'

Thrasymachus, whatever his other faults, is not this sort of skeptic. He is skeptical about the value of justice—we will soon see that he thinks it is a vice rather than a virtue—but he is not skeptical about the importance of consistency. Let us assume that Thrasymachus recognizes the argument as logically valid. (Since it wasn't until Aristotle that anyone worked out the notion of logical validity, it is anachronistic

---

3   Ralph Waldo Emerson, *Essays* (New York: Harper Perennial, 1995), p. 41.
4   F. Scott Fitzgerald, *The Crack-Up* (New York: New Directions Publishing, 2009), p. 69.
5   Emerson, p. 41.
6   Fitzgerald, p. 69.

to speak of Thrasymachus as recognizing the argument's validity, but doing so seems a harmless aid to clarity.) If he wants to resist its conclusion—which presumably he does, since it says that his account of justice is false—he must think at least one of the premises is false. P1 seems unassailable: at least insofar as strength is understood in terms of political power, the law-making rulers are stronger than their subjects. P2 is never challenged by Thrasymachus or anyone else, despite Socrates' bringing it up almost half a dozen times. I cannot help but think that these are winks or gentle nudges to prod readers to look more closely at P2. Thrasymachus agrees that 'it is just to obey the rulers' (1.339b), a proposition that he repeatedly assents to: 'it is just for their subjects to do whatever their rulers order' (1.339d); 'it is just for the others to obey the orders they give' (1.339e); 'it is just to obey the orders of the rulers' (1.340a). While obeying the law is typically just, we might ask whether it is always, unconditionally, just to do so, just as Socrates questioned Cephalus' definition. Many readers will think that there is a presumption in favor of obeying the laws of our communities: obedience is the default position. But fewer will think that this presumption is exceptionless, for there seem to be times when this presumption does not hold—for example, if a law is unjust. Some thinkers, among them Thomas Aquinas and Martin Luther King, go even farther and think that unjust laws are not *really* laws at all but are counterfeits, and that we should no more obey them than we should accept a $20 bill we know to be counterfeit.

P2, as I have stated it, does not merely claim that legal obedience is just; it claims that that is what justice is. It is a subtle but important difference, apparently unnoticed but accepted by Thrasymachus. When Socrates asks him, 'And whatever laws they make must be obeyed by their subjects, and this is justice ((τὸ δίκαιον) [*to dikaion*]: the just)?', he replies 'Of course' (1.339c). By adding the definite article τὸ—'the' in English—the adjective, 'just', gets promoted to a noun, 'the just', which is a typically Platonic way to talk about justice itself. On this view, all there really is to justice is obeying the rules, regardless of their content. Justice on such a view is merely a matter of convention: there are no mind- or culture-independent facts about whether something is really just or not. The only fact that makes something just is that it is a rule of one's community. If the laws of one's community mandate racial segregation, then justice requires obedience to them. Some readers—though fewer now than sixty years ago—will agree with this, holding that one should always obey the law, even laws one considers unjust, though one can work within the system to change unjust laws. Notice, too, that the conventionalism about justice expressed in P2 implies that there really is no standard by which to assess the laws of one's community as just or unjust. All there is to justice on such views is following whatever rules there are, regardless of their content, and there is no way to assess that content morally. Different communities have different rules, but if this deep cultural conventionalism or relativism is correct, no community's rules are better than any others, they are just different—and the same goes *within* a community over time: if a community allows slavery at time t_1 but abolishes it at t_2, the new legal code is not better, it is just different. This is something that few people are willing to accept, upon reflection. When we associate conventionalism and relativism with open-mindedness and tolerance of other cultures' practices and norms, they can seem attractive, but they often seem significantly less so when we examine their implications.

To draw on some vocabulary developed in the previous chapter, this conventionalism about justice is an anti-realist view: there are no culture-independent moral facts by which to morally assess the laws and norms of one's culture. The contrast between nature and convention—between what is mind- and culture-independent and what is mind- and culture-dependent—is a pervasive theme in the *Republic*. The border between Illinois and Wisconsin seems purely conventional, the result of a decision to draw the line in a particular place. The border between Wisconsin and Minnesota seems more natural, since the Mississippi and St. Croix rivers are natural objects, existing whether we think they do or not. But even this boundary is not completely natural, since it is the border only because people decided it was.

We have spent a lot of time on a view no one in the *Republic* mentions because I think Plato wants us, his readers, to do what his characters do not do, to think through issues that are ignored or given short shrift in the text. If we pause and double-click here, so to speak, examining the issues more thoroughly than Socrates' interlocutors do, we will be doing philosophy for ourselves. And if we do, we might well think that P2 is false or at least in need of serious revision, even if no one in the *Republic* questions it.

Despite Socrates' repeated prompting, Thrasymachus ignores P2. He will reject P3, which he initially assented to but now, on reflection, finds problematic. But before Thrasymachus addresses P3, Cleitophon tries to come to his rescue, suggesting that Thrasymachus' view is that justice is what the stronger *believe* to be to their advantage. In short, Cleitophon is suggesting that the Error Argument is irrelevant, since it misunderstands Thrasymachus' view. Polemarchus objects that is not what Thrasymachus said. It is telling how Socrates responds here: 'If Thrasymachus wants to put it that way now, let us accept it' (1.340c). This suggests that, contrary to what Thrasymachus says about him, Socrates is not primarily interested in winning an argument; he is interested in getting at the truth. If Cleitophon's revision more accurately reflects what Thrasymachus thinks, then that is what we should attend to, Socrates thinks. *What he meant* is more important than *what he said*, for Socrates. To think otherwise would be a foolish consistency indeed.

Thrasymachus declines to go through the door Cleitophon has opened for him, however. Instead, he does what philosophers often do: he makes a distinction between different senses of a key term or concept. Here, Thrasymachus distinguishes between the *ordinary* and *precise* senses 'ruler', claiming that P3 is true in the ordinary sense of 'ruler' but false in the precise, philosophical sense. Thus he can consistently reject the argument's conclusion, since he thinks that P3, the seemingly plausible claim that rulers sometimes err and make laws that are not to their own advantage, is false, *strictly speaking*. In the strict or precise sense, rulers do not make mistakes, he claims. 'Do you think I'd call someone who is in error stronger at the very moment he errs?' (1.340c), Thrasymachus asks.

For all his bluster and swagger, Thrasymachus shows himself capable of subtle, philosophical thought when he distinguishes between the precise and ordinary senses of terms. 'When someone makes an error in the treatment of patients', Thrasymachus asks rhetorically, 'do you call him a doctor in regard to that very error?' (1.340d) The same goes for accountants, grammarians, and any person said to possess a craft. A craftsperson, after all, possesses expertise and knowledge; the names for possessors of such expertise—carpenter, shepherd, doctor, teacher, etc.—are not merely descriptive but are to an extent normative, indicating that their possessor has earned the right to be so called. Someone might be on the roster as quarterback or employed by the university as a teacher. But if they are so bad at their jobs, we might want to withhold the name: 'He's no quarterback', says the disgruntled football fan of a now-departed player. The fan is not saying that, say, Jay Cutler did not play that position; they would be likelier to say 'he is not a quarterback' if the description is factually incorrect, if say the player were a linebacker and not a quarterback. Typically, 's/he is no *x*', where *x* is a term for a craftsperson, makes the *normative* claim that the person in question is not good enough at their craft to merit the title. It is a normative issue, rather than a descriptive one, and it extends beyond names for craftspeople, as when someone says of rap—or rock and roll or jazz, in their early days—'that's not music'. This issue, by the way, is an important one in Confucianism. Confucius and especially his follower Xunzi were concerned with the 'rectification of names (*zhengming*)', given the importance of social roles to their thinking. Someone who regularly fails to display the required filial piety does not deserve to be called a son—or, as Thrasymachus would put it, is not a son in the precise sense.

So Thrasymachus thinks that while P3 of the Error Argument is true in the ordinary, descriptive sense of 'ruler', it is false in the precise, normative sense—and that is the relevant sense here. There is a certain logic to his view. Since a craftsperson is so called because they possess the requisite knowledge, when they make a mistake, they seem to lack this knowledge—or at least they are unable to act on it at that moment. 'It is when his knowledge fails him that he makes an error', Thrasymachus says, 'and in regard to that error he is no craftsman. No craftsman, expert, or ruler makes an error at the moment when he is ruling, even though everyone will say that a physician or a ruler makes errors' (1.340e). When he agreed with P3 earlier (1.339c), he had the ordinary, imprecise sense in mind. But on the precise account—and Socrates is 'a stickler for precise accounts' (1.340e)—P3 is false, since 'no craftsman ever errs.'

There is certainly something to what Thrasymachus says. But is he overstating his case in holding that any error renders the craft-title in question inapplicable? Does expertise really require such infallibility?

A baseball player need not throw a perfect game in to be called *pitcher* in the precise sense. If Thrasymachus were right, there have only been twenty-three genuine pitchers in the history of major league baseball. It is not just that perfect games depend on more than the pitcher's skill. And it is not just a matter of human imperfection. Rather, it seems that some level of failure is consistent with possessing the relevant expertise, which is rarely an all-or-nothing matter. The best hitters in baseball, after all, make outs more often than they get hits. What level of imperfection is acceptable varies by craft: a batter who gets a hit only a third of the time is an excellent hitter; an orthopedic surgeon who successfully sets a broken bone for only a third of their cases seems far from competent.

Thrasymachus' distinction between the precise and ordinary senses of 'ruler' allows him to avoid accepting the conclusion that his definition of justice is false, since it allows him to claim, with some reason, that one of the argument's premises is false. Socrates does not challenge Thrasymachus' distinction between the ordinary and precise senses of 'ruler' (and, presumably, of other terms for experts in various crafts). Instead, he turns the distinction back against Thrasymachus in what we will call the Craft Argument.

The Craft Argument (1.341c–348b)

The heart of the Craft Argument is Socrates' insistence that craftspeople, in the strict sense, always seek to benefit their subjects, never themselves. Doctors, for example, insofar as they are doctors, seek to heal their patients; horse-breeders seek to raise healthy horses; etc. If we think of craft-knowledge as a kind of strength—as cognitive-practical strength rather than physical strength—then the expertise the craftsperson possesses is a kind of strength; thus 'crafts rule over and are stronger than the things of which they are the craft' (1.342c). Stated in premise-conclusion form, the Craft Argument begins thus:

P1   All crafts seek to benefit the objects over which they rule, not their practitioners.

P2   All objects over which a craft rules are weaker than the craft, which is stronger.

C1   So, all crafts seek to benefit the weaker, not the stronger.

The argument is valid, and though Socrates has given only a few examples in support of P1, Thrasymachus accepts it. So far, so good. Now, to get to his desired conclusion that Thrasymachus' account of justice is false, Socrates has to assume that justice is a craft; there is no way to get to a conclusion about justice without a premise about justice. Since Socrates needs to make this assumption, let us state it clearly in the second half of the Craft Argument:

P3   Justice is a craft.

C2   Therefore, justice seeks to benefit the weaker, not the stronger.

C3   Therefore, justice is not the advantage of the stronger.

This half of the argument is valid, too. C2 follows from C1 and P3 by plugging 'justice' into the general claim that all crafts seek to benefit the weaker. And then C3 follows from C2, because if justice seeks to benefit the weaker, then justice is not the advantage of the stronger.

Thrasymachus' initial reaction to the conclusion is a lesson in how *not* to react rationally to an argument: 'Tell me, Socrates do you still have a wet nurse? [...] Because she is letting you run around with a snotty nose, and does not wipe it when she needs to!' (1.343a). Needless to say, such insult-ridden responses, sadly not uncommon in cyberspace, do not pass philosophical muster. And Thrasymachus' second response is not much better. For rather than challenging one of Socrates' premises, as one should do when one rejects the conclusion of a valid argument, Thrasymachus does what many of us often do: he simply repeats his view, loudly and more stridently: 'justice is really the good of another, the advantage of the stronger ruler, and harmful to the one who obeys and serves' (1.343b). His merely repeating his view rather than engaging with Socrates' objections to it echoes Polemarchus' reminder in the opening scene that one cannot be persuaded to change one's mind if one will not listen.

Thrasymachus' responding as he does is not terribly surprising when we remember his profession: he is a sophist, a wandering teacher of rhetoric, who teaches students how to make speeches in law courts. If he is any good at his job, he can teach his students to make a speech for or against any view. 'You want to argue that the defendant is guilty? Here's how you do that. You want to argument that the defendant is innocent? Here's how you do that. You want to figure out whether the defendant is really guilty or not? Not my department.' He is a master of the art of disputation, engaging in what Plato calls *eristic*, the etymology of which is telling: *Eris* was the Greek goddess of strife; but for her rolling an apple engraved 'to the fairest' at a divine wedding reception, the Trojan War might not have happened. To be ἐριστικός (*eristikos*) is to be fond of strife, to enjoy combat—at least the verbal variety. However effective good speeches are at persuading one's listeners of pre-determined conclusions, they are not especially effective for arriving at philosophical conclusions. Socrates thinks his method of *elenchus*, the method of question-and-answer that proceeds from premises his interlocutor agrees to, is a better way to get at the truth. Now if you already know—or, like Thrasymachus, think you know— the truth about an issue, a rhetorically sound speech (or op-ed piece or book) may be the best way to bring your audience around to your view. But if, like Socrates, you do not think you know the answer to the question, Socratic cross-examination seems a better way to get at the truth, whatever it will turn out to be. 'Whatever direction the argument blows us', Socrates says a bit later in the *Republic*, 'that is where we must go' (3.394d). Where Thrasymachus draws on his rhetorical skills to get to that pre-determined end, Socrates will accept 'the [answer] that seems right to me after I have investigated the matter' (1.337c). This difference between their approaches is ultimately the difference between indoctrination and inquiry.

It is a shame that Thrasymachus is unwilling or unable to query Socrates' argument, for it is not as airtight as Socrates seems to think it is. As is often the case in the *Republic*, we will have to do for one of the interlocutors what they cannot or will not do for themselves. For starters, Thrasymachus might question P1, the claim that all crafts seek to benefit their objects, not their practitioners. The trouble here is not that the argument Socrates gave in support of P1 is too brief, although it is that. From just a few examples of crafts that aim at the benefit of their objects rather than their practitioners, Socrates arrives at a general conclusion that all crafts are like this. Perhaps more examples would strengthen this inductive argument.

A more serious problem with the Craft Argument is that Socrates himself provides a counterexample to its first premise when he introduces 'the craft of wage-earning' (1.346c). Crafts are distinguished by their different ends and their different means for achieving their ends—that is, by their different functions: 'every craft differ[s] from every other in having a different function' (1.346a). The function of a doctor, *in the precise sense,* is healing patients, not making money. And similarly for the other crafts Socrates lists: navigation, horse-breeding, etc. Making money is the function of a different craft, the craft of wage-earning or money-making. If doctors and horse-breeders and ship-captains and teachers benefit financially from practicing their crafts, it is because they possess another craft, the craft of wage-earning. Many readers will be familiar with chefs and carpenters and doctors who are truly expert at their crafts but who lack business sense. At the other end of the spectrum are those 'famous for being famous' celebrities whose only discernible skill is money-making, an ability to monetize their otherwise-devoid-of-accomplishment existences. By now the point is probably obvious: the craft of money-making is practiced for the benefit of the practitioner. While medicine and teaching are other-focused, wage-earning is self-focused: it benefits the craftsperson. And it is true that you might practice this craft altruistically, as when you want to earn more money so you can better provide for your family or community, but the craft itself aims to benefit the craftsperson.

So right off the bat, Thrasymachus has grounds to resist the conclusion that his definition is false. Of course, the conclusion of an unsound argument might still be true. Just as there is nothing inconsistent about a juror thinking the defendant actually committed the crime in question but voting to acquit because the state did not prove its case beyond a reasonable doubt, there is nothing inconsistent in believing that the conclusion of an unsound or invalid argument is true. If Thrasymachus were more fair-minded, he might concede that his definition of justice might *be* false but insist that Socrates has not *shown* that it is.

Another and perhaps better option for Thrasymachus is to cast doubt on P3, the claim that justice is a craft. As noted above, this is an implicit assumption of the argument, not an explicit claim—though Socrates did assert it earlier, in arguing against Polemarchus: 'what does the craft we call justice give, and to whom or what does it give it?' (1.332d) This would be a good move for Thrasymachus to make, since we already have good reason to think that P3 is false: while crafts and character virtues are similar in many ways, crafts are morally neutral whereas character virtues are not. If justice is not a craft, then the general claim that crafts are other-focused would not apply to it. Now it looks like the argument is doubly unsound, since we have good reason to doubt both P1 and P3, so Thrasymachus is not rationally compelled to accept its conclusion. Socrates might reply that even if justice is not a craft, ruling is. But then the Craft Argument's conclusion needs to be changed as well, which stymies Socrates' attempt to make progress toward understanding what *justice* is by showing what it is not. The argument so modified would not be a refutation of Thrasymachus' definition of justice but rather of the view that rulers, in the precise sense, seek not their own benefit but rather the benefit of those they rule. We might think this is true, at least of *good* rulers, but Thrasymachus could here raise the problems with P1, reminding Socrates that his own example of wage-earning is a counterexample to the general claim that crafts are not practiced primarily for the benefit of the craftsperson. Why not think ruling is analogous to wage-earning, Thrasymachus could ask, and aims at the benefit of the ruler? At the very least, Socrates has not given him compelling reasons to think that it is not.

An important lesson here is how interlinked the arguments of the *Republic* are. Earlier I suggested that the important conclusion to draw from Socrates' attempted refutation of Polemarchus was not the one he explicitly drew but rather that justice and other moral virtues are not crafts. Whether this was the lesson Plato hoped we'd learn is beside the point, at least to the extent that one goal in reading the *Republic* is to do philosophy ourselves, to engage in imaginary dialogue with Socrates as we try to get at or at least close to the truth of the matter. If the assumption that justice is a craft is false, its reappearing as a premise here undermines the Craft Argument.

The Outdoing Argument (1.348b–350d)

Even if the Craft Argument is unsound, it explicitly raises the *Republic's* second main question of whether the just life is happier than the unjust life. This question's urgency leads Socrates to leap-frog the more theoretical question of the nature of justice in favor of the practical question of 'which whole way of life would make living most worthwhile for each of us' (1.344e).

Modern moral philosophy often focuses on particular actions, especially choices in dilemmas. Sometimes the dilemmas are intentionally artificial, to bring out larger moral principles lurking in the background. Many readers will be familiar with 'the trolley problem' and its numerous variations: is it permissible to divert a runaway trolley car onto a track where it will kill one worker if doing so will save five people working on the track the trolley is on? Other times, the dilemmas are more the stuff of everyday life: is aborting a pre-viability fetus permissible or not? Socrates' question is far more general than these, as it concerns *whole ways of life* rather than particular actions. It concerns not so much what we ought to do as 'the way we ought to live' (1.352d). Socrates' approach focuses on persons rather than actions and takes the unit of evaluation to be lives rather than choices and actions. This approach, known as Virtue Ethics, has enjoyed a resurgence among moral philosophers in recent years, and though virtue ethicists often look to Aristotle for inspiration, we see its roots in the ethical thought of Plato and Socrates. This virtue-centric concern comes to the fore almost immediately in the third of Socrates' arguments against Thrasymachus, the Outdoing Argument, to which we now turn.

Since Socrates has shifted his attention from the first to the second of the *Republic*'s main questions, his aim now is not to refute Thrasymachus' definition of justice but rather Thrasymachus' claim that 'complete injustice is more profitable than complete justice' (1.348c). The question of whether a just life is happier than an unjust one has great practical implications, given the overwhelmingly plausible assumption that each of us wants to be happy. Few of us would dispute that the just life is *morally* better than the unjust life; the issue here is whether the just life is *prudentially* better—whether, as we put it in the Introduction, having a good life requires leading a good life. Thrasymachus thinks not, since 'a just man always gets less than an unjust one' (1.343d). If Thrasymachus is right about which life is happier, then each of us has a strong reason to act unjustly: if a just or morally good life is always at odds with happiness, living a just life will inevitably frustrate a core desire each of us has. Socrates argues that, despite its apparent plausibility, Thrasymachus' view is profoundly mistaken, since morality and happiness are *not* fundamentally at odds with each other. Far from being an impediment to happiness, a just life is at least a necessary condition of a happy life, on Socrates' view, since we cannot be happy unless we are just.

Thrasymachus understands happiness in terms of material success, in terms of power and its trappings. On his view, the more a person *gets*, the happier they will be. Life is a competition between people striving to outdo each other where the winner is the person who is able to bend others to their will. Few people, I trust, try to inculcate Thrasymachus' materialism and egoism in their children. Socrates' last words, nearly, to the jury that found him guilty of impiety and sentenced him to death, are a request for a favor:

> When my sons grow up, gentlemen, if you think they are putting money or anything else before goodness, take your revenge by plaguing them as I have plagued you; and if they fancy themselves for no reason, you must scold them as I scolded you, for neglecting the important things and thinking they are good for something when they are good for nothing. If you do this, I shall have had justice at your hands, both I myself and my children.[7]

Despite his profound disagreement with Thrasymachus' materialistic conception of human flourishing, Socrates does not argue *directly* against it but instead, in a pattern that by now is familiar, he tries to show Thrasymachus that a key premise he believes in—here, that the unjust person 'outdoes everyone else' (1.344a)—does not support and in fact is at odds with the conclusion Thrasymachus holds.

This notion of *outdoing* is central to the Outdoing Argument. The Greek word is πλεονεξία (*pleonexia*); etymologically it is a combination of *pleon* (more) and *echein* (to have). Thrasymachus' unjust person wants to have more than anyone else and recognizes no legitimate moral constraints on his pursuit of his goal. Fans of classic cinema will find a fine example of *pleonexia* in John Huston's 1948 film, *Key Largo*, starring Humphrey Bogart, Lauren Bacall, and Edward G. Robinson. In a confrontation between Frank McCloud (Bogart) and Johnny Rocco (Robinson), McCloud tells captive innkeeper James Temple (Lionel Barrymore), that he knows what Rocco wants:

---

7   *Plato: Five Dialogues: Euthyphro, Apology, Crito, Meno, Phaedo,* trans. by G. M. A. Grube (Indianapolis: Hackett Publishing, 1981), p. 44 (41e–42a).

McCloud:	He wants more, don't you, Rocco?
Rocco:	Yeah. That's it. More. That's right! I want more!
Temple:	Will you ever get enough?
McCloud:	Will you, Rocco?
Rocco:	Well, I never have. No, I guess I won't. You, do you know what you want?
McCloud:	Yes, I had hopes once, but I gave them up.
Rocco:	Hopes for what?
McCloud:	A world in which there is no place for Johnny Rocco.[8]

Rocco's insatiable desire for more is the heart of *pleonexia*. It is almost as though the object of this desire is secondary: whatever people want, the pleonectic person wants more of it, wants to outdo everyone else. The rest of us, not strong enough to bend others to our wills to get what we want, live in fear of the Johnny Roccos of the world, those amoral creatures who are strong enough to bend us to their will to get what they want. Glaucon, playing devil's advocate, will soon articulate the Thrasymachan view that justice is a deal the weak make to protect themselves against the caprice of the stronger. 'Those who reproach injustice', Thrasymachus says, do so not because they are afraid of doing it but of suffering it' (1.344c). If enough of us weak folk band together and gain political power, we can make laws that protect us against the Thrasymachuses and Roccos of the world. After all, that is all justice is, in the conventionalist view Thrasymachus articulated at the outset: the rules the politically powerful make to serve their own interests.

We should note, though, that Thrasymachus shifts gears at the outset of the Outdoing Argument and articulates a view that does not square with his conventionalism. For he counts injustice not as a vice but as a virtue:

Socrates:	Do you call one of the two a virtue and the other a vice?
Thrasymachus:	Of course.
Socrates:	That is to say, you call justice a virtue and injustice a vice?

---

8   *Key Largo*, dir. by John Huston, prod. by Jerry Wald (Warner Bros., 1948).

Thrasymachus:	That is hardly likely, since I say that injustice is profitable and justice is not...
Socrates:	Do you really include injustice with virtue and wisdom, and justice with their opposites?
Thrasymachus:	I certainly do. (1.348c–e)

Thrasymachus is here articulating *immoralism*, the view that what most people think of as the wrong way to act is actually the right way: what are conventionally thought to be character vices are actually virtues. Unlike the conventionalism Thrasymachus expressed earlier, immoralism is a realist view: there are mind-independent moral facts that provide standards by which to evaluate a society's conventions and norms. Athenian culture takes justice to be a virtue and injustice to be a vice. Here, Thrasymachus is saying that Athenian culture get this backwards, since injustice is really the virtue and justice the vice.

Thrasymachus' immoralism makes sense when we pair the last chapter's discussion of what a virtue is with his materialistic conception of human flourishing. A virtue is the condition that enables a thing to perform its function well. So a knife's virtue is sharpness, since that is what enables the knife to cut well. If our function is to outdo others, to get more stuff, then of course injustice is a virtue and justice is a vice, since injustice enables and justice prevents our getting more than others: 'a just man always gets less than an unjust one' (1.343d).

Socrates notices the challenge posed by Thrasymachus' shift to immoralism: 'it is not easy to know what to say' (1.348e) in light of Thrasymachus' jettisoning the moral order that would usually serve as the background of a conversation like this. But he cannot simply presuppose the usual background without begging the question—that is, without assuming the truth of what he is trying to prove—against Thrasymachus: he needs to *argue* against Thrasymachus' immoralism, not just *assume* it is wrong and that the traditional moral order, on which justice is a virtue and injustice a vice, is correct. Socrates' direct target in the Outdoing Argument is Thrasymachus' immoralist view that justice is the vice and injustice is the virtue; if he can show this, he will knock out the support for Thrasymachus' view that the unjust life is happier than the just life.

Thrasymachus thinks that an unjust person tries to outdo everyone—and if they are sufficiently good at being bad, they will succeed. He thinks that the just person, by contrast, is a simpleton, easily duped by the more crafty and complicated unjust person. Socrates gets Thrasymachus to agree that the just person seeks to outdo only unjust people, but Thrasymachus is skeptical that the person will succeed at this, being so 'polite and innocent' (1.349b). Socrates once again appeals to the analogy between crafts and virtues: a craftsperson, he argues, tries to outperform the person lacking the craft in question, while the craft-lacking person tries to outdo everyone. Thrasymachus agrees to this, and also to Socrates' claim that a craftsperson is wise and good, which makes sense at least with respect to the craft in question. A skilled carpenter possesses a kind of technical wisdom, knowing how to build a wrap-around deck or a roll-top desk, for example. The person who lacks the craft, by contrast, is ignorant and bad: they lack the craftsperson's knowledge and are not, for example, a good carpenter—they are not properly called a carpenter at all, if Thrasymachus' earlier point about the precise sense of craft-terms is correct. The craftsperson, Socrates thinks, wants to perform the craft in question better than someone who lacks it, not someone who possesses it: they want to outdo those unlike them, not those like them. The craft-lacking person, by contrast, wants to outperform everyone, both those like them and those unlike them. Similarly, the just person wants to outdo unjust people, those unlike them, while the unjust person wants to outdo everyone, both those like and those unlike them.

If all of this is correct, the just person resembles the craftsperson, since each wants to outdo only those unlike them, the unjust and craft-lacking person, while the unjust person resembles the craft-lacking person, wanting to outdo everyone, both those unlike them and those like them. Since 'each of them has the qualities of the people he is like' (1.349d) and Thrasymachus has agreed that the craftsperson is good and wise, while the craft-lacking person is neither, it follows that the just person is good and wise while the unjust person is neither; from there it is a short trip to the conclusion that 'justice is virtue and wisdom and that injustice is vice and ignorance' (1.350d).

Since most of us, I assume, are not immoralists, we will agree with Socrates' conclusion. But as often is the case in Book I, Socrates' argument for his conclusion is problematic. The first problem is that the argument relies on the analogy between crafts and virtues, a troublesome analogy that bedevils much of Book I. Given the difference between character virtues and crafts—the latter are morally neutral while the former are not—why should Thrasymachus accept the claim that 'each has the qualities of the one he resembles' (1.350c)? After all, the kinds of knowledge the just and skilled persons require are very different. In possessing a skill, the craftsperson possesses a morally neutral knowledge of how to do certain things. As Socrates noted in his argument with Polemarchus, the craftsperson can use their skills for good or ill: a doctor can use their medical expertise to heal or kill. Even someone who possesses a skill that seems intrinsically bad— imagine, say, an assassin—can use that skill for good ends as well as bad: assassinating Hitler seems a good thing. The lesson here is that arguments from analogy rise and fall on the presence of relevant similarities and dissimilarities, respectively, between the things being compared. Given the important dissimilarity between crafts and virtues, Thrasymachus would be right to push back on this premise.

Another problem with the Outdoing Argument, which many readers will have already noticed, is that its very first premise, the claim that the skilled person seeks to outdo only the unskilled person rather than another skilled person, seems to be not merely false but obviously false. Socrates is probably correct that when it comes to *tuning* the lyre, the lyre-player wants to do better than a non-musician. Where there is one correct way to do something, genuine experts will do that thing in the same way. But when it comes to *playing* the lyre, for example, rather than merely *tuning* it, a skilled musician does not merely want to play better than a non-musician—that is not much of an achievement—they want to outperform another lyre-player. Readers might be puzzled by Socrates' confident assertion that 'a doctor [...] when prescribing food and drink [...] want[s] to outdo a nondoctor' (1.350a), given how competitive doctors can be. Some doctors are better diagnosticians than others, some cellists are better at playing Bach than others, some philosophers are better at interpreting Plato than others, some investors are better at spotting under-valued companies than others, etc. Developing these skills is often fueled at least in part by competition and a desire to outperform—to outdo, as Socrates puts it—other experts: the desire to be the best at x-ing, whatever x may be.

So even setting aside the *dis*analogy between crafts and virtues, the Outdoing Argument flounders because its key premise is false or at least highly questionable; at the very least, it needs more defense than it gets.

Even if we agree with Socrates that Thrasymachus' immoralism is mistaken, we can see that the Outdoing Argument is far from conclusive against it. Perhaps a lesson here is that being too personally invested in one's views, as Thrasymachus seems to be, can get in the way of adequately defending them. If I see your argument as refuting *me* rather than refuting a view I hold, as attacking me as a person rather than a premise or principle I subscribe to, I may well react as Thrasymachus does. Earlier he responded to the Error Argument with a literally snotty put-down of Socrates; here he is tamer in defeat, blushing and producing 'a quantity of sweat that was a wonder to behold' (1.350d). But clearly a more dispassionate attitude would serve him better. After all, if the goal is to discover the truth about justice, seeing that one's view was mistaken is actually something to welcome, since by clearing away false views we get closer to the truth. Such an attitude is a tall order for most of us, but even if we think it is not fully achievable, given human nature, it does present an ideal to which we can aspire.

The Common Purpose Argument (1.350d–352d)

There is a discernible change in Thrasymachus' demeanor after the Outdoing Argument, one noted by Glaucon towards the beginning of Book II: 'I think that Thrasymachus gave up before he had to, charmed by you as if he were a snake' (2.358b). Thrasymachus thinks his immoralism, a view he regarded as bold and daring, has been refuted, and since speech-making has been ruled out, he announces that he will just agree with Socrates from here on. In again urging Thrasymachus not to answer 'contrary to his own opinion' (1.350c), Socrates reminds us of the nature of Socratic cross-examination, which is personal in the sense of its aiming to help the person being questioned to discover the truth by examining how well their views hang together or if they hang together at all. Especially when the topic is an important one like justice, being in error can have disastrous consequences. In the conclusion of Book I of his *Treatise of Human Nature* David Hume famously said,

'Generally speaking, the errors in religion are dangerous; those in philosophy only ridiculous'.[9] Socrates could not disagree more, since so much hangs on the philosophical question of whether the just life is happier than the unjust life. (Hume, in response, would think that philosophical questions have far less effect on how we live our lives than Socrates thinks; far from being able to govern our conduct, 'reason is and ought only to be the slave of the passions, and can never pretend to any office than to serve and obey them'.[10]) If Thrasymachus is mistaken that the unjust life is a happier life, this mistake is not merely theoretical or conceptual or abstractly philosophical, for 'the argument concerns no ordinary topic but the way we ought to live' (1.352d); it is a mistake that will have profound implications for the quality of one's life. If Socrates is right about justice, then Thrasymachus' view is a prescription for a life of glittering misery.

So it is a shame that Thrasymachus gives up, for the final two arguments of Book I deserve more scrutiny than they get. The first of these is the Common Purpose Argument, which aims to refute Thrasymachus' claim that 'injustice is stronger and more powerful than justice' (1.351a). This claim is implied by the immoralist view that Socrates tried to refute with the Outdoing Argument. Thrasymachus thinks that injustice empowers its possessor to outdo everyone, to take control of and rule a city-state. Socrates argues that Thrasymachus has woefully misidentified injustice's power: 'injustice has the power, first, to make whatever it arises in—whether it is a city, a family, an army or anything else—incapable of achieving anything as a unit, because of the civil wars and differences it creates, and, second, it makes that unit an enemy to itself' (1.351e).

Socrates' idea is that even a criminal gang cannot successfully achieve its goals unless some kind of justice regulates the gangsters' dealings with each other. Spelled out in premise-conclusion form, the Common Purpose Argument goes something like this:

P1   If x enables successful common action and y prevents this, then x is stronger than y.

---

9   David Hume, *A Treatise on Human Nature*, ed. by L. A. Selby-Bigge, 2nd ed., rev. by P. H. Nidditch (Oxford: Clarendon Press, 1987), p. 272 [Book I, Part iv, Section 7].

10   Hume, *Treatise*, p. 415 [II.iii.3].

P2   Justice enables and injustice prevents successful common action.

C   Therefore, justice is stronger than injustice.

The argument is logically valid—its conclusion must be true if its premises are true—and its premises seem in fact true, so it is sound, to boot. As the preceding arguments have all been problematic, this success almost seems worth celebrating. But before Socrates and company start with the ancient Athenian equivalent of high-fiving, they would do well to pause and note that even if the argument is sound, the conclusion it establishes seems too weak, for it shows that justice is merely instrumentally good, useful for any group to achieve its goals, be they just or unjust. Socrates thinks that justice (and especially a reputation for possessing it) is instrumentally good, but presumably he wants to show that justice is also intrinsically good—that its goodness is internal and not dependent merely on the external benefits it brings about, that all by itself it makes its possessor better off. If justice helps a criminal enterprise be more unjust, then it is hard to see how it is a moral virtue; instead, it seems to be just another skill or craft and merely conditionally good: it is good when aimed at good ends and bad when aimed at bad ends.

So even though the Common Purpose Argument is sound, it does not seem to prove what it ought to prove. It is a shame that Thrasymachus' wounded pride prevents him from challenging the Common Purpose Argument. If he had, Socrates might have given it up, or perhaps on reflection he might have regrouped and responded that the argument shows at least that Thrasymachus' immoralism is incorrect. After all, Thrasymachus thinks injustice is a virtue and justice is a vice because the former enables and the latter prevents its possessor from achieving happiness: immoralism implies that injustice is stronger than justice. So in showing that the opposite is true, that justice is stronger than injustice, Socrates shows that immoralism is false. So even if the Common Purpose Argument comes to the wrong conclusion about the nature of justice, it still packs a punch against Thrasymachus' immoralism.

The Function Argument (1.352d–354c)

The last argument in Book I reprises and repurposes some concepts employed earlier in Book I and discussed in the last chapter, especially the nature of a virtue. Socrates seems to regard it as a knock-down argument that the just life is happier than the unjust life, but we will see that even he is ultimately dissatisfied with it.

The ideas of *virtue* and *function* came up earlier in Book I, in one of Socrates' arguments against Polemarchus' view that justice is helping friends and harming enemies. A thing's function is its goal-directed purpose, the activity characteristic of things of its kind. So a knife's function is cutting, a heart's function is pumping blood, etc. Socrates 'define[s] the function of a horse or anything else as that which one can do only with it or best with it' (1.352e). So even though one can cut with a spoon or a fingernail, cutting is a knife's function since a knife cuts best. A virtue, we have seen, is what enables a thing to perform its function well: 'anything that has a function performs it well by means of its own peculiar virtue and badly by means of its vice' (1.353c). Thus a knife's virtue is sharpness, because sharpness enables a knife to cut well. Since we make knives and other tools to perform certain tasks, it is easy to see an artifact's function and virtue. But natural objects like hearts, eyes, and kidneys, have functions, too. And indeed, in the Function Argument, Socrates is concerned about the function and virtue of the soul (ψυχή [*psuchê*], whence the word 'psyche' (the upsilon is often transliterated as a 'y', so *psuchê* becomes *psyche,* for example)). Though Socrates will later argue that the soul is immortal, it is best not to read any religious beliefs into 'soul' here. Instead, think of a soul as a life-force. All living things have souls on this view. Indeed, Aristotle will distinguish between vegetative souls, which enable metabolic processes, sentient souls, which enable feeling and locomotion, and rational souls, which enable thought. Humans, he thinks, have all three, and non-human animals have the first two. Thus Socrates asks, 'What of living? Is not that a function of a soul?' (1.353d) He then claims, and Thrasymachus half-heartedly agrees, that 'justice is a soul's virtue and injustice its vice' (1.353e). He made this claim earlier, in the argument with Polemarchus: 'But is not justice human virtue?' (1.335c). Just as a sharp knife cuts well, a just soul lives well. And what is happiness but living well? Thus Socrates concludes that 'a just person is happy, and an unjust one is wretched' (1.354a). Spelled out in premise-conclusion form, the Function Argument looks like this:

P1   A thing's virtue enables its function to be performed well. (1.353c)

P2   Living is a function of the soul. (1.353d)

P3   Justice is a soul's virtue, injustice a vice. (1.353e)

C1   So, the just person lives well; the unjust person lives poorly. (1.353e)

P4   Happiness is living well; unhappiness is living poorly. (1.354a)

C2   So, the just person is happy; the unjust person is unhappy. (1.354a)

The argument is logically well constructed: if its premises are true its conclusions must be true. But even if we agree with Socrates that its premises are true, we might wish that Thrasymachus would push back a bit, for it is not clear that we are justified in thinking them true.

P1 is unproblematic: it is just a definition of what a virtue or excellence is. But we might worry that P2 is weaker than it needs to be: living needs to be *the* function of the soul, not merely *a* function of the soul, for the argument to work. While one cannot be just—or unjust, for that matter—if one is not alive, it is hard to see how mere biological life is the issue here. A deeper worry is P3, which Thrasymachus is already on record as rejecting: on his immoralist view, injustice is the virtue and justice the vice. While we might agree that Socrates was right to reject Thrasymachus' immoralism, if we are fair-minded we should concede that his argument for doing so leaves much to be desired, relying on both a false equivalence between skills and virtues and on the false premise that the skilled person seeks to outdo only the unskilled person. The Common Purpose Argument gives an indirect reason for thinking P3 is true and thus that Thrasymachus' immoralism is false, but it is overly dependent on the bad analogy between skills and virtues. What Thrasymachus should do, but does not do, is to push back and argue that Socrates may well be correct that the just life is happier, but the Function Argument does not prove it, since two of its key premises may well be false and at the very least Socrates has not given us reasons for thinking they are true. Book I would be very different if Thrasymachus gave Socrates more of a run for his money.

Socrates himself is dissatisfied at the end of Book I, and he seems to implicitly acknowledge that his arguments—especially the last one—rely on premises that Thrasymachus finds doubtful and that even sympathetic but fair-minded readers wish were better supported. Moreover, Socrates recognizes a flaw in his procedure: he started to address the *Republic*'s second question of which life is happier before answering the first question on the nature of justice. It is a moment of typical Socratic insight: 'the result of the discussion, as far as I am concerned, is that I know nothing, for when I do not know what justice is, I will hardly know whether it is a kind of virtue or not, or whether a person who has it is happy or unhappy' (1.354c).

So Socrates himself realizes that he is not really justified in asserting the Function Argument's key premise, P3. It is not that he thinks it is false; he has not gone over to Thrasymachan immoralism. But he recognizes that he has not given the immoralist a good reason to change their mind, and he has not given himself a good reason to believe what he believes.

Several years ago, Donald Rumsfeld's talk of 'the known unknown' was held up to some ridicule or at least befuddlement in the popular media. But one need not approve of Rumsfeld's role in the Second Gulf War to appreciate the essentially Socratic nature of the point he was making. There are things that we know, and we know that we know them: our names, where we live, etc. And there are things that many of us do not know—what the capital of Belarus is, Ted Williams' lifetime batting average, how to play the cello—and we probably know that we do not know them. But it is those things that we do not even know that we do not know that can be a source of trouble, as any student who discovers, during an exam, that they now know that they do not know something... Had they come to this higher-order awareness before the exam, they could have asked their professor or a classmate for help. As is so often the case in other areas of life, timing is everything in moving from not knowing that we do not know something to knowing that we do not know it.

Coming to this kind of higher-order knowledge is often an epiphany; it certainly was for Socrates when he realized that his wisdom consisted in his not thinking he knew what he did not know—in his knowing what he did not know (*Apology* 20d–21e). And the same goes at the end of Book I, when he realizes that he does not yet know what justice is, and thus that the arguments he is given that the just life is happier rely on premises he is really not entitled to assert. He is displaying a kind of intellectual humility that is sadly in short supply in our age (as it was in his). Even if his interlocutors have not challenged him when they could have and should have, Socrates does not let himself get away with thinking he knows something he does not know.

While Book I ends on a down-note, we will see in the next chapter that there is reason yet for optimism.

Some Suggestions for Further Reading

For an excellent discussion of the notion of virtue, interested readers should see Heather Battaly, *Virtue* (Malden, MA: Polity Press, 2015).

Readers interested in Confucius' views on the strict senses of terms will find them in Book 13, chapter 3 of his *Analects*. *The Analects of Confucius: A Philosophical Translation*, trans. by Roger Ames and Henry Rosemont (New York: Ballantine Books, 1998) is excellent and includes a very helpful introduction. The later Confucian Xunzi (aka Hsun Tzu) explores the issue in greater depth in chapter 22 of the text that bears his name. Interested readers should see *Xunzi: The Complete Text*, trans. by Eric Hutton (Princeton: Princeton University Press, 2014), https://doi.org/10.2307/j.ctt6wq19b

Readers interested in the historical Thrasymachus will find fragments of his work in *The Greek Sophists*, ed. by J. Dillon and T. Gergel (New York: Penguin Books, 2003).

There are many discussions of Socrates' encounter with Thrasymachus. An excellent one to start with is Roslyn Weiss, 'Wise Guys and Smart Alecks in *Republic* 1 and 2', in *The Cambridge Companion to Plato's 'Republic'*, ed. by G. Ferrari (New York: Cambridge University Press, 2007), pp. 90–115, https://doi.org/10.1017/ccol0521839637.004

Readers interested in relativism might start with chapters two and three of James Rachels and Stuart Rachels, *The Elements of Moral Philosophy*, 8th ed. (New York: McGraw-Hill, 2014).

Thomas Aquinas, *Treatise on Law*, trans. by Richard J. Regan (Indianapolis: Hackett Publishing, 2000), is the *locus classicus* for the view that unjust laws are not really laws; interested readers will also want to see Martin Luther King Jr., 'Letter from Birmingham Jail', in *Why We Can't Wait* (New York: Signet Classics, 2000), pp. 76–95, for a modern application of that view.

Readers interested in a scholarly treatment of Socrates' method might start with Gregory Vlastos, 'The Socratic *elenchus*—Method Is All', in Vlastos, *Socratic Studies*, ed. by Myles Burnyeat (New York: Cambridge University Press, 1994), pp. 1–29.

For readers intrigued by the concept of irony, there is no better place to begin than the first chapter of Gregory Vlastos, *Socrates, Ironist and Moral Philosopher* (Ithaca: Cornell University Press, 1991), pp. 21–44.

Franz Caucig, *Socrates with a Disciple and Diotima* (1810). Photograph
by Sporti (2014), Wikimedia, Public Domain, https://commons.
wikimedia.org/wiki/File:Franc_Kav%C4%8Di%C4%8D_-_
Sokrat_z_u%C4%8Dencem_in_Diotimo.jpg#/media/File:Franc_
Kavčič_-_Sokrat_z_učencem_in_Diotimo.jpg

3. A Fresh Start

Book II

Socrates is not the only one who is dissatisfied with the results—the non-results, really—of Book I. Glaucon and Adeimantus feel let down, too. It is not that they have been convinced by Thrasymachus. Quite the contrary. They agree with Socrates that the just life is happier than the unjust life, but they do not find Socrates' arguments persuasive and thus they recognize that they cannot defend or justify that belief, to themselves or others. We could put their predicament thus: they *believe* that the just life is happier, but they do not *know* that it is—and they know that they do not know this.

When thinking about knowledge—more precisely, about propositional or factual knowledge, the kind of knowledge involved in knowing *that* certain claims are true, in contrast to the knowing *how* to do certain things, the sort of knowledge that is distinctive of the skills and crafts discussed in earlier chapters—a good place to start is to think of knowledge as a matter of justified true belief. On the JTB conception of knowledge, so-called because it defines knowledge as Justified True Belief, I *know* that the White Sox won the 2005 World Series because I *believe* that they won, my belief that they did is *justified* (since it is based on good reasons: I watched (and re-watched) the deciding game, I have confirmed their victory on various reliable websites, etc.), and that belief is *true*. We all have various beliefs that are true but unjustified and beliefs that are false but justified. For example, looking at the usually reliable and accurate clock on my office wall, I form the belief that it is half-past eight and thus that I still have time for some last-minute preparation and

     https://doi.org/10.11647/OBP.0229.03

perhaps another coffee before my nine o'clock class. But unbeknownst to me the clock is malfunctioning because of a power surge, and it is actually a quarter past nine (and most of my students have given up on me). Even though my belief is false, it seems justified, since my evidence is a clock that has always been reliable. More on point, though, are cases in which my belief is true but unjustified. Suppose that I know that my clock is wildly inconsistent, speeding up and slowing down with no rhyme or reason. Even so, I come to believe that it is eight o'clock after glancing at the clock. Even if it is eight o'clock, I am inclined to think that I do not know that it is eight o'clock, because my belief, while true, is not justified: it is based on evidence I myself regard as unreliable. Similarly, suppose I 'just have a feeling' that the White Sox will win today, and suppose further that my gut-feelings about the outcomes of baseball games are not especially reliable, being wrong at least as often as they are right. Even if the Sox win, you would be right to disagree when I say, 'I knew they would win today!', since a crucial element in knowledge, namely justification, is missing.

Even though the JTB conception of knowledge does not feature in the *Republic,* it has its roots in another of Plato's dialogues, the *Theaetetus,* where Socrates and Theaetetus consider (among other things) whether 'it is true judgment with an account (λόγος [*logos*]) that is knowledge' (201d).[1] They ultimately reject the JTB account because, ironically, they cannot come up with a satisfactory account of what an account or reason is. We will see in Chapter Eight that Socrates has a very different conception of knowledge in the *Republic.* But even though the JTB conception of knowledge lacks Platonic *bona fides* (not to mention contemporary philosophical disagreements about what justifies beliefs and indeed about whether knowledge is best thought of as JTB), it is helpful in understanding the dynamics of Books II and III. Glaucon and Adeimantus, having been raised properly, have (let us assume) a true belief about the relation between justice and happiness. But they recognize that they lack a justification for this true belief, and they hope Socrates can help provide them with one. We saw in the previous chapter that Socrates' arguments in support of this belief leave a great deal to be

---

1   As before, '201d' refers to the page in the standard edition of Plato's works. Translations of the *Theaetetus* are from *Plato: Theaetetus,* trans. by M. J. Levett, rev. by Myles Burnyeat, ed. by Bernard Williams (Indianapolis: Hackett Publishing, 1992).

desired, a fact of which Socrates as well as Glaucon and Adeimantus are painfully aware. Thrasymachus, for his part, would insist that Glaucon and Adeimantus do not know that the just life is happier, not because they lack a justification for their true belief, but because their belief is false: the just life is *not* happier than the unjust life, on his view.

The most striking feature of their request for help is their asking Socrates *not* to proceed as he did in Book I and 'give us [yet another] theoretical argument that justice is stronger than injustice' (2.367b). Nor are they asking Socrates to become more like Thrasymachus and give long speeches. But they also do not want him to crank out argument after argument, as he did in Book I. They are reasonably bright young men, but they are not philosophically sophisticated, and want something that is convincing without being too abstract.

Glaucon's approach in seeking a justification for his belief that the just life is happier is twofold. First, he makes a distinction between three different kinds of goods, which will help them clarify the kind of good Socrates should show justice to be. Second, he articulates three claims or theses that he thinks capture the heart of Thrasymachus' position, adopting the role of devil's advocate. It is not, Glaucon assures Socrates, that he believes any of these Thrasymachan claims (2.358c, 2.361e). But if Socrates can show him how to refute these theses, Glaucon's belief that the just life is happier will inch closer to being justified.

Three Kinds of Goods (2.357a–358a)

There is healthy scholarly disagreement about the details of Glaucon's division of goods, but we can get a good sense of the division without getting tripped up in a scholarly tangle. For the sake of clarity, I will depart slightly from Glaucon's ordering, switching the second and third categories.

The first kind of good comprises *intrinsic goods*, which 'we welcome not because we desire what comes from it, but [...] for its own sake—joy, for example, and all the harmless pleasures that have no results beyond the joy of having them' (2.357b). The idea is that we value certain things, experiences, and activities in and for themselves and not for their consequences. This way of putting it is not quite right, though. Possessing these goods makes our lives go better, and having one's life go better because one possesses x seems to be a consequence of possessing x. We can get clearer about what Glaucon means if we think of the relation between such goods and a good life as a part-whole relation, rather than a means-end relation. Enjoying a sunset is not a means to having a good life, it is part of a good life. To modify an example from the philosopher John Akrill (which he made in a different but related context), driving to a golf course is a means to playing a round of golf that is external to the game: I drive to the course in order to play a round. I drive the ball off the tee and putt in order to play a round of golf, but these activities are not external means to playing golf, as driving to the course is; they are constituent elements or internal parts of playing a round of golf. So Glaucon's intrinsic goods are constituent parts or elements of a good life conceived as a whole; they are not external, instrumental means to such a life.

Where first category goods are best thought of in terms of the part-whole relation, the second category (which Glaucon takes third) contains things, activities, and experiences that are best thought of as means to an end external to them. We can think of such goods as *instrumental* rather than intrinsic goods. Glaucon takes them to be 'onerous but beneficial' (2.357c), valued not in themselves but for 'the rewards and other things that come from them' (2.357c). Physical training and medical treatment (and, it will later turn out, governing) are offered as examples of such instrumental goods. There is a certain subjectivity here, though, as some people find physical training enjoyable in itself, even apart from its instrumental benefits. Some people love running, for example, enjoying the activity itself; others loathe it, valuing it only for the benefits it brings. We might put the difference this way: the lovers enjoy running, while the loathers enjoy having run. Flossing one's teeth seems an everyday example of an 'onerous but beneficial'—i.e., purely instrumental—good: we do it not because it is enjoyable in itself, but because of its good results: healthier gums and fewer lectures about the importance of flossing from finger-wagging dentists. But a person who enjoys the activity itself is not making a mistake; they merely have preferences and tastes that are not widely shared.

The third kind of good (which Glaucon takes second) is mixed, comprising intrinsic and instrumental goods: 'a kind of good we like for its own sake and also for the sake of what comes from it' (2.357c). For some people, physical exercise is completely a second-category good, onerous but beneficial: instrumentally good but intrinsically bad. But for others it belongs to this third, mixed category: one recognizes the health benefits of running five miles every day, but one also enjoys the activity itself. And perhaps watching that sunset relaxes you and lowers your blood pressure, so it too might be a mixed good. Glaucon and Socrates regard goods of this third category as the best kind of goods, since they combine both intrinsic and instrumental goodness. It might be that the drive to the golf course is lovely and thus valuable both intrinsically, since you enjoy it in itself, and also instrumentally, since it is an efficient way to get to the golf course.

Where does justice belong? Most people, Glaucon says on behalf of Thrasymachus, place it in the second category of things and acctivities that are intrinsically bad but instrumentally good, to be valued not for their intrinsic features but for the external benefits they bring— especially the benefits of having a reputation for being just: 'most people [...] say that justice belongs to the onerous kind, and is to be practiced for the sake of the rewards and popularity that come from having a reputation for justice, but is to be avoided because of itself as something burdensome' (2.358a). Socrates and Glaucon, by contrast, think justice is the best kind of good, belonging in the third, mixed category, 'to be valued [...] both because of itself and because of what comes from it' (2.357e). Even though acting justly will not always be easy, its being challenging does not make it onerous, something one wishes one did not have to do, any more than running a marathon is onerous and to be avoided in virtue of its being difficult or challenging.

The question of justice's proper categorization shapes the rhetorical strategy of the rest of the *Republic* in an important way. Most people only halfway agree with Glaucon's classification of justice. They concede the instrumental value of having a reputation for justice, of *seeming* to be just, but they deny justice's intrinsic value, holding that *being* just is not by itself good. Thus what Glaucon and Adeimantus want from Socrates is to show them that a just life is intrinsically good: all by itself, it makes its possessor's life go well. There is no need to try to show that a reputation for it is instrumentally good, since that is conceded on all sides—even Thrasymachus could agree with this. To show that justice is intrinsically good, they need to find a way to bracket off and ignore its instrumental value; if they do not do this, they cannot be sure that justice is being valued intrinsically, in and for itself, rather than for its extrinsic benefits. Thus it will not be enough to compare the just and unjust persons. To ignore the instrumental benefits a reputation for justice brings, Socrates must draw on the distinction between *being* and *seeming* and saddle the just person with a reputation for *in*justice. If he can show that the person who *is* just but *seems* unjust is happier than the person who *is* unjust but *seems* just, he will have shown that justice is intrinsically good—that all by itself it makes its possessor's life better.

Glaucon's Three Thrasymachan Theses (2.358a–362c)

Let us now turn to the second prong of Glaucon's challenge, his devil's advocacy of Thrasymachus' view. We should pause to appreciate what good intellectual practice Glaucon models here. To understand an opponent's view well enough to be able to state it clearly and forcefully and fairly is not easy, but it is a hallmark of intellectual fairness. Most of us are more familiar with someone's arguing against a view by presenting and then rejecting a caricature of the view in question. To argue this way is to commit what is known as the strawman fallacy (so-called because strawmen and -women are so easy to knock over). To take an obvious contemporary example, consider arguments about the morality of abortion. Most of us have probably heard arguments like these: 'Of course abortion is immoral; those who think it is not seem to think it is okay to murder babies' and 'Of course abortion is permissible; those who think it is not seem to think a woman should have no right at all to decide what happens to her body'. Both of these arguments commit the strawman fallacy: it is a safe bet that no defender of the moral permissibility of abortion takes pleasure at the thought of murdering babies; nor does the typical opponent relish the opportunity to interfere with a woman's bodily autonomy. Indeed, the phrase 'they seem to think that…' is a fairly reliable indicator that a strawman fallacy is coming your way. Now it may be that strawman characterizations are rhetorically effective; they are no doubt good ways to 'energize the base.' But they are intellectually debased ways of providing reasons in support of one's view, whatever that view may be. There is nothing wrong with arguing for one's view by arguing against an opponent's view, but intellectual integrity requires that we characterize the opponent's position fairly and charitably, such that they will recognize it as theirs and that it appears to be a view that a reasonable person might hold, rather than—as seems sadly typical—a view that only a morally corrupt, irrational person would find compelling.

Thrasymachan Thesis #1: Justice is Conventional, Not Natural (2.358e–359b)

The distinction between nature (φύσις [*phusis*], whence the word 'physics') and convention (νόμος [*nomos*], whence words like 'economics') is common in the *Republic*. In one sense, what is natural is what is real or true independently of what anyone thinks or does, while what is conventional is true or real only in virtue of a decision one or one's culture makes. The difference between rivers and trees is a natural difference, not a conventional one; but borders between states are matters of convention, even when the border is a natural object such as a river. In a different but related sense, a thing's nature is what makes it the kind of thing it is—a knife rather than a fork, a plant rather than an animal, etc. In his *Physics,* Aristotle said that a thing's nature is its internal principle of change and stability, and what is natural to the thing is to follow this internal principle.[2] Although most acorns will not become oak trees, becoming an oak tree is natural to an acorn in this sense. In claiming on behalf of Thrasymachus that justice is not natural but a matter of convention, Glaucon is suggesting that *in*justice is what comes naturally to us; left to our own devices, we strive to outdo our fellows without regard to the propriety of doing so. But since we weak folks fear being treated unjustly, we band together and take power, inventing the rules of justice to protect ourselves against the more powerful, who are fewer and can be subjugated by the many. Thus justice is conventional, not natural: it is an invention, imposed upon us from without, existing only as the result of intentional human activity and choice.

The basic picture will be familiar to readers acquainted with the great seventeenth-century British philosopher, Thomas Hobbes. Imagine a world before law and civilization. In this state of nature, Hobbes

---

2   Aristotle, *Physics,* II.1 192b20–23.

thought, we have complete freedom to do whatever we want to do; there are no moral or legal restrictions on one's conduct. The good news, then, is that you can do whatever you want to do: take someone else's stuff, kill them if you feel so inclined, etc. The bad news, of course, is that everyone else can do so as well. Life in the state of nature, Hobbes said, is 'solitary, poor, nasty, brutish, and short'. There is no right to life in the state of nature, understood as a claim-right or entitlement not to be killed, which imposes a duty on others not to kill. But most of us, Hobbes plausibly thought, are willing to give up some of the total freedom we have in the state of nature in exchange for the sort of security a right to life brings. I agree not to kill you and take your stuff but only on the condition that you agree to do the same for me. Thus is civil society, and indeed morality, born. Justice, on this view, is the result of a bargain; it is an invention, and thus conventional rather than natural. Only a fool, Thrasymachus and Hobbes think, would altruistically refrain from killing and taking from others without getting a corresponding guarantee in return. Most of us find it to our advantage 'to come to an agreement with each other neither to do injustice nor to suffer it' and thus we 'make laws and covenants, and what the law commands [we] call just and lawful' (2.359a). (Hobbes takes an additional step not mentioned by Thrasymachus or Glaucon, holding that there must be an authority to settle disputes and enforce the social contract, but we need not linger over this point.)

On this Thrasymachan view, justice is not natural in either sense distinguished above. Far from being mind- or culture-independent, it is something we invent rather than discover, and there is nothing more to it than the rules agreed to. Thrasymachus expressed such a view in Premise 2 of the Error Argument back in Book I. Moreover, it is injustice, he holds, and not justice, that comes naturally to us. Injustice 'is what anyone's nature naturally pursues as good' (2.359c), on the Thrasymachan view. The ideal of masculinity implicit in this view of justice will seem to many a toxic one: 'a true man', Glaucon says, wearing his Thrasymachan mask, 'would not make an agreement with anyone not to do injustice in order not to suffer it' (2.359b). He would not make such an agreement because he would not have to: the Thrasymachan man is able to impose his will on his fellows in the state of nature; *he* has no need of rules restraining his natural inclinations to outdo others, since he is powerful enough not to fall victim to others' attempts to outdo him. (Later in the *Republic* Plato will criticize this picture of masculinity, but for now it is part of the Thrasymachan picture Glaucon is painting.) Even though most of us lack this kind of strength and power, if enough of us band together we might be more powerful than the Thrasymachan 'true man'. If so, we can make rules to protect ourselves against him, since morality—or, rather, "morality"—is merely the mechanism by which the powerful protect their interests. But if this group of individually weak but collectively strong people is driven by self-interest, it is unlikely to extend the protections of morality to those whom it can exploit for its own ends. This brings us to the second thesis.

Thrasymachan Thesis #2: Those Who Act Justly Do So Unwillingly (2.359b–360d)

The second thesis is intimately connected with the first. Since injustice comes naturally to us and justice is unnatural and artificial, acting justly is contrary to our natural inclinations; it goes against our grain because 'the desire to outdo others and get more and more [...] is what anyone's nature naturally pursues as good' (2.359c). On this view, people who act justly do so unwillingly; if they could get away with acting unjustly, they would. And in fact the artifice of justice does not merely go against our nature, it distorts it: 'nature is forced by law into the perversion of treating fairness with respect' (2.359c).

This is a pretty bleak view of human nature and of the nature of morality, but it has an undeniable plausibility. But Glaucon does not rely merely on forceful language to garner agreement, he gives a famous argument for it: the Ring of Gyges Argument, important both for its content but also for the kind of argument it is. The ring in question belongs not to Gyges but to an ancestor of his, so the argument is misnamed—but that does not really matter to the point at hand, which is Thrasymachan Thesis #2. Gyges' ancestor happens upon a ring with magical powers: when he turns it in a certain direction, he becomes invisible. What does he do with his newfound power of invisibility? He seduces the queen, kills the king, and takes over the kingdom. The key move in the argument happens next: imagine, says Glaucon, that there is another such ring; what do you think its wearer would do? Would they be so thoroughly, incorruptibly moral that they would not take advantage of the situation to enrich themselves at the expense of others? If you think the wearer would act unjustly because they can do so with impunity, you should agree that the second thesis is true. We act justly only because we think we have to, Thrasymachus thinks, not because we want to; if we could act immorally and get away with it, we would do just what Gyges' ancestor did.

Glaucon has offered a thought-experiment, which is a very common way of doing philosophy: here is a fanciful scenario, what do you think about it? What is the right thing to do? Philosophical inquiry is rife with thought-experiments: Would you throw the switch to divert a runaway trolley car from a track on which it will kill five workers to a track on which it will kill only one? If you were kidnapped by the Society of Music Lovers and awoke with your kidneys connected to those of a famous violinist who will die if you disconnect yourself, are you morally permitted to disconnect yourself, resulting in the violinist's death?[3] Etc. There is certainly a place for thought-experiments in philosophical thinking, and their artificiality is no objection to them; they are not intended as realistic situations we encounter in our everyday lives but rather bear certain similarities to situations we *do* encounter in ordinary life: if you think disconnecting yourself from the violinist is permissible, should not you also think that it is permissible for a woman to terminate an involuntary pregnancy? Thought-experiments are common in philosophy—and in theoretical physics, too (just ask Schrödinger's cat)—but when fundamental claims about human nature are at issue, perhaps thought-experiments should yield to fields like evolutionary biology and psychology. That the Thrasymachan takes it to be obvious that most people think they would act as Gyges did if they had the chance might tell us a lot about the culture these Thrasymachans inhabit, even if it does not establish any trans-cultural truths about human nature. But that is probably all it is intended to do here: Thrasymachan Thesis #2 articulates a widely-held view of human nature, one that Glaucon thinks is false and that he wants Socrates to refute.

---

3   Judith Jarvis Thomson, 'A Defense of Abortion', *Philosophy & Public Affairs*, 1 (1971), 47–66 (pp. 48–49).

Thrasymachan Thesis #3: The Unjust Person is Happier than the Just Person (2.360e–362c)

This of course is Thrasymachus' answer to the second of the *Republic*'s two main questions, whether the just or unjust life is happier, which Socrates realized that he'd tried to answer before answering the first one. What is most relevant here are the constraints Glaucon proposes for answering it. If the unjust person is really going to outdo everyone, they will find that having a reputation for justice will greatly help them use the rules of justice to exploit others: they will find that they are more effective at *being* unjust if they *seem* just. No one who thought that Bernard Madoff was a conman running a Ponzi scheme would have invested with him; his cheating his investors out of billions of dollars was made possible in no small part by his sterling reputation.

The last third or so of the *Republic* is devoted to assessing this third Thrasymachan thesis; Glaucon is here stating it, not arguing for or against it (though we do know that he actually thinks it is false, devil's advocacy aside). Instead, he is setting the parameters for how Socrates is to defeat this thesis. Harking back to the distinction between kinds of goods, Socrates and company think that most people regard justice as onerous but beneficial: bad intrinsically but good instrumentally, especially the reputation for justice. Glaucon and Socrates think justice is both intrinsically and instrumentally good, but since even skeptics agree with them about its instrumental value, what Socrates needs to do is to show that justice is intrinsically good: that all by itself, a morally good life benefits the person living it, and indeed is better for them than a morally bad life, even if they do not get any of the extrinsic, instrumental benefits. We need to bracket off the instrumental benefits of having a reputation for justice because if we do not find a way to ignore them, we cannot be sure that we are valuing justice intrinsically, in and of itself, and not for the instrumental benefits a reputation for justice brings:

> we must take away his reputation, for a reputation for justice would bring him honor and rewards, so it would not be clear whether he is just for the sake of justice itself or for the sake of those honors and rewards. We must strip him of everything except justice and make his situation the opposite of an unjust person's. Though he does no injustice, he must have the greatest reputation for it, so that his justice may be tested full-strength and not diluted [...] (2.361c)

So in settling the question of which life is happier, we must draw not only on the distinction between intrinsic and instrumental value but also on the distinction between appearance and reality. Glaucon will regard his belief that the just life is happier as justified only if Socrates can show him that the person who really *is* just but *seems* unjust is happier than the person who *is* unjust but *seems* just.

It is quite a tall order, as Socrates recognizes, but it is the only way they can think of to separate off the intrinsic goodness of justice from its instrumental, reputational benefits. If Socrates can show us that the really just but apparently unjust person is happier than the really unjust but apparently just person, he will have shown us that justice is intrinsically good, since he will have shown that being just in and of itself makes one better off. If he can do this, he will have justified Glaucon's presumably true belief that the just life is happier and thereby transmute his belief into knowledge.

Adeimantus Ups the Ante (2.362d–367e)

Glaucon's brother Adeimantus thinks that Glaucon has left out 'the most important thing' (2.362d), which he takes to be the way justice is treated in Athenian popular culture. Adeimantus' attention to culture shapes the *Republic* by anchoring Socrates' focus on education in the ideal city that they will soon start constructing, if only in theory. His complaint is that Athenian culture and Greek culture more broadly, 'don't praise justice in itself, [but] only the high reputations it leads to and the consequences of being thought to be just' (2.363a). He worries about the effect of such a culture 'on the souls of young people' (2.365a), when they see through their culture's shallow platitudes to the deeper antirealist view that 'injustice [...] [is] shameful only in opinion and law' (2.364a) and not in itself. Agreeing with Thrasymachus about the value of *being* unjust but recognizing the importance of *seeming* just, they will become cynical and hypocritical, desiring to cultivate only 'a façade of illusory virtue' (2.365c) rather than a genuinely virtuous character.

The stories Athenian culture tells about the gods, such as the ones we find in Homer's *Iliad* or *Odyssey* or Hesiod's *Theogeny*, suggest that the gods can be influenced by prayers, sacrifices, and offerings. It is more profitable, on the Thrasymachan view of individual happiness, to reap the benefits of acting unjustly, and then toward the end of one's life to seek absolution by building a temple or making many sacrifices, thus avoiding the just deserts of a life of injustice. Although there will be a few people of 'godlike character who [are] disgusted by injustice' (2.366c), most of us will find the allure of material success too attractive to resist. Some of us will feel guilty or ashamed, but others—perhaps *because* we will feel guilty or ashamed—will 'laugh aloud' when we hear justice praised (2.366b), since, like Thrasymachus, we think 'justice' is for suckers.

Thus it is vital, Adeimantus thinks, for Socrates to show that justice is intrinsically good and to ignore any benefits that might accrue to someone with a reputation for justice. He wants Socrates to swim against the tide of Athenian culture and show them that 'injustice is the worst thing a soul can have in it and that justice is the greatest good' (2.366e). Only if Socrates does this will Glaucon and Adeimantus be justified in their belief that the just life is happier—only then will that belief become knowledge.

Socrates' Plan: Investigate Personal Justice by Investigating Political Justice (2.367e–369a)

Socrates' way of responding to Glaucon and Adeimantus' request for a fresh defense of the just life will resonate with anyone who needs drugstore reading glasses to deal with a restaurant menu. Just as it is easier to read larger than smaller letters, Socrates argues (2.368d), it will be easier to figure out the nature and value of justice if we see it on a larger scale. So the plan is to examine the nature and value of justice writ large, in a *polis* (city-state), in order to see what it tells us about justice in a person: 'let us first find out what sort of thing justice is in a city and afterwards look for it in the individual' (2.369a). This method of investigation is apt to strike many readers as odd, since it assumes an analogy between persons and cities that will seem a stretch to many. The analogy has certainly intrigued philosophical commentators on the *Republic*. Socrates is assuming that justice in individuals and justice in city-states do not differ in any relevant ways. A person (more properly, their soul) and a *polis* differ in size and thus so too does the *amount* of justice each contains, but the amount of justice is not relevant to its nature, Socrates assumes, any more than a glass of water differs in nature from a gallon of water: water is water, regardless of how much of it there is.

As we move forward, we will want to keep in mind the big *if* at the heart of Socrates' method: *if* people and city-states are relevantly similar, then what we learn about the nature of justice in the latter can be mapped onto the former. We will see in Book IV that Socrates will try to do more than just *assume* they are similar; he will *argue* that they are. But for now, let us grant the analogy and see what Socrates does with it.

A False Start: Socrates' Rustic Utopia (2.369b–373a)

Socrates plans to 'create a city in theory from its beginnings' (2.369c), but of course it cannot be just any city; for the plan of the *Republic* to work, it must be a just city. And this city must not only *be* just, if they are to determine the truth about the nature and value of justice, it must also *seem* just to Glaucon and company, if they are to be persuaded that the just life is the happier life. Once all agree that the theoretically constructed city is just, the task will be to determine the nature of the virtue of justice, or what makes it just. We should note too that since Plato wants his readers to imaginatively participate in the dialog, readers will have to determine for themselves whether they find the city Socrates has created to be just (which, remember, is synonymous with being morally good, generally). Readers who do not think the ideal city is just or who are not sure can still follow the argument in a hypothetical way: 'Well, *if* this were a just city, does Socrates plausibly explain what makes it just?'. But this will be less than fully satisfying, especially if, like Glaucon and Adeimantus, we want Socrates to provide us with reasons we find plausible that would justify the belief, if indeed we hold it, that the just life is a better and happier life than the unjust life.

The origin of any community, Socrates thinks, is that 'none of us is self-sufficient' (2.369b). It is not just that we have needs, but we have needs that we cannot ourselves always meet. Thus, he thinks, communities are formed: 'people gather in a single place to live together as partners and helpers' (2.369c). This idea of cities as essentially cooperative is an attractive one, and it is at odds with the Thrasymachan view of cities as sites of competition rather than cooperation, where citizens are always trying to outdo each other. Perhaps Thrasymachus could agree with Socrates about the cooperative origins of any *polis* while thinking that people will strive to outdo each other once a city is up and running. People will always strive to exploit others' neediness for their own advantage, and crafty Thrasymachans will be more successful at doing so than others.

Socrates next argues for a division-of-labor principle that will not only organize the city's economic life but will ultimately have profound ethical implications, as it will be the basis of the definition of justice he arrives at in Book IV. We are all born with different natural aptitudes and preferences, he thinks, each of us having a distinctive ἔργον [*ergon*] or natural task or function, a notion we met in Book I, most notably in the Function Argument. Since we are born with different aptitudes, Socrates advocates a division of labor: 'more plentiful and better-quality goods are more easily produced if each person does one thing for which he is naturally suited [...] and is released from having to do any of the others' (2.370c).

At least two things about the argument for what we will call the Specialization Principle are worth attending to. The first is the way Socrates appeals to what he takes to be natural facts in arguing for it, facts which many readers will find quite plausible. Many readers will have known people who have always been good at math, or who can quickly master a variety of musical instruments, or who have a knack with machines, or who excel at certain sports, etc. Though hard work and discipline are necessary for success in such areas, there usually is a natural aptitude at the core that can be developed and perhaps perfected by diligent practice and education—but without the natural aptitude as the raw material which nurture can develop, the chances of high-level success seem slim indeed. The second feature is that Socrates advocates the Specialization Principle because it benefits the community as a whole, not because it enables individual flourishing. This is perhaps the first inkling of Socrates' communitarian inclinations: he is likelier to think of the needs and good of the community first, in relatively sharp contrast to the tendency many contemporary Westerners—especially Americans—have to think individualistically. On this individualistic view, individuals are morally primary and communities exist primarily to enable individual flourishing or perhaps to protect the natural rights individuals possess. The distinction between communitarian and individualistic thinking is a matter of degree and often context: a baseball team or string quartet comprising dyed-in-the-wool individualists who care more (or only) about their own individual successes will surely be less successful than teams or quartets with more group-minded members.

In the riveting opening chapter of his novel, *Enduring Love*, Ian McEwan writes of 'morality's ancient, irresolvable dilemma: us, or me'.[4] If McEwan is right, the fundamental moral question is not *us versus them* or *me versus you* but rather *me versus we*: do the needs and interests of the community trump the individual's? Far from regarding the dilemma as 'irresolvable', Plato and Socrates resolve it in favor of *we* over *me*. I suspect that many, if not most, readers will often find themselves resistant to and put off by Socrates' communitarian, *we*-favoring impulses. Even so, there is much value in being confronted with thinking that is fundamentally different from one's own, as this not only provides alternative perspectives but also might force one to play Glaucon and Adeimantus and try to justify deeply-held beliefs that one takes for granted.

There will be many occupations in the ideal city: farmers, builders, carpenters, shepherds, weavers, and cobblers, to name a few. There will also be importers and exporters, merchants, retailers, and physical laborers. Very quickly, in just a couple of pages, we learn that the ideal city is complete: 'our city [has] grown to completeness [... So] where are justice and injustice to be found in it?' (2.371e). As Socrates begins to answer this question by examining the sort of lives its citizens lead, Glaucon objects—to the surprise of many readers—to the food. The food is of 'the sort they cook in the country' (2.372c), he complains, unsuitable for a young Athenian aristocrat, but perhaps suitable 'if you were founding a city for pigs' (2.372d). Most readers are apt to be misled by this charge, since to modern ears talk of pigs suggests gluttony and perhaps uncleanliness. But this is not the connotation for ancient Athenians, for whom, Myles Burnyeat points out, 'the pig was an emblem rather of ignorance [...] "Any pig would know" was the

---

4   Ian McEwan, *Enduring Love* (New York: Anchor Books, 1998), p. 15.

saying. What Glaucon means is, "You describe the feasting of people who do not know how to live. It is *uncivilized.*"[5]

Socrates acquiesces and agrees to develop 'a luxurious city' (2.372e) better suited to his young friends' expectations about what a good life involves. He does not agree with them, as he quickly makes clear: 'the true city [...] is the one we have described, the healthy one' (2.372e). But he goes along with them because the plan of the *Republic* demands it. Glaucon and Adeimantus, remember, want Socrates to provide them with good reasons for a belief they sincerely hold but recognize to be unjustified, the belief that the just life is the happier one. If this requires that they give up their conception of what a good life is—if justice requires that they live the simple, rustic life Socrates depicts—they are unlikely to be convinced by what he has to say. There is some interesting scholarly disagreement about whether and how seriously to take Socrates' praise of the first city. Its benign anarchy—there is no mention of any political structures or governmental offices—will appeal to many readers, as will its simplicity, its communal bonds, and its relative self-sustainability. But the ideal city they ultimately develop is structured by 'three *natural* classes' (4.435b (italics added)), which suggests that the first city, which lacks them, is not natural after all.

In any event, Socrates agrees to sketch a luxurious city, replete with the sorts of delicacies Glaucon and Adeimantus insist upon and, going well beyond the more basic necessities found in the first city, to include perfumes, prostitutes, and pastries (2.373a). More striking, though, than what the luxurious city includes is what follows in its wake: war. Having 'overstepped the limit of their necessities' (2.373d), the citizens now require resources they do not possess, and now possess goods that other city-states might envy and seek for themselves. It is striking that Plato finds 'the origins of war' (2.373e) not in an innately aggressive human nature; the explanation is social and economic rather than biological: communities come into conflict with each other when they exceed a simple, natural life and grasp for luxury (and here *pleonexia* rears its ugly, Thrasymachan head). If the first, rustic city is a real possibility,

---

5   Myles Burnyeat, 'Culture and Society in Plato's "Republic"', in *The Tanner Lectures on Human Values,* vol. 20 (Salt Lake City: University of Utah Press, 1999), p. 231. Italics in the original. (Burnyeat's lecture and dozens of others can be found online at https://tannerlectures.utah.edu/lecture-library.php).

then acquisitive, me-first *pleonexia* is not what comes naturally to human beings.

Obviously, with warfare comes the need for soldiers, but Socrates eschews the idea of citizen-soldiers in favor of a professional army. 'Warfare is a profession' (2.374b), he argues, and according to the Specialization Principle only someone with a natural aptitude for warfare should become a soldier. But the ideal soldier must naturally be 'both gentle and high-spirited' (2.375c), tough with foes but gentle with friends. Socrates initially despairs of finding such a combination, worrying that these traits are so at odds with each other that 'it seems impossible to combine them' and thus 'that a good guardian cannot exist' (2.375c). His despair vanishes, though, when he thinks of dogs, whom he delightfully regards as 'truly philosophical' (2.376b), since their conduct is knowledge-based. Dogs treat people differently based on whether they know the person or not: friends are proper objects of gentleness, while strangers or foes are not.

Of course, not all dogs make good watchdogs: some are too gentle and sweet by nature, others too aggressive, even with family members. Since gentleness and high-spiritedness are often at odds with each other, proper education will be crucial to the soldier-guardians' proper development and thus to the flourishing of the city. So once we have found someone who seems to possess a natural aptitude for guarding the city (in the case of soldiers) or the home (in the case of dogs) the question is this: 'how are we to bring him up and educate him?' (2.376c). This is the question to which we turn in the following chapter.

Some Suggestions for Further Reading

Readers interested in a philosophically sophisticated account of Glaucon's division of kinds of goodness will find C.D.C. Reeve, *Philosopher-Kings: The Argument of Plato's 'Republic'* (Indianapolis: Hackett Publishing, 2006), pp. 24–32 challenging but rewarding.

I first encountered the distinction between instrumental and constitutive means in J. L. Ackrill, 'Aristotle on *Eudaimonia*', in *Essays on Aristotle's Ethics,* ed. by Amélie Oksenberg Rorty (Berkeley and Los Angeles: University of California Press, 1981), pp. 15–33. The golf example appears on p. 19.

Readers interested in Hobbes' political philosophy will find helpful Sharon Lloyd and Susanne Sreedhar, 'Hobbes' Moral and Political Philosophy', in *The Stanford Encyclopedia of Philosophy*, ed. by Edward N. Zalta, https://plato.stanford.edu/entries/hobbes-moral/

Readers interested in the scholarly discussion of the city-soul analogy will find no better place to start than Bernard Williams, 'The Analogy of City and Soul in Plato's *Republic*', in *Plato's 'Republic': Critical Essays*, ed. by Richard Kraut (Lanham, MD: Rowman & Littlefield, 1997), pp. 49–59. G. R. F. Ferrari, *City and Soul in Plato's 'Republic'* (Chicago: University of Chicago Press, 2005) devotes itself to the city-soul analogy as well as 'attempt[ing] to say what Plato is getting at in the *Republic*' (p. 9), which it does in lucid, lively prose.

For readers interested in the scholarly debate around the first city, an excellent place to start is Rachel Barney, 'Platonism, Moral Nostalgia and the City of Pigs', *Proceedings of the Boston Area Colloquium in Ancient Philosophy*, 17 (2001), 207–27, https://doi.org/10.1163/22134417–90000032.

Readers interested in making sense of Glaucon's food-based objection to the first city in particular and Athenian life around Plato's and Socrates' time in general will delight in James Davidson, *Courtesans and Fishcakes: The Consuming Passions of Classical Athens* (New York: St. Martin's Press, 1997), which is lively and engaging.

Figure of a boy writing on a kylix, 480 B.C. Photograph by Reame (2019), Wikimedia, CC BY-SA 4.0, https://commons.wikimedia.org/wiki/File:Figura_ragazzo_che_scrive_su_kylix.jpg#/media/File:Figura_ragazzo_che_scrive_su_kylix.jpg

4. Blueprints for a Platonic Utopia
Education and Culture
Books II and III

In having Socrates work out the proper education for the would-be guardians—which at least initially must include all the city's children—Plato engages in the philosophy of education for the first time in the Western philosophical tradition. He is not the first philosopher to do so, as readers familiar with non-Western philosophy will know. Confucius' *Analects,* which predates Plato's *Republic* by almost a century, devotes considerable attention to the nature and value of education and in fact begins by celebrating it; indeed, the first word 'The Master' is quoted as saying is *xue* (學), which means learning or study. Education is a topic of sustained focus in the *Republic*. In Books II and III Plato sees education as a two-pronged endeavor, comprising 'physical training for bodies and music and poetry for the soul' (2.376e). A little later, he will reconsider this way of thinking about education's objects, holding that physical training and poetic education are 'both chiefly for the sake of the soul' (3.410c). Later in the *Republic,* while developing the famous Allegory of the Cave in Book VII, Plato has Socrates give an account of *formal* education involving arithmetic, geometry, astronomy or physics, and dialectic, a sort of philosophical logic, more or less inventing what has come to be known as liberal education. In Books II and III, however, the focus is on education's less formal aspects, education in the wider sense of the Greek word παιδεία (*paideia*): upbringing or enculturation.

  https://doi.org/10.11647/OBP.0229.04

Supervising the Storytellers: Musical and Poetic *Content* (2.376c–3.392c)

Socrates is especially concerned with the effects of popular culture on the development of character, both of the would-be soldier-guardians and of the citizenry at large. We begin absorbing our culture, which is carried by the songs sung in the home and in public, so Socrates first focuses on the stories—literally the myths (μῦθοι [*muthoi*])—children hear in the songs sung to and around them. Many readers will shrink at Socrates' insisting that the first thing he and his fellow theoretical architects must do is 'supervise the storytellers' (2.377b). But even those of us who value freedom of speech and artistic expression—two values conspicuous by their absence in the *Republic*—probably do not think that all books or movies or television shows or videogames or music are appropriate at all ages. But while most readers will likely think this is a private matter, to be determined by parents, for Plato it is too important to be left to individual discretion (and thus is another of those places where his community-mindedness is evident). After all, the explicit point of education is to develop good soldier-guardians, which is surely a matter of public and not merely private concern.

At the root of Plato's educational program is a belief in the malleability of the human psyche, especially at young ages: 'You know, don't you, that the beginning of any process is most important, especially for anything young and tender? It's at that time that it is most malleable and takes on any pattern one wishes to impress upon it' (2.377b). Hence the need to regulate the stories children hear, both their content and their form. Socrates focuses first on the former, on *what* the stories say, and then in Book III he focuses on *how* the stories are told, on their form.

The most important restriction on the content of stories is that they must not convey *true falsehoods*, which are 'falsehoods [...] about the most important things' (2.382a). The phrase 'true falsehood' is easy to trip over, since it suggests the idea of stories that are literally false but convey moral truths. This is emphatically *not* what Socrates means; 'true' here means 'real' or 'genuine'; a true falsehood is something that is deeply, genuinely false. Socrates is not anti-fiction; he is not opposed to nursery rhymes that contain literal falsehoods, or what he calls 'falsehood in words' (2.382c). That there never was a person who lived in a shoe or a race between a tortoise and a hare is not important, so long as the story's underlying moral message is not radically false.

There are three categories of stories whose content should be regulated: stories about the gods, stories about epic heroes, and stories about people. Socrates rightly avoids regulating the last kind of story at this stage of the *Republic*. Presumably, he regards Thrasymachus' claim that the unjust life is happier than a just life as a true falsehood: it is deeply, profoundly mistaken and soul-distorting, and it ruins anyone who steers their life by it. But to rule out such stories now, before the *Republic*'s two questions have been satisfactorily answered, would beg the question—that is, it would assume the truth of what he should be trying to prove. It would be intellectually unfair to adopt a regulation banning such stories in his ideal city, since he is not yet entitled to claim that Thrasymachus is mistaken.

As the gods are among the most important things, we must be on guard against true falsehoods regarding the gods. There are two restrictions on stories about the gods: first, that the gods are not the cause of everything but only of good things (2.380c); second, that the gods are not shape-shifters or deceivers who 'mislead us by falsehoods in words or deeds' (2.383a). Since a god is by nature good, and what is good cannot cause something harmful and bad, a god cannot be the cause of bad things. So any story saying otherwise is promoting a true falsehood and should be disallowed, even if Homer or Hesiod or any canonical Greek poet is its author. The same goes for stories depicting gods as deceivers. Since 'the best things are least liable to [...] change' and the gods are among the best things, they would not alter their appearances or have any need to speak falsely (2.380e).

We might question the chains of argument by which Socrates arrives at these conclusions. For example, he never considers the possibility that there are no gods, or the possibility that a god might lie for good reasons. But the real take-aways here are not the particular content of any rules he arrives at, but rather three key ideas: first, that one should not uncritically accept the norms and values of one's culture; second, that reason provides a perspective from which cultural norms and values can be assessed; and third, that if there is a conflict between culture or tradition and reason, we should follow the dictates of reason. Although his community-first ethos is often associated with a kind of conservatism that prizes tradition and the wisdom embodied therein, Socrates is no conservative. Far from it. He is a radical rationalist, believing that rationality affords a perspective from which a tradition's practices and values can be assessed. Socrates loves Homer, but he thinks that his passion for poetry must give way to what reason tells him about it. Hence he goes through Homer and Hesiod with an editor's pen, striking passages that cannot stand up to rational scrutiny, much as someone might go through the Bible or Koran striking out passages they took to express true falsehoods. (Thomas Jefferson seems to have been up to something similar in *The Life and Morals of Jesus of Nazareth*, in which he excised all mention of Jesus' divinity, his performing miracles, resurrection, etc.)

Much as censoring stories about the gods is designed to foster the virtue of piety, censoring stories about epic heroes is meant to foster the secular virtues of courage and moderation. If would-be guardians are to acquire the courage-grounding belief that there are things that are worse than death—slavery and dishonor, to name two—they must not be exposed to stories about the horrors of Hades or of heroes lamenting the loss of loved ones. The same goes for moderation (also known as temperance): if young people are to become temperate, they must have exemplars to imitate, which they will not have if they are exposed to stories showing heroes over-indulging in food, drink, and sex, or desiring money or acting arrogantly or being overcome by anger or even laughter. Socrates' point here is that one's culture provides models of appropriate behavior, models that we internalize from a very young age. Although the reasoning is not conscious, the process seems to go something like this: we hear stories of gods acting dishonestly or heroes wailing about death and infer that these are appropriate ways for *us* to behave. 'Everyone will be ready to excuse himself when he is bad', Socrates argues, 'if he is persuaded that similar things [...] have been done in the past by "close descendants of the gods"' (3.391e).

Hence it is vitally important that one be exposed to good models right from the start, where 'good models' does a double duty: good models of good people. That Athenian culture fails in this regard, that its stories traffic in models of clever people acting unjustly and getting away with it, is Adeimantus' complaint.

Supervising the Storytellers: Musical and Poetic *Style* (3.392c–401d)

One of the fascinating features of Socrates' account of education broadly construed is that it attends not merely to the *content* of stories and songs, as we might expect, but to their *form* or *style,* as well. The main idea is that a song's musical mode—not exactly equivalent to our notion of key but close enough for our purposes—and its meter or rhythm affect us independently of its words. This issue is connected to a longstanding debate in the philosophy of music about whether music contains emotions or merely excites them—whether, for example the second movement of Schubert's Sonata in A major is sad in itself or whether the sadness is merely evoked in us by the music, which is itself emotionally unladen. How music could encode emotions is a fascinating question, but it is one we need not address here, since what Plato has Socrates say does not require—though it is consistent with—the view that music contains and encodes emotion rather than merely evoking it in listeners.

While Greek musical modes are not identical to keys in Western music, thinking about keys can help us get a sense of how different modes have different emotional tones. The internet can be a great help here, since YouTube is rife with songs in which the key has been shifted from major to minor or minor to major. Consider the Beatles' classic, 'Hey Jude', originally written in F major. Transposed to F minor, it is a very different song: sad, pensive, almost dour. Upbeat pop songs like Cyndi Lauper's 'Girls Just Want to Have Fun' or Cheap Trick's 'I Want You to Want Me' sound sad and ironic when transposed from their original major to the corresponding minor key. Regardless of whether one stands or kneels for 'The Star-Spangled Banner' before a professional football game, it seems like a different song when sung in a minor key. It works the other way, too: R.E.M.'s 'Losing My Religion' sounds happy and optimistic when modulated into A major, as does the theme from *The Godfather.* The lesson here is that the key—or, for Plato, mode—in which a song is sung matters.

So in addition to wanting to 'delete the lamentations and pitiful speeches of famous men' (3.387c), since they cultivate cowardice and indulgence rather than courage and temperance, Socrates also wants to do away with 'the lamenting modes' (3.398e) in his ideal city, since even without lamenting lyrics, these modes will convey or cultivate these vices, too. The 'soft modes suitable for drinking parties' (3.398e) are out, too. What remains are 'the mode that would suitably imitate the tone and rhythm of a courageous person who is active in battle' and 'another mode, that of someone engaged in a peaceful, unforced voluntary action [...] acting with moderation and self-control' (3.399b), since these modes will cultivate the emotions and thus virtues proper to the would-be guardians.

Socrates pays similar attention to rhythm and meter, aiming to cultivate grace and avoid gracelessness (3.400c). It is important to see that the restrictions on form and style are not afterthoughts, secondary to the restrictions on content. They are in fact more basic, since we are exposed to music well before we can understand the words of the songs our families and fellow-citizens sing to and around us. 'Rhythm and harmony', Socrates says, 'permeate the inner part of the soul more than anything else' (3.401d). Before we can understand the words of songs, we are shaped by their modes and rhythms, and indeed the shaping done by rhythm and harmony is even more important, Socrates thinks, since it begins to work on us at once. The point of proper aesthetic education here is not to come to have knowledge *about* the beautiful, but rather to come to know it directly, to recognize it when we hear and later see it.

The Aesthetically Beautiful and the Morally Beautiful (3.401d–403c, 412b–e

At least three other features of Plato's account of aesthetic development are worthy of our attention. The first is that our aesthetic education is in fact the beginning of our moral education. Plato does *not* draw a sharp line, as we moderns tend to, between the beautiful and the morally good. While other approaches to ethics focus on duty and action (for example, the ethics embodied in the Ten Commandments, replete as it is with *Shalts* and *Shalt Nots*, and in the modern era Kant's duty-based deontology), Plato's ethics takes virtue to be central. For a virtue-centered ethics, the fundamental question is not 'What should I do?' but 'What kind of person should I be?' Where duty is essentially imperative, placing demands upon us, virtue is essentially attractive, expressing ideals of character that we can approach by degrees—and, if Plato is right, that we are drawn to precisely because it is beautiful (κᾰλον [*kalon*]). Where Kant thought one should be motivated by duty to do one's duty, Plato—and here I am making the safe bet that he would agree with his student Aristotle, who is much more explicit about this than his teacher—holds that the proper moral motivation for performing a certain action is that the action is fine or noble or beautiful—that it is *kalon*, which seamlessly combines aesthetic and moral notions.

Our moral education begins with our aesthetic education because, Plato thinks, proper exposure to beautiful modes, harmonies, and rhythms will cultivate 'the right distastes' and tastes (3.401e) in young people. This is not so they will become cultured aesthetes devoted to the aesthetically beautiful, but rather so they will be able to recognize and become devoted to the morally beautiful. In learning to recognize ugly sounds as ugly we come to learn to recognize shameful actions as shameful. It is no accident that the same Greek word αἰσχρός (*aischros*) means both ugly and shameful. Socrates regards doing injustice as shameful, but the Thrasymachan strongman—and anyone whose moral sensibilities have not been properly cultivated—'has no scruples about doing injustice' (2.362b), since he does not find the very idea repellant. Without radically altering the kind of upbringing and education Athenian popular culture will produce, young people will not be 'disgusted by injustice' (2.366d) but will try to get away with it when they can.

A second important feature is that proper musical education will inculcate correct moral beliefs 'while [we are] still young and unable to grasp the reason' (3.401a). In other words, we will learn *that* certain traits and actions are admirable while others are not—but this will not teach us *why* the morally admirable traits are admirable. For that, we need philosophy. As I have noted already, this is essentially Glaucon's and Adeimantus' position: they believe that justice trumps convenience and self-interest, that the just life is happier than the unjust life, etc., but they recognize that they cannot justify these beliefs. But this underlying moral substrate of proper tastes and distastes—in a word, proper moral sentiments or feelings—is absolutely essential, on Socrates' view. Children who develop in a musically corrupt culture will fail to acquire the correct moral beliefs, because of the false models of beauty they will internalize.

A third feature, closely related to the second, is that properly educated children will love what is beautiful and good. 'Education in music and poetry', says Socrates, 'ought to end in the love of the fine and beautiful (καλοῦ ἐρωτικά [*kalou erôtia*])' (3.403c). It is well worth noting that the 'love' there is *erotic* love: they are in love with what is noble and fine, with what is morally beautiful. So, underlying any cognitive, philosophical grasp of justice is a pre-rational, emotional attachment to it. This comes to the fore later in Book III when Socrates, in addressing the question of who should rule, separates off the guardians from the auxiliaries. We will say more about this in a bit, but it is worth bringing out the connection between love and governing. 'The rulers must be the best of the guardians' (3.412c), Socrates thinks. But in the Book I conversation with Polemarchus he said that the best guardian of something is also its best thief (1.334a). What keeps these guardian-rulers from stealing the city—from 'going Thrasymachan', so to speak, and using their power to benefit themselves—is that they love the city? 'The right kind of love' (the *orthos erôs*) that is the product of proper musical education is 'the love of order and beauty' (3.403a). In loving the city, the guardians identify its good with theirs: 'someone loves something most of all when he believes that the same things are advantageous to it as to himself and supposes that if it does well, he will do well, and that if it does badly, then he will do badly too' (3.412d).

Love certainly has an affective or phenomenological dimension: it *feels* a certain way. The variety of poems and pop songs devoted to what love feels like attests to the difficulty of describing the feeling in a non-metaphorical way: love is like a heatwave, love is a flame, etc. But in stressing the belief at the core of love, Plato plays down its affective dimension and plays up its cognitive dimension. We should note an asymmetry to the belief at the heart of Socratic love. In loving you, I identify my wellbeing with yours: I take what is good for you to be good for me. Taking what is good for me to be good for you is another way of creating an identity between your wellbeing and mine, but it is a defective form of love if it is a form of love at all. Many readers know— sadly, some know through first-hand experience—parents who force or at least foist their wellbeing and conceptions of what a good life is onto their children, insisting that the child act for the sake of the parent. In addition to this asymmetry in belief, we should note that love requires something more than this belief and a feeling of fondness. In addition to love's cognitive and affective dimensions, there is also what we might call (for lack of a better word) its conative dimension, for loving another involves commitment to the other's wellbeing and thus taking actions to promote it, often actions that seem to go against the lover's interests. If I merely believe that your good is thereby also my good but I do nothing to promote your good when I am able to do so, it is hard to take seriously my claim that I love you.

The upshot and real point of proper musical education, then, is that the guardians love the city. Where for Thrasymachus there is a clear gap between *what is good for me* as a ruler and *what is good for the city,* Socratic love for the city closes this gap. That a certain course of action might benefit me as a ruler at the expense of the city gets no traction if I have been properly educated; there just is not any space for such considerations to have any pull. The properly educated ruler would be baffled at the thought that they could gain from selling out the city, since the city's good *is* their good, just as no amount of money would induce a good parent to sell their child into sex slavery.

As we will see momentarily, the city's founders must find ways to test the would-be guardians to discover which of them cannot be induced to give up their love of the city; they must 'make sure that neither compulsion nor magic spells will get them to discard or forget their belief that they must do what is best for the city' (3.412e).

Physical Education—and Food (3.403c–405a)

Plato says significantly less about physical education, the other prong of the would-be guardians' education. Given that the Greek word here is γυμναστική (*gumnastikê*, from which we get the English word 'gymnastics'), we might expect a discussion of various kinds of exercises, but 'detailed supervision of the body' (3.403d) is not really necessary, Socrates thinks, as a well-cared-for soul will be able to figure out what is appropriate for the body. He will return to the topic of physical education, especially as it concerns soldiering, in Book V.

But here Socrates does offer a of bit detail where food is concerned, with examples drawn from Homer. The soldier-guardians will eat roasted but not boiled meats, presumably because this requires less equipment to be lugged around. There will be no fish, which as we noted above is a luxury item, no sweet desserts, and no Syracusan or Sicilian delicacies (ὄψον [*opson*]) (3.404d)—though this time Glaucon raises no objection. The guardians' lifestyle should be simple, both musically and physically. Simple music conduces to personal in the soul and simple food conduces to bodily health.

Symptoms of Poorly Educated Cities: Too Many Lawyers and Doctors (3.405a–408c)

Given how frequently one hears jokes about lawyers and complaints that American society is overly litigious (Google's fascinating Ngram Viewer shows a twofold increase in the use of the word 'litigious' in American English in the last half of the twentieth century), it is likely that many readers will agree with Socrates that an overabundance of lawyers is a symptom of something amiss, bemoaning those who 'take pride in being clever at [...] exploiting every loophole and trick to [ensure that their clients] escape conviction' (3.405c). Fewer, I suspect, are likely to bemoan the presence of doctors, as Socrates does. At least as regards illness resulting from idleness and dubious dietary choices, we may concede that he has a point. But many readers will find what Socrates says about disease and disability shocking and indeed morally abhorrent. His remarks about those who are chronically, incurably ill are apt to make one shudder: 'as for the ones whose bodies are naturally unhealthy or whose souls are incurably evil [...] let the former die of their own accord and put the latter to death' (3.410a).

One reason Socrates' attitude can seem horrifyingly wrongheaded is that it seems driven by the Specialization Principle and his community-mindedness: 'everyone in a well-regulated city has his own work to do and [...] no one has the leisure to be ill and under treatment all his life' (3.406c). Since the chronically ill cannot contribute to the city, the argument seems to go, caring for them would just be a drain on resources. Many readers will insist that individuals have a value that transcends their usefulness or instrumental worth, and that treating them as dispensable cogs in a great machine is profoundly immoral, as it fails to recognize and respect their inherent dignity. Here we seem to find the starkest of clashes between individualism and communitarianism. Without seeking to defend

Socrates' attitude, it is worth noting that this is only half the story, for he also appeals to the perspective of the diseased individual: 'such a person would be of no profit either to himself or to the city' (3.407e); 'his life is of no profit to him if he does not do his work' (3.407a). While this might blunt the sharp edges of Socrates' view, it does so in a way that many people, informed by contemporary thinking on disability or by their own life experiences, will find offensive and profoundly mistaken. For it seems to take as its guide not the perspective of those who are chronically ill or disabled but rather the perspective of healthy people imagining how they would react to permanent disability. Empirical research suggests that the perhaps commonsensical assumption that disabilities make the lives of the disabled significantly if not disastrously worse is mistaken, and many readers will themselves have lives well worth living or will have friends and family members whose lives are well worth living despite their physical and cognitive limitations. We might share some of Socrates' wariness about 'excessive care [and attention] to the body' (3.407b), being aware, as he is not, of the corrosive dangers of cultural norms of physical perfection, without sharing his attitude toward the disabled.

And many will regard Socrates' attitude as not only morally abhorrent, but philosophically suspect, as well. On the medical model of disability, a disability is thought of as an abnormality, such as an inability to walk that in itself significantly impairs its possessor's chances for a happy, flourishing life. But the social model of disability, which is now the standard view in the field of disability studies, challenges the medical model. It distinguishes impairments from disabilities, regarding the inability to walk, for example, as atypical rather than abnormal. It is an impairment, but it is a disability only in a society that is inhospitable to and stigmatizes those who cannot walk. On the social model, being disabled is largely a social fact, turning on the ways in which a society is structured with respect to various impairments. While it might seem 'obvious' that deafness, for example, is a disability, many regard it instead as a difference, and treasure it as part of their identity.

This brief discussion is not meant to suggest that the social model is correct, but rather that thinking about disability has advanced significantly since Socrates' time, and the medical model he assumes to be obviously correct has been called into serious doubt in recent decades.

Harmony between Musical and Physical Education
(3.410a–412b)

As we noted above, Socrates initially said that musical education treats the soul while physical education treats the body (2.376e) but towards the end of Book III he corrects himself, holding that both are 'chiefly for the sake of the soul' (3.410c). And here he hints at the distinction he will make in Book IV between the parts of the soul, suggesting that physical training aims at properly arousing 'the spirited part of one's nature' while musical education tends 'the philosophical part' (3.410d). His overriding concern is that the two parts be brought into harmony or balance. Remember that guardians must be both gentle and high-spirited, traits that are typically not found together and that are in tension when they are. Too much *gumnastikê* and one ends up savage and harsh rather than spirited; too much *mousikê* results in softness rather than gentleness. As noted earlier, the *Republic* is written in the decades following Athens' defeat by Sparta in the nearly three-decades-long Peloponnesian War. It is not a stretch to see Plato here trying to find a balance of the best of the Spartan and Athenian temperaments while avoiding their excesses.

Towards the end of Book III, the artistic culture of the ideal city has been morally purified, lest citizens be harmed by being exposed to 'images of evil' (3.401b), like cows grazing 'in a meadow of bad grass' (3.401c). The potential guardians are subjected from youth on to a series of tests designed to see whether 'their belief[s] that they just do what is best for the city' (3.412e) can survive the blandishments of pleasure, the pressures of compulsion, and the effects of time and rhetoric. Here and elsewhere in Book III Socrates is concerned with changes that escape notice. A potential guardian who can be persuaded by a sophist, such as Thrasymachus, will not pass muster, since clever rhetoric can 'take away their opinions without their realizing it' (3.413b).

After describing the tests employed, Socrates distinguishes 'complete guardians' from the auxiliaries, resulting in a city with three classes: guardians or rulers, auxiliaries, and craftspeople. As will become clear, these are not socioeconomic classes but rather political classes, distinguished not by wealth but by political authority. The rulers and their helpers— that is, the guardians and the auxiliaries—live a spare, communal lifestyle, owning no private property, and living together in military-style barracks, as befits 'warrior athletes' (3.416e). Though it might be tempting to think that those who pass these exacting tests are guardians while those who do not are merely auxiliaries, this clearly will not do: the auxiliaries must also be 'guardians of this conviction [...] that they must do what is best for the city' (3.412e). The difference is age and experience: the auxiliaries are 'young people' (3.414b), while presumably the guardians, like good judges, are older and have more experience. A good judge, Socrates thinks, 'has learned late in life what injustice is like and who has become aware of it not as something at home in his soul, but as something alien and present in others, someone who, after a long time, has recognized that injustice is bad by nature, not from his own experience of it, but through knowledge' (3.409b). We will soon see that a crucial difference between auxiliaries and guardians is that the auxiliaries have unshakable and true *beliefs* about what is best for the city, the guardians have something even firmer: they have *knowledge* of what is best for the city

The Noble Falsehood (3.414b–417b)

The structure of the ideal city now set, Socrates offers a three-part foundational myth for the ideal city, which he calls the 'noble falsehood' (3.414b). He imagines telling the first-generation citizens of the now-completed city that they are born from the earth, which is their mother. They literally are of the soil—the soil of *this* place. This presumably will make them eager to defend their city-state, as one would be eager to defend one's mother. The second part of the myth follows from the first: since they are born of the same soil, they are all related, all brothers and sisters. Thinking of one's fellow citizens as family, he thinks, will bind the city together as one, making the citizens love each other as family members ideally do. For many of us, family bonds transcend reasons in an interesting and important way: whether one's siblings *merit* one's love seems beside the point; the basis of family affection is the bare fact of being related: that someone is your brother or sister itself provides reasons for action. Some philosophers are suspicious of the kind of loyalty that is grounded in pure relations rather than reasons, since it can lead to immoral or illegal actions, as many a *Law & Order* episode will attest. While we might expect Socrates to explore and question such loyalty, instead he exploits it, finding unifying power in familial love. Readers will remember that among the restrictions on stories about the gods is that no stories about gods hating or fighting each other will be allowed, since 'we want the guardians of our city to think that it is shameful to be easily provoked into hating one another' (2.378b), which is 'impious' (2.378c).

The last element of the Noble Falsehood is the famous Myth of the Metals: 'the god who made you mixed some gold into those who are adequately equipped to rule [...] He put silver in those who are auxiliaries and iron and bronze in the farmers and other craftsmen' (3.415a). So each class of the city is distinguished by the kind of metal that dominates the souls of its members. This is one of the most interesting as well as objectionable parts of the *Republic*. Its interest, I think, is its indicating Plato's awareness of the importance of myth in public life, especially myths of origin. Though humans are rational, we are not entirely rational. Earlier, Socrates appealed to the love the guardians have for the city as the glue binding them to it, although it is a love more cognitive than affective. And we just saw that the primary purpose of the second part of the Noble Falsehood is to cause the citizens to love each other. In having Socrates offer the Noble Falsehood, Plato is acknowledging the power and importance of myth, not just to human self-understanding but to the formation of *a* people of a nation or, here, a city-state. What the Myth of the Metals does is to provide a narrative understanding and mythic justification of the ideal city's three-part and decidedly non-egalitarian structure. The guardians' most important task, Socrates says, is to guard against 'the mixture of metals in the souls of the next generation' (3.415b), for 'the city will be ruined if it ever has an iron or bronze guardian' (3.415c). Oddly, there is no claim that letting the silver-souled auxiliaries rule would have this destructive power.

It is clear that Socrates must think of the Noble Falsehood as a merely verbal falsehood, 'one of those useful falsehoods' (3.414b) mentioned at the end of Book II, rather than a true or genuine falsehood, which is a falsehood 'about the most important things' (2.382a). Thrasymachus' belief that the unjust life is the happier life would be a true falsehood, on Socrates' view. It is not a true *lie*, since lying requires intentional deception, trying to get others to belief what you regard as false, and there is nothing to suggest that Thrasymachus does not sincerely hold the view he espouses. But, on Socrates' view, anyway, it is a true falsehood. It is not just factually false, but morally false and profoundly damaging to someone who believes it, since someone who lives their life by it cannot be happy (a claim he will try to prove in the last third of the *Republic*). Like the allowable stories about the gods and heroes, the Noble Falsehood is factually false—the citizens are *not* in fact born from the soil and are not actually distinguished by the kinds of metals in their souls. But its message, Socrates thinks, is deeply true.

This is where the Noble Falsehood is apt to seem most objectionable, for the profound claim it expresses, cloaked in mythic garb, is that human beings are *not* created equal. The guardians are simply more valuable than the craftspeople, Socrates holds, in the same way that the sexist thinks that men are just more valuable than women and the racist thinks that white people are just more valuable, possess more intrinsic worth, than non-whites. Anyone who subscribes to the fundamental moral and political equality of human beings will have to regard Socrates' Noble Falsehood as not merely a verbal falsehood but rather a true falsehood, with profoundly harmful consequences to those who believe it. If it is a compelling myth, a craftsperson will see nothing amiss in not having a voice in how the *polis* is governed; it is just not their place. Much of the power of myth is ideological: making what is contingent and constructed seem natural and necessary. In a memorable passage from *My Bondage and My Freedom,* Frederick Douglass recalls having been

> taught from the pulpit at St. Michael's, the duty of obedience to our masters; to recognize God as the author of our enslavement; to regard running away an offense, alike against God and man; to deem our enslavement a merciful and beneficial arrangement [...] to consider our hard hands and dark color as God's mark of displeasure, and as pointing us out as the proper objects of slavery.[1]

---

1   Frederick Douglass, *Autobiographies: Narrative of the Life of Frederick Douglass, an American Slave/ My Bondage and My Freedom/ Life and Times of Frederick Douglass*, ed. by Henry Louis Gates (New York: Library of America: 1994), p. 306.

Douglass, being Douglass, is able to pierce the veil of racist ideology in which slavery is clothed. He recognizes that, the Bible (or supposedly authoritative interpretations of it) notwithstanding, he is *not* a proper object of slavery: no one is. But such is the power of ideology and myth to make a contingent institution like slavery seem to be metaphysically necessary and ordained by God.

I suspect that most readers will agree that the Noble Falsehood is in fact a true falsehood, rather than the beneficial verbal falsehood Socrates takes it to be, since it denies the fundamental equality of all persons. I should stress that to believe in human equality is not to believe that all humans are equally able to do calculus, hit a curveball, nurture their children, etc. It is not a belief in *factual* equality. It is a belief in *moral* equality, in the equal dignity of all persons.

There are many places where the *Republic* butts up against deeply held but often implicit and perhaps unjustified beliefs many of us have. And though there are times when we are likely to arch our eyebrows and wonder if Plato is not really onto something in thinking as he does, I do not think this is one of those times.

Some Suggestions for Further Reading

Readers interested in philosophical issues raised by music will find Peter Kivy, *Introduction to a Philosophy of Music* (Oxford: Clarendon Press, 2002) well worth their time.

Less is known about ancient Greek music than one might expect, but interested readers should see M. L. West, *Ancient Greek Music* (Oxford: Clarendon Press, 1994).

Readers interested in Jefferson's Bible can find it at the Smithsonian Institute's webpage: http://americanhistory.si.edu/jeffersonbible/.

Readers interested in issues around disability will find Andrew Solomon, *Far From the Tree: Parents, Children, and the Search for Identity* (New York: Scribner, 2012), especially its first chapter, well worth reading. For a clear-headed, clearly written contemporary philosophical take on disability, see Elizabeth Barnes, *The Minority Body: A Theory of Disability* (New York: Oxford University Press, 2016).

Readers interested in exploring conceptual and ethical issues about deception and lying might start with Sissela Bok, *Lying: Moral Choice in Public and Private Life* (New York: Vintage Books, 1999).

Josef Abel, *Socrates Teaching his Disciples* (1807). Photograph by Jarash (2015), Wikimedia, Public Domain, https://commons.wikimedia.org/wiki/File:Josef_Abel_1807_Socrates_teaching_his_disciples.jpg

5. Starting to Answer the First Question

The Political Virtues

Book IV

In Book IV Socrates answers the *Republic*'s first question, *What is justice?* Keeping to the plan devised in Book II, he first tells us what *political* justice—justice in the *polis* or city-state—is and then, arguing that the ideal *polis* and the human soul (*psuchê*) share the same three-part structure, he applies his definition of political justice to the *psyche*, arriving at his definition of *personal* justice. His definition is interesting in many ways, not least of which is its accounting for justice not as a matter of outward behavior, as Cephalus' and Polemarchus' definitions did, but rather as an inward matter of psychic harmony.

Happiness: Parts and Wholes, Individuals and Communities (4.419a–421c)

Book IV begins with Adeimantus jumping back into the conversation with a concern that brings to the fore the tension between individualism and communitarianism. He worries that the guardians and auxiliaries will not be especially happy, given the lifestyles Socrates described at the close of Book III: communal living, no privacy, not much money, etc. 'The city really belongs to them', Adeimantus says, 'yet they derive no good from it' since they lack 'the things that are thought to belong to

   https://doi.org/10.11647/OBP.0229.05

people who are blessedly happy' (4.419a). This is certainly a plausible view about what the best kind of life is like. The Greek verb translated as 'thought' is νομίζεται (*nomizetai*), which is cognate with νόμος (*nomos:* custom or law), and thus indicates what is thought or deemed or customarily taken to be the best life—not necessarily what actually *is* the best life.

Plato has Socrates give a twofold response to Adeimantus. First, he suggests that far from being unhappy, the guardians may well be the happiest group in the ideal *polis*. They are performing the task or function for which they are best suited, after all, and if they are performing it well, they are probably delighting in it. It is another reminder that while the good of the community is Socrates' primary concern, it is not his only concern. Socrates then reminds Adeimantus of the plan they have adopted, to investigate the nature of *personal* justice and its connection to *personal* happiness by discovering the nature of *political* justice and its connection to happiness. His focus, then, is on *political* happiness, on 'making the whole city happy' (4.420c); he does not aim to make 'any one group outstandingly happy, but to make the whole city so' (4.420b). Even though he seems to be doubling down on the holistic or communitarian ethos that is regularly contrasted with the individualism which many readers will find intuitively more attractive, his communitarianism here is largely methodological, a useful device to get to his ultimate concern, which is individual happiness. In Book V he will suggest that individual wellbeing depends in no small way on whether the *polis* one lives in is just, which suggests a more modest community-first ethos than he has been espousing heretofore.

The Ideal City: Finishing Touches (4.421c–427d)

After giving a warning about the damage economic inequality can wreak in a city—a theme to which he will return in Book VIII—Socrates reminds Adeimantus of the importance of the guardians' preserving the educational system as they have received it, lest it be corrupted by seemingly minor and innocuous changes.

Many readers will have witnessed versions of such cultural conservatism in their lifetimes, for example, panicked responses to the threats posed by jazz, Elvis, the Beatles, and rap music. But lest Plato seem like just another cranky old fuddy-duddy bemoaning music he did not grow up with, we should remember that the ideal city's music was chosen intentionally and with great care, since it is meant to cultivate traits of character necessary to the city's thriving. The worry is that 'lawlessness easily creeps in [...] unnoticed' (4.424d), so, given how malleable young people are (a fact of human nature that is highly relevant to the educational system developed in Books II and III) it is important that music and culture generally provide sustenance to young souls. Children will absorb lawfulness or lawlessness—Plato mentions no neutral third option—from the games they play and the songs they sing and hear, so it is vital that the healthy system be preserved. Changes of mode and meter can seem trivial and morally neutral, but they are not, on Plato's moral-aesthetic conception of character development. Even if we do not share Plato's worry that 'changing to a new form of music [...] threatens the whole system' (4.424c), keeping in mind his beliefs in the malleability of young minds and the inseparability of morality and aesthetics should render his worry at least less curmudgeonly.

Though there are several other things worth discussing in this part of Book IV, I will mention just one, what we might call Plato's legislative minimalism. It is foolish, Socrates says, to think that legislation can overcome failures of education. Though some of his examples are trivial—regulating hairstyles and clothes—others are not: how the young treat the old and how they care for their parents, for example. This brief stretch of the *Republic* might seem little more than harrumphing about 'kids today', but Plato is doing more than mere griping here. He might not agree with the details of Ed Tom's diagnosis in Cormac McCarthy's *No Country for Old Men*—'*It starts when you begin to overlook bad manners. Any time you quit hearin Sir and Mam the end is pretty much in sight. I told her, I said: It reaches into ever strata.*'[1]—but in principle they seem to be of one mind. Communities are held together by more than rules and laws; they are held together by shared values and affections. Education in Plato's broad sense is primarily *character* education, after all, and there is something to his point that legislation cannot repair defective character

---

1   Cormac McCarthy, *No Country for Old Men* (New York: Vintage Books, 2006), p. 304. Spelling, syntax, and italics as in original.

education. Still, we might worry that his view ignores the expressive function of law—the law's power to say something about the shared norms and values that bind a community together. If, in addition to governing behavior, the law can also shape attitudes and beliefs, then it may have a contribution to make to character education, if only an ancillary one.

In my home state of Wisconsin, adultery is a crime—a felony, in fact. Prosecutions are extremely rare—there have been none in the last thirty years—but presumably that is not because there have been so few violations of Wisconsin Statute §944.16. I know of no empirical studies of this law's efficacy in reducing adultery, but it seems unlikely that potential adulterers would be deterred by it, especially given its non-enforcement. But even if there is no direct causal link between criminalizing adultery and reducing extramarital adventuring, its criminalization may yet serve an important function: expressing the citizenry's collective disapproval of adultery. If the law plays this expressive role, striking the adultery statute from the books might seem to signal, if not the community's approval of adultery, at least its non-disapproval, and it is not implausible that this would have negative behavioral consequences, by changing attitudes and feelings about the importance of marital fidelity, promise-keeping, etc. So there may be a dimension to the law that Plato is missing here. On the other hand, a law's remaining on the books because of its expressive function might cultivate the sort of cynicism and hypocrisy Adeimantus complains about in Book II: many citizens make a great show of the importance of the values just mentioned, because it is important to *seem* just, but in practice their conduct suggests a preference for *being* unjust.

The Political Virtues (4.427d–434d)

Now that the ideal city is complete, it is time to look for justice in it. But before we do that, I bring up a seemingly minor point that, as is so often the case with Plato, is surprisingly deep upon examination, carrying more philosophical weight than initial appearances suggest.

In announcing the completion of the ideal city, which paves the way for the inquiry into the nature of justice, Socrates says to Adeimantus, 'your city might now be said to be established' (4.427d). This seems innocuous enough, but up to this point, Socrates' possessive pronoun of choice has been the first-person plural: he speaks of 'our city' and 'our citizens' (2.370d, 2.371e, 2.373b, 2.378b, 3.387e, 3.394d, 3.397d). At the corresponding point in Book II, at the completion of the first city, Socrates says, 'Well, Adeimantus, has our city grown to completeness, then?' (2.371e; emphasis added) Why the shift here from *our* city to *your* city? Perhaps it is merely stylistic variation on Plato's part. After all, within just a few lines Socrates shifts back to 'our city' (4.427e), and then it is soon back again to 'your city' (4.431c). I suspect that the shift in pronouns is Plato's way of reminding us that Socrates, despite being the chief theoretical architect of the just-completed ideal city, still regards the first city, the rustic utopia rejected by Glaucon as 'a city for pigs' (2.372d), as 'the true city [...] the healthy one' (2.372e). Perhaps Plato hopes his readers will pick up on Socrates' ambivalence and reflect further on his allegiance to his rustic utopia. That city, which has been all but forgotten by this point in the *Republic,* was without guardians and auxiliaries and indeed without classes of any kind. The just-completed city is not only structured by political classes but in fact, we will soon see, has the same structure as the human soul. This is a perfect place to remind attentive readers of the second-best nature of the ideal city, if only to make us think through how seriously to take Socrates' attitude toward it.

So what seems a matter of mere style may turn out to be really a matter of substance, though we will not pursue so fine a point any further. Hopefully, though, this brief discussion reminds us of what a subtle work the *Republic* is and why it rewards repeated rereading.

Cardinal Virtues

If the city is well founded, Socrates argues, it will be 'completely good' (4.427e) and thus it will not be missing any of the moral virtues. For Socrates and Plato, there are four primary virtues: courage, moderation, wisdom and justice. Aristotle had a much longer list, including friendliness, wit, generosity, and proper pride, among others. Philosophers often speak of Plato's four virtues as 'the cardinal virtues', which suggests at a minimum that the virtues are important or paramount. But in another, stronger sense, to call a virtue a *cardinal virtue* is to say that it is theoretically basic: there are no virtues more basic than it and any non-cardinal virtue is somehow reducible to or a version of the cardinal virtue in question. Socrates says that 'there are four virtues' (4.428a) and that together they make the city 'completely good' (4.427e), which suggests that these virtues are cardinal in the stronger, theoretically basic sense. To see what is at stake here, consider the attention paid earlier in the *Republic* to cultivating the virtue of piety by regulating stories about the gods—and consider Plato's having devoted an entire dialogue (the *Euthyphro*) to investigating the nature of piety. If piety is not a cardinal virtue, perhaps it can be subsumed under justice, since piety concerns what is owed to the gods and justice is plausibly thought of as giving to each what they are owed. Viewing piety as a requirement or form of justice would preserve the cardinality of Socrates' four virtues. One problem with this view, however, is that in Book I Socrates casts doubt on defining justice in terms of what is owed, and we will soon see that the definition of justice Socrates proposes is *not* couched in terms of giving to each what they are owed. Another, related, worry is that what goes for piety can also go for the other virtues. If courage, for example, can be thought of as what soldiers owe the city, then like piety courage is not itself a distinct virtue but instead a kind of justice. So by seeking to preserve the cardinality of the four cardinal virtues we end up destroying their cardinality.

This concern about piety is in a sense *internal* to Plato's moral thinking and to the account of virtue he is offering here: he seems committed to piety's being a genuine, stand-alone virtue and yet he excludes it from his 'official' list. A different kind of concern is *external*: when looking at Plato's list *we* might think he is excluding some traits *we* take to be virtues. Many readers will think of kindness and generosity, for example, as virtues of character, and thus think Plato's list is mistaken not because of an internal inconsistency or tension but because it fails to include traits that belong on the list. When thinking about the attitudes Socrates expresses toward the disabled in Book III, many readers will think that the virtue of compassion is in short supply in his ideal city. It would be difficult to subsume generosity under justice, since generosity is at least in part a matter of giving which goes *beyond* what is owed.

Yet another worry concerns the argument Socrates gives for the complete goodness of the ideal city:

P1   If our city has been correctly founded, it is completely good. (4.427e)

P2   Our city has been correctly founded.

C   Therefore, our city is completely good.

While we might question why correctness must imply completeness, P1 seems plausible. But many readers, noting the absence of individual liberty and equal political rights in the ideal city, will have grave doubts about P2. Socrates' more community-minded interlocutors raise no such objections, but as thoughtful readers we will want to engage in philosophical dialogue with our author by thinking through the issues for ourselves, in both senses of *for ourselves.* We want to think about these issues independently, not merely relying on what Plato or Socrates or whoever has to say. And we want to think about what Socrates' claims mean *to us.* As he reminds his readers at various points, Socrates' method depends upon his interlocutors' 'saying what [they] really think' (1.349a). Good philosophical reading often requires adopting another's point of view, examining whether the claims an author makes from within that point of view are consistent with it. But good philosophical reading also requires scrutinizing that point of view itself, not just for its internal consistency but also for its substantive correctness. Of course, there is a danger here of taking our own points of view as sacrosanct and beyond criticism and rejecting points of view at odds with them. But one of the values of reading a book like the *Republic,* which expresses perspectives very different from our own, is that they can prod us to think through our deeply-held but not always carefully, critically scrutinized beliefs.

As usual, there is more to be said here and by no means am I suggesting that Plato has no plausible responses to these worries. But in questioning the adequacy of his claim about how many virtues there are we honor him by doing the thing he most wants of us: to think philosophically and critically.

Wisdom (4.428a–429a)

The first virtue discovered in the city, wisdom (σοφία [*sophia*]), is the virtue of a particular class: the guardian-rulers. Wisdom is often thought of as an intellectual virtue, rather than a character virtue, as it is a kind of knowledge. Aristotle distinguished the intellectual and character virtues (although he ultimately thought that some of them were mutually dependent). While this is not a distinction Plato explicitly makes, it is a helpful one, both in itself and for the light it will shed in Book VII of the *Republic,* when Plato is busy distinguishing philosophers from non-philosophers.

Wisdom is a kind of knowledge, Socrates thinks, but not just any old kind of knowledge and certainly not the kind of knowledge that craftspeople possess. Nor is it the kind of abstract, theoretical knowledge a mathematician might possess. It is more general than the craftsperson's know-how and more practical than the mathematician's know-that. It is knowledge of what is best for the city as a whole (4.428c). Although many readers are leery of Socrates' holism and communitarianism, here they seem unproblematic: wisdom is knowledge of what is best for the city *as a whole,* not what is best for any particular group of citizens. If the city is to function well, it must be unified, and it can only be unified if its rulers aim at the good of the whole, rather than at what is good for a particular part of it at the expense of the whole. Socrates has already implied that good rulers will strive to minimize economic inequality, given its dis-integrating effects. Some economic inequality is to be expected and may well be beneficial, but too much leads to there not being 'a city [...] [but] two cities at war with one another, that of the poor and that of the rich' (4.422e [italics in the original]). Just as the ideal city's founders aimed not to 'make any one group outstandingly happy but to make the whole so, as far as possible' (4.420b), its rulers must aim at the good of the city as a whole.

It should make sense that this is the virtue distinctive of the guardians, if we remember the earlier account of a virtue as what enables its possessor to perform its function well. Since the function of the rulers is—unsurprisingly—to rule, they can rule well only if they possess wisdom. A ruler who makes only lucky guesses, or even educated guesses, about what is best for the city is less likely to rule well than a ruler who *knows* what is best for the city. Now of course we can agree that rulers require wisdom to rule well without agreeing with Socrates' conception of it or with his belief that only a few citizens are capable of it. One might be skeptical that *knowledge* about what is best for a city-state or country is really possible, settling instead for experience-grounded *beliefs*. And one might think wisdom is at least in principle within the grasp of ordinary citizens. We have already seen, and will see in more detail in Books VIII and IX, that Socrates is no fan of democracy—presumably because he is skeptical that ordinary citizens are capable of the sort of knowledge needed to rule well.

Courage (4.429a–430c)

Courage, like wisdom, is also a virtue distinctive of a particular class: the soldiering auxiliaries. It becomes clear that the guardians, who emerge from the auxiliaries, will also possess courage, but their *distinctive* (rather than sole) virtue is wisdom, not courage. As above, their possessing courage makes sense when we remember that the auxiliaries' function is to protect the city, which they can do well only if they possess courage. A surprising way in which courage is similar to wisdom is that courage, at least as Socrates characterizes it, is at root a cognitive affair: it is 'th[e] power to preserve through everything the correct and law-inculcated *belief* about what is to be feared and what is not' (4.430b [emphasis added]). Attentive readers will have noticed that the wisdom the guardians possess is a kind of *knowledge*, but the auxiliaries' courage is a matter of *belief*, not knowledge. Making clear how knowledge and belief differ will be a central focus of Books V, VI, and VII. It might be helpful to bring the JTB (justified true belief) conception of knowledge into play again (reminding ourselves that it is not Plato's view but rather a heuristic to help us make sense of some features of the *Republic*). The auxiliaries believe that certain things are worse than death—slavery and dishonor, for example—but the guardians know *why* these things are worse than death: they have, in addition to a true belief, a justification for their true belief. While the auxiliaries' beliefs lack the intellectual backing the guardians possess, this in no way prevents their holding it firmly and unshakably. Their belief that there are fates worse than death must be dyed-in-the-wool, in Socrates' memorable metaphor: dyed in so deeply that 'the color is fast—no amount of washing [...] can remove it' (4.429b). If the Spartan soldiers holding the pass at Thermopylae against Persian invaders—an event that, until the film *The 300*, was the province of classicists and history nerds—valued their own lives over the good of the community, they would have thrown down their weapons and run for safety. The opening pages of Book III, attentive readers will remember, were rife with constraints on stories and poetry designed to cultivate courage. Any would-be auxiliary who believes that their death would be the worst thing that could happen believes a true falsehood, a belief that is radically false and distorts an important dimension of reality. The auxiliaries' education, both poetic and physical, is meant to cultivate the virtue of courage.

We should note a subtle but important refinement Socrates makes to his definition of courage. He first describes courage as the auxiliaries' 'power to preserve through everything its belief about what things are to be feared' (4.429b), but he quickly adds a qualifier: courage is 'preservation of the belief *that has been inculcated by the law through education* about what things and sorts of things are to be feared' (4.429c [emphasis added]), a qualification he repeats a page later: '*the correct and law-inculcated belief*' (4.430b). He is making a distinction between what Aristotle will later call *natural virtue* and *virtue proper*. Some people and indeed many animals seem by nature courageous, born with correct beliefs about what is properly feared and with the power to preserve those beliefs in the face of danger. But unless these beliefs are the product of education, what is present is not 'courage but something else' (4.430b). Socrates does not elaborate, but presumably he thinks this because proper courage's natural analog may misfire without the guidance of reason and education. We have already seen that too much physical education and not enough musical education results in a person's becoming 'hard and harsh' (3.410d) rather than courageous.

Moderation (4.430d–432b)

Unlike courage and wisdom, moderation is *not* distinctive of any particular class in the city; instead, 'moderation spreads throughout the whole' (4.432a). Socrates starts with the commonsense connection between moderation (also called temperance) and self-control. If you decline and I insist on a third slice of cheesecake, you seem to have and I seem to lack the virtue of moderation. But explaining this in terms of self-control is puzzling, Socrates thinks, since what does the controlling and what is controlled is the very same thing. The puzzle is solved when we realize that our souls have better and worse parts, with the better part comprising our capacities for reason and choice and the worse part our appetite and desires. In the self-controlled person, 'the naturally better part is in control of the naturally worse' (4.431a), so they decline that third slice of cheesecake while I do not.

There is something problematic about Socrates' procedure here. The plan is to figure out the nature of the *political* virtues in order to discover the nature of the *personal* virtues. But here he is appealing to the structure of the soul or person in trying to understand the nature of the *political* virtue of moderation, so he is building into the *polis* the psychic structure he will soon claim to find there. As a grad school professor once wrote in the margins of a paper of mine, 'if you are going to try to pull the rabbit out of the hat, it is best if you are not seen putting it in'. But perhaps there is no big problem here. After all, Socrates is simply appealing to an ordinary belief about moderation as a kind of self-control; he is not importing any high-level psychological theory, and he may well have been able to arrive at his conclusion—that 'something in which the better rules the worse is properly called moderate and self-controlled' (4.431b)—without the appeal to commonsense psychology.

The ideal *polis* is self-controlled and thus moderate, Socrates thinks, because it is ruled by the guardians, who are the best part of the *polis*. But there is more to it than that. A city in which the guardians only tenuously hold power over the rebellious craftspeople is not moderate, nor would Socrates think it is, for it is lacking the harmony distinctive of true self-control. In a moderate or self-controlled *polis,* the three classes 'all sing the same song together' (4.432a): there is 'agreement between the naturally worse and the naturally better as to which of the two is to rule' (4.432a).

As with the wisdom and courage, Socrates plays up the cognitive nature of this virtue: 'ruler and ruled [...] share *the same belief* about who should rule' (4.431d [italics added]). They are in agreement, not in the way in which a good drawing or measurement agrees with its object or in the way in which some food agrees with my finicky stomach but other food does not, but in the way that only rational creatures can be: consent. We should tread carefully here, however, for the idea of *consent* can be misleading. Socrates is not offering the modern, liberal view that the legitimacy of a government turns on the consent of the governed. The consent Socrates has in mind is a *symptom* of good government, not a condition of its legitimacy. Presumably, in a well-governed city, the craftspeople consent to being governed by the guardians because things are going well for them economically; they are happy with the arrangement and are happy to be left alone to their cobbling, baking, doctoring, etc., and their family lives. The entitlement of the guardians to rule depends not on the consent of those they govern but on their possessing the relevant virtue, wisdom.

A word or two about the 'spread out' nature of moderation is in order. Unlike wisdom and courage, which are what we might call *particular* virtues, which are virtues distinctive of particular classes, moderation is a *holistic* virtue, a virtue of the whole city, not of any of its particular classes. This is a subtle point, easily misunderstood. Although a city is wise because its rulers are wise and brave because its auxiliaries are brave, Plato is *not* saying that the city is moderate because every class is moderate. Moderation does not work that way. By way of analogy, think of a basket containing red balls, green balls, and yellow balls. The collection of balls has a property which none of its members has: the property of being multi-colored. The collection is multi-colored because of the colors of the individual balls: if the basket contained only green balls, the collection would not exhibit the property of being multi-colored. But none of the individual balls in the basket is multi-colored: each is either red or green or yellow. (Of course, nothing prevents individual balls from being multi-colored: a particular ball might be red, green, and yellow—but none of the balls in our example has this property.) So the collection's having this property depends upon the members having certain properties—but it is the collection, and not its members, that has the property of being multi-colored. Being multi-colored, in this example, is a holistic property, depending on the nature of the individuals but not reducible or equivalent to them.

The political virtue of moderation, as Socrates conceives of it, is the same kind of holistic property, belonging to the whole and not to the parts. It is *not* the case that the city is moderate because each class is moderate; rather, the city is moderate because the different classes agree about who should rule, just as the basket of balls is multi-colored even though none of the balls are.

Socrates' talk of better and worse parts may be easier to hear when the parts in question are parts of the soul rather than the city. Thinking of the guardians as 'naturally better' than the craftspeople has a dissonant ring to egalitarian ears. As we noted when discussing the Noble Falsehood, the kind of equality that most readers will insist on (and which Plato has Socrates denying) is not factual equality. Some people can run or swim faster than others; some people are better at knitting than others; some people are better at differential equations than others. What is at issue is *political* equality, the belief that all citizens have equal rights to participating in the political life of their communities. We will see in the next chapter that Socrates expresses the view that being a woman does not in itself disqualify a person from being a guardian. But he certainly does not think that all women, or all men, are capable of being guardians, since so very few of us are capable of acquiring the requisite virtue, wisdom.

We will return to this topic in the next chapter and then again when discussing Plato's attitudes toward democracy in Chapter 12, so for now the egalitarians among us should merely note our disagreement with Plato. But we should also be thinking of how we might go about trying to convince him, drawing on premises he himself would accept, that he is mistaken to reject political equality. It is not an easy task. But, as I have said before, one of the great benefits of carefully reading the *Republic* is that doing so can lead us to wrestle with difficult tasks like this, to question and defend propositions that seem self-evident *to us* but do not so appear to others.

Justice (4.432b–434d)

Since three of the four cardinal virtues have been identified, Socrates thinks that justice must be whatever is left. 'Justice: it's what is left over' does not exactly inspire confidence, either as a bumper-sticker or a philosophical methodology. But Socrates' point is that the answer to the *Republic*'s first question is staring them in the face, so to speak. They have been talking about it without even knowing it, he thinks, because justice is based on, and indeed seems to be a moralized version of the Specialization Principle: 'justice', he says, 'is doing one's own work, and not meddling with what is not one's own' (4.433a).

Although it is initially stated in terms of individual behavior, justice as a virtue of the *polis* is really a matter of each *class* doing its work: the craftspeople produce and exchange goods, the auxiliaries protect the city, and the guardians govern it. If this is indeed what justice is, Socrates' earlier insistence that the guardians' most important task is to protect against the mixing of the metals grows in importance. If their task is to ensure justice and prevent its opposite, then they must prevent the craftspeople from ruling, since, the Noble Falsehood informed us, 'the city will be ruined if it ever has an iron or a bronze guardian' (3.415c). When cobblers bake and bakers cobble, the city will have suboptimal bread and sandals (and not enough of them), since this violates the Specialization Principle, which requires specialization as a way of producing 'more plentiful and better-quality goods' (2.370c). But occupation-switching is disastrous, and not merely suboptimal, when bakers and guardians switch roles. A baking guardian who lacks the baker's skill will produce bread that is not very good, but a ruling baker who lacks the guardian's wisdom will produce disaster, on Socrates' view.

Justice as non-meddling has intriguing parallels in Confucius' *Analects*. When asked about good governing, Confucius replies, 'The ruler must rule, the minister minister, the father father, and the son son' (12.11). Underlying Confucius' somewhat odd way of making his point is that roles are not merely descriptive but rather normative, providing rules and norms of conduct. (This echoes the discussion of the 'precise sense' of craft-terms such as 'ruler' back in Book I.) A widely heard complaint about contemporary American parenting is that too many parents seek to be their children's friend (searching Google or Yahoo for 'be a parent not a friend', for example, yields millions of hits). But even without investigating the complaint's merits, we see its point, which is both a Platonic and Confucian one. We each inhabit many roles: citizen, friend, neighbor, mother, cousin, customer, boss, etc., and it may not always be clear which role is appropriate in a given situation. To a great degree, practical wisdom is a matter of seeing which role is appropriate in the circumstances so one can then act accordingly. And of course it is not always clear what the role requires, even when one determines which role is called for. It may be that in interacting with a particular employee on a particular day, being a friend rather than a boss is what is called for. But it may be that a different situation calls for just the opposite.

Although this idea of the normative status of roles is plausible and intriguing—indeed, Confucianism is often thought of as a kind of role ethics—many readers will be understandably uncomfortable with the *political* implications of Plato's role-based account of justice, rejecting the idea of assigning to a fellow citizen 'the rank appropriate to his nature' (3.415c), for it seems an easy, morally problematic slide from here to insisting that others 'know their place'. Role ethics is a fascinating topic, but exploring it in more depth would take us too far afield. So instead, let us briefly explore two arguments Socrates makes in support of his definition of political justice.

The first argument is explicitly marked in a way that should garner our attention: 'Look at it this way if you want to be convinced' (4.433e), Socrates says. The argument turns on the proper role of a judge, which is not surprising, given the focus on roles. The ideal city's rulers will also be judges, Socrates argues, and a judge's 'sole aim' is that 'no citizen should have what belongs to another or be deprived of what is his own' (4.433e)—because this, intuitively, is just. Therefore, Socrates concludes, 'the having and doing of one's own would be accepted as justice' (4.434a). This seems plausible, and Glaucon finds it so. But a more critically disposed reader might question the sudden appearance of 'doing one's own' in the conclusion, when the premises have concerned only *having* one's own. Socrates' argument is commonsensical and intuitive because it concerns property: justice requires that I not be wrongfully deprived of my property. Is what one *does* properly thought of something one *has?* Are one's roles to be counted among one's property? Perhaps, but if *being, doing,* and *having* are distinct metaphysical categories, we should be leery of fusing them into each other.

The second argument is also simple and straightforward. Since 'meddling and exchange between these three classes'—that is, the mixing of the metals—'is the greatest harm that can happen to the city' and injustice is the worst thing one can do to one's city, it follows, Socrates argues, that 'meddling is injustice' (4.434c). And if meddling is injustice, it must follow that its opposite, not meddling, is justice. A reader who suspects that this argument begs the question—that it assumes the truth of what it is trying to prove—seems to be on the mark. Only someone who already accepts the proposed definition of justice would accept the argument's first premise, that meddling is the worst evil that could befall the city. And even waiving that worry, egalitarian-minded readers who are friendly to democracy are likely to think that the first premise is simply false. They are likelier to think that the hierarchical, elitist structure of Socrates' ideal city is among the worst evils that can befall a political community. And sharp-minded readers will wonder whether Socrates is confusing cause and effect, thinking that even by Socrates' lights the meddling itself is not the great evil but rather is the *cause* of the evil, which presumably is the disintegration of the city. Many such readers will be skeptical that meddling or metals-mixing will cause the great harm Socrates claims for it.

In addition to these external worries about Socrates' definition of justice, there is an *in*ternal worry about it—that is, a worry from *within* Socrates' point of view—concerning the cardinality of the cardinal virtues. Piety, the reader will remember, is treated elsewhere in the *Republic* (and elsewhere in Plato's dialogues) as a distinct virtue in its own right. But Socrates does not count it as a cardinal virtue (or even mention it) in Book IV. Earlier I suggested that attempting to regard piety as a form of justice (and thus retaining Socrates' view that there are only four moral virtues) did not pan out. Here, the concern is that justice, as Socrates describes it, and moderation are so similar that it is difficult to count them as *two* virtues. A city is moderate when all three classes 'share the same belief about who should rule' (4.431de) and it is just when each class does its own work, but it is hard to see how those are really different, since each class doing its own work seems to be the embodiment of the agreement. Although making an agreement and acting on it are not the same thing—as anyone who has had a contractual dispute or, to choose a homier example, anyone who has experienced a child not being willing to go to bed at the agreed-upon time, can attest—the difference here does not seem sufficient to justify viewing moderation and justice as distinct cardinal virtues. If we are tempted to insist that the difference between agreement and action *is* sufficient to justify claims of cardinality, we might find our position turned against us. After all, an opponent might argue, could not the same be said about courage? Surely a *belief* that *x* is an appropriate object of fear and *acting* on that belief are not the same thing, even if they are closely related. If so, there would need to be another virtue, related to but distinct from courage; and if that is the case, then Socrates is mistaken that 'there are four virtues' (4.428a).

While Socrates does not wrestle with this problem directly, his view that justice is a sort of meta-virtue might implicitly solve his problem. The prefix 'meta-' suggests a higher-level or higher-order aboutness. Meta-cognition is cognition about cognition: thinking about thinking. Though it is often more at home in psychological contexts, there is a sense in which *we* are engaged in meta-cognition here: we are thinking about Plato's thinking about justice. So to call justice a *meta*-virtue is to suggest that it is a virtue *about* the other virtues. Even so, there is a sense in which thinking of justice as a meta-virtue can be misleading. Cognition comes before meta-cognition: there is no thinking about thinking unless there is first some thinking to think about! But on Socrates' view, justice comes before the other virtues: it is the condition of their possibility, 'the power that makes it possible for them to grow in the city and that preserves them when they have grown for as long as it remains there itself' (4.433b). It is worth emphasizing the word 'power' in this description (the Greek word is δύναμις (*dunamis*), from which the English word 'dynamic' derives). Justice is a power that enables agreement about who should rule; it is what makes it possible for there to be an agreement in the first place. Justice so conceived is not merely everyone's doing his own work, but is rather '*the power* that consists in everyone's doing his own work' (4.433d [emphasis added]). Similarly, courage is not merely the correct belief about what is appropriately feared, but is '*the power* to preserve through everything [the] belief about what things are to be feared' (4.429c). Earlier, I emphasized the *belief* at the center of courage, to draw a contrast with the *knowledge* that constitutes wisdom. Indeed, that is what enabled the imaginary interlocutor above to drive a wedge between belief and action. Reminding ourselves that courage is not merely a belief, but rather the power to preserve that belief through thick and thin, closes that gap.

Socrates' idea that justice is what makes the other virtues possible certainly makes sense for moderation, especially if we remember that the shared agreement about who should rule is a symptom of a well-governed city, and not, as we moderns tend to think, the ultimate condition of the government's legitimacy. It seems initially to make less sense for courage and wisdom, since they are particular rather than holistic virtues (virtues distinctive of particular classes rather than of the city as a whole). Would would-be rulers and auxiliaries still possess their distinctive virtues even if justice did not prevail in the city? Those capable of ruling would still know what is best for the city as a whole even if they are not in fact ruling, and the same would seem to go for would-be auxiliaries. Indeed, just these sorts of situations arise as the ideal city begins to disintegrate, as described by Socrates in Books VIII and IX. Perhaps. But the time and attention Socrates has devoted to education in the ideal city suggests that while wisdom and courage can be defined and understood independently of justice, they cannot be manifested or made real in its absence. Much of the program of education Socrates spells out in Books II and III is devoted to educating the auxiliaries. He will return to education in Book VII, but there his focus will be on educating the guardians, sketching out a program that will ultimately enable them to grasp the nature of goodness itself, which they will need if they are to *know* what is best for the city as a whole and not merely have correct beliefs about this. So even if we can understand what courage and wisdom *are* independently of justice, we can imagine Socrates saying, those virtues will never come to be without the rigorous educational program of Books II, III, and VII, which is why it is so crucial for the guardians to defend it and resist all attempts to change it even slightly. In Book III Socrates indicates that the guardians' most important task is to prevent the mixing of the metals described in the Noble Falsehood: 'there is nothing that they must guard better or watch more carefully than the mixture of metals in the souls of the next generation' (3.415b). What he says in Book IV initially seems to conflict with this, since there he suggests that their most important task is to 'guard the one great thing [...] education and upbringing [...] [that] those in charge must cling to education [...] guarding it against everything' (4.423d–24b). It seems that these distinct tasks cannot be the *one* most important task. But indeed, they really are one and the same task, since the only way to prevent the mixing of the metals is to preserve the educational system. Indeed, as we will see when Socrates describes the disintegration of the ideal city in Books VIII and IX, the decay begins when 'they have less consideration for music and poetry than they ought [... and] then they will neglect physical training' (8.546d). These changes to education are quickly followed by '[t]he intermixing of iron with silver and bronze with gold' (8.546e).

So while justice is *conceptually* distinct from the other cardinal virtues, they depend upon it for their coming into being in the city. Justice and the other virtues, while conceptually distinct, are not *really* or *existentially* distinct: justice is the condition of their coming into existence. Thus it is a tad misleading to call it a 'meta-virtue', since it is *about* the other virtues in a distinct way: it is the condition of their reality. It is their basis—their ἀρχή (*archê*) or foundation.

Some Suggestions for Further Reading

Readers interested in Plato's other Socratic dialogues on the virtues will want to read the *Euthyphro* (on piety), the *Charmides* (on temperance), and the *Laches* (on courage), all of which are available both online and in print form. Excellent translations of all of Plato's dialogues and letters can be found in *Plato: Complete Works,* ed. by John Cooper (Indianapolis: Hackett Publishing, 1997).

Readers interested in the ethics of virtue generally and the question of the cardinal virtues in particular might start with Rosalind Hursthouse and Glenn Pettigrove's excellent overview in the Stanford Encyclopedia of Philosophy: https://plato.stanford.edu/entries/ethics-virtue/.

Readers interested in role ethics will find a good overview in John Ramsey, 'Confucian Role Ethics: A Critical Survey', *Philosophy Compass,* 11 (2016), 235–45, https://doi.org/10.1111/phc3.12324.

Readers interested in the expressive function of law might start with Cass Sunstein, 'Law's Expressive Function', *The Good Society,* 9 (1999), 55–61.

Bust of Athena, of the 'Velletri Pallas' type (inlaid eyes are lost). Copy of the 2nd century CE after a votive statue of Kresilas in Athens (ca. 430–420 BCE). Photograph by Aavindraa (2010), Wikimedia, Public Domain, https://commons.wikimedia.org/wiki/Category:Athena#/media/File:Bust_Athena_Velletri_Glyptothek_Munich_213.jpg

6. The *Republic*'s First Question Answered at Last

Personal Justice

Book IV

Whatever worries or quibbles we might have about Socrates' definition of political justice, Glaucon finds it satisfactory: 'I agree. Justice is that and nothing else' (4.434d). A reminder about methodology might be in order here. Back in Book I, Socrates opted for question-and-answer over speechifying as the preferred method for investigating the nature of justice. Crucial to this method is 'seeking agreement with each other' (1.348b), arriving at a conclusion from shared premises, and then in turn treating that conclusion as a premise from which to derive new conclusions. Sometimes Glaucon and others seem too ready to agree with Socrates, and they often fail to critically scrutinize his claims, but an important feature of Socrates' method is its cooperative, agreement-securing nature. (This is perhaps surprising in light of cinematic and televisual depictions of 'the Socratic method' as a matter of antagonistic intellectual combat between a knowing professor and a terrified first-year law student.) So before putting the definition of *political* justice to work in order to understand *personal* justice, Socrates wants to be sure that Glaucon accepts the conclusion of their investigation into the nature of political justice. Given the focus on theoretical city-building, it is easy to forget that the political theorizing is not an end in itself but rather a means to grasping what justice is for the individual. Now Socrates must

    https://doi.org/10.11647/OBP.0229.06

make good on the promissory note he wrote in Book II and justify the assumption that city and soul are sufficiently analogous so that what is true of the former is also true of the latter.

Platonic Psychology: The Divided Soul (4.434d–441c)

If Socrates is to 'apply what has come to light in the city to an individual' (4.434e), he first needs to show that city and soul have the same structure. He has been proceeding on the assumption that they do, and now it is time to make good on the big *if* he has been operating with: 'if an individual has these same three parts in his soul' (4.435b). In a few pages, he thinks he has done the job, noting 'we are pretty much agreed that the same number and the same kinds of classes as are in the city are also in the soul of each individual' (4.441c). How does he get there?

Earlier, when discussing personal, Socrates suggested that the commonsense idea of self-control was puzzling, for it seems 'ridiculous' (4.430e) that something could control itself. But he makes sense of this intuitive account of moderation by positing that the soul has parts. In a moderate person's soul, a better, rational part is in charge, governing by 'calculation in accordance with understanding and correct belief' (4.431c) the worse part, which contains 'all kinds of diverse desires, pleasures, and pains' (4.431c). He now makes explicit the principle by which he arrived at this distinction, which I will call the Opposition Principle: 'the same thing will not be willing to do or undergo opposites in the same part of itself, in relation to the same thing, at the same time. So, if we ever find this happening in the soul, we will know that we are not dealing with one thing but many' (4.436b).

To get a sense of the Opposition Principle, suppose you have one hand in a bucket of hot water and the other in a bucket of cold water. It seems that you are both hot and cold—but how could that be, since hot and cold are opposites? The Opposition Principle tells us you must have parts, which indeed you (obviously) do: one of your parts is hot while the other is cold. Another example: if I am standing in one spot, but nodding my head, am I moving or not? The answer seems to be both yes and no: I am not changing my location, so in that sense I am not moving, but in another sense, I am moving, since I am moving my head. The Opposition Principle tells us that I must have parts, since I can simultaneously undergo or instantiate incompatible opposites.

Most of us have had the experience of wanting to do something but not doing it, even when we are able. I am really hungry and there is a piece of pizza right in front of me, but I do not eat it—perhaps because I see that it is *your* pizza, not mine, and I think that I should not take what is not mine. I am really jonesing for a cigarette, yet I do not light up—not because there are no cigarettes available, but because I am trying to quit. Whatever the details, the question is essentially the same: what explains my having a desire or appetite that I am able to fulfill but do not? It might be that I have another desire and that both of these desires cannot be satisfied at the same time. If I am really, really hungry and really, really, really tired, whichever one is stronger—whichever has more 'really's—will probably determine what I do. A conflict of desires shows that I have many desires, but not that my soul is divided. But the kinds of cases Socrates discusses are not like that: they are cases in which I *choose* not to act on my desire because I have a *reason* not to do so. In these sorts of cases the Opposition Principle tells me that my soul must have at least two parts, one appetitive and one rational. But Socrates soon comes to see that there must be a third part, as well:

> Do we do these things with the same part of ourselves, or do we do them with three different parts? Do we learn with one part, get angry with another and with some third part desire the pleasure of food, drink, sex, and the others that are closely akin to them? Or, when we set out after something, do we act with the whole of our soul, in each case? (4.436a)

Now he suggests there is a third part, spirit, in addition to reason and appetite. In contrast to the rational part, which is 'the part of the soul with which it calculates' (4.439d), and the irrational appetitive part, which is 'the part with which it lusts, hungers, thirsts, and gets excited by other appetites' (4.439d), there is also 'the spirited part$_{[,]}$ by which we get angry' (4.439e)—both at others, when we have been treated unjustly, and also at ourselves, when we have acted unjustly. To illustrate this, Socrates offers the rather disturbing example of Leontius' necrophilia:

> He had an appetite to look at them but at the same time he was disgusted and turned away. For a time he struggled with himself and covered his face, but, finally, overpowered by the appetite, he pushed his eyes wide

open and rushed towards the corpses, saying, 'Look for yourselves, you evil wretches, take your fill of the beautiful sight!' (4.439e)

Leontius' spirited element 'makes war against the appetites' (4.440a) but ultimately loses, giving in to a desire that Leontius himself is disgusted by—which results in his self-directed anger.

Let us pause for a moment and consider the role disgust plays in the *Republic*. Socrates has praised the person 'of godlike character who is disgusted by injustice' (2.366c), in contrast to the unjust person who 'has no scruples about [—i.e., is not disgusted by] doing injustice' (2.362b). The would-be guardians are being educated to 'disdain to act' (3.388a)—to be disgusted to act—as Thrasymachus would. We have already remarked upon the moral point of their aesthetic education, the point of which is to acquire 'the right distastes' (3.401e). It is the same Greek word in all these passages, δυσχεραίνω (*duschertainô*): to be unable to endure, to be disgusted with. Disgust at rotting meat seems to be a universal human reaction, one we come to naturally, without learning. But moral disgust is a product of education and upbringing. Someone raised on the Thrasymachus plan will fail to be appropriately disgusted at wrongdoing and other modes of moral ugliness. And unlike its physiological counterpart, moral disgust is conceptual. It is not the *thought* of rotting meat that disgusts us, it is the smell of the rotting meat itself (although physical revulsion may well arise if I imagine rotting meat robustly enough). I should be morally disgusted at witnessing an outrageous act of injustice, but—if I have been properly raised—I should also feel moral disgust at the thought of injustice and be angry about it.

Leontius was disgusted both by the corpses and by his attraction to them, which suggests that his problem is not that he 'lacks the right distastes' (3.401a). His problem, rather, is that his soul is not properly aligned: his spirited part is not strong enough to overcome his appetites and thus it sides with them rather than with reason. A conflict between reason and desire, between what we think we *ought* to do and what we *want* to do, is a common feature of the human condition. On Plato's psychology—literally, his *logos* of the *psychê*—the conflict requires a third party for its resolution: spirit, which sides with reason in a well-ordered soul, and with appetite in a poorly ordered one. Spirit is 'by nature the helper of the rational part', Socrates says, but to call the arrangement natural is not to say that it will occur all by itself, without outside help, but rather that this is what spirit's function is. Spirit will perform its natural function 'provided that it has not been corrupted by a bad upbringing' (4.441a).

It is telling that spirit is defined as the part of the soul 'we get angry with', for anger of a particularly moral type—resentment or indignation—can be the appropriate emotional response to injustice suffered or witnessed, respectively, just as shame, a kind of moral self-disgust, is the proper emotional response to having acted unjustly. Spirit, like reason but unlike appetite, is evaluative, but its evaluative scope is narrower than reason's. Spirit seeks to protect its distinctive good, honor, and views the actions of oneself and others through this lens. Many philosophers agree with Jeffrie Murphy's view that wrongdoing can communicate the demeaning message that it is permissible for the wrongdoer to treat the victim as they do, and that the victim's anger, which often involves a desire to retaliate, can be seen as a way of denying the wrongdoer's demeaning message.[1] While spirit is able to see what is good and bad for *it* and to defend its own turf, it is not able to see what is good *all things considered*—that is reason's task. When one has been wronged, the spirited part of the soul typically burns with anger and a desire for revenge, to negate the demeaning message the wrongdoing seems to encode. 'It would be good to harm him in return!' it seems to say. But spirit is 'the part that is angry without calculation' (4.441c). Where spirit is passionate and hot, reason is detached and cool, seeking 'what is advantageous for each part and for the whole soul' (4.442c) rather than for any particular part. Reason might offer an alternative interpretation of the event that has angered passion, suggesting perhaps that the wrongdoer did not mean it that way or that it was an accident, etc., and thus that spirit's anger is unjustified, so retaliation is inappropriate in this case. Or reason might reject retaliation altogether since 'it is never just to harm anyone' (1.335e), as Socrates argued in Book I.

The upshot of all this is that spirit is distinct from appetite and reason, though it shares affinities with each. In a well-ordered soul, spirit can be 'called to heel by the reason within [...] like a dog by a shepherd' (4.440d). Of course, this order must be cultivated from an early age, by the proper

---

1   Jeffrie Murphy, 'Forgiveness and Resentment', in Jeffrie Murphy and Jean Hampton, *Forgiveness and Mercy* (New York: Cambridge University Press, 1988), p. 25.

balance of musical and physical training. Overdoing physical training results in someone who is under-responsive to the demands of reason and who, like a rogue soldier, is unable or unwilling to obey orders. Underdoing physical education results in someone unable to subdue the appetites and passions. Readers familiar with Freud's psychology will see an intriguing parallel between the roles reason, appetite, and spirit play in Plato's psychology and the roles ego, id, and super-ego play in Freud's.

The Personal Virtues (4.441c–444e)

Having secured agreement that the soul has the same three-part structure as the ideal city, Socrates has justified to his companions' satisfaction the dangling *if* at the heart of their method of investigating personal justice. If the assumption that city and soul are isomorphic—that they have the same three-part structure—were false, then we would have no reason to think that anything we have discovered about the nature of the political virtues tells us anything about the nature of the personal virtues. But having justified the hypothesis that underlies their method—at least to the satisfaction of Glaucon and Adeimantus—they can now 'apply what has come to light in the city to an individual' (4.434e).

Socrates makes quick work of the first three personal virtues, each of which is parallel to the corresponding political virtue. Just as political courage involves preserving law-inculcated beliefs about what are appropriate objects of fear, personal courage is not the preservation of innate or natural or accidentally acquired beliefs about what is to be feared but rather 'the declarations of reason about what is to be feared and what is not' (4.442c). In a well-ordered soul, the rational part is the part making these declarations, since *it* is the part capable of 'knowledge of what is advantageous for each part and for the whole soul' (4.447c), which is wisdom. As with political wisdom, personal wisdom requires the capacity to see the big picture.

We encounter a problem when we try to map political moderation onto the individual soul. Like political moderation, personal moderation involves harmony—the Greek word is συμφωνία (*sumphônia*), whence the English word 'symphony'—between the rational and appetitive parts of the soul. With political moderation, this agreement is not merely practical, as when we say things like, 'cabin life really agrees with him', or when subject and verb agree in a grammatically coherent sentence. It is also *cognitive:* 'the ruler and the ruled believe in common that the rational part should rule' (4.442c). But in the soul, the irrational appetites are parties to the agreement, and it is hard to see how mere appetites like hunger and thirst can agree with anything in the cognitive sense. One implication of the otherwise puzzling claim that 'each appetite itself is only for its natural object' (4.437e) is that the appetites are non-cognitive, non-evaluative drives incapable of belief, judgment, and agreement. There is no corresponding head-scratching about the craftspeople agreeing with the guardians that the latter should govern the *polis,* since the craftspeople are *people* and thus capable of agreeing and disagreeing with claims or propositions. Personifying the parts of the soul helps us to make sense of Socrates' account of moderation as a personal virtue, but in addition to the weirdness of thinking of appetites as being like persons, capable of forming beliefs and of making agreements, personifying the parts of the soul puts us on the road to an infinite regress: a person's soul comprises three parts, each of which is itself a miniature person or is like one; but then each of these miniature sub-persons would comprise even more miniature sub-sub-persons, and on and on. Like the poet Walt Whitman, we contain multitudes, apparently.

Perhaps Socrates' talk of agreement between the rational and irrational parts should be taken metaphorically. Socrates regularly appeals to metaphors in the *Republic,* such as the famous Allegory of the Cave and the less famous (but no less important) metaphors of the Sun and the Divided Line, which we will soon be exploring. But while thinking of personification metaphorically staves off the looming infinite regress, it leaves unexplained just how the irrational and rational parts come to an agreement. Are we letting Socrates off the hook too easily if we accept his metaphorical explanation?

Albert Camus raised a parallel worry about metaphorically explaining the atom by appealing to the solar system:

> You tell me of an invisible planetary system in which electrons gravitate around a nucleus. You explain this world to me with an image. I realize that you have been reduced to poetry [...] So that science that was to

teach me everything ends up in a hypothesis, that lucidity founders in metaphor, that uncertainty is resolved in a work of art.[2]

Though I understand his complaint, it seems that Camus fails to appreciate the cognitive power of metaphor, which is odd, given the centrality of the metaphor of Sisyphus to his account of the human condition. Are metaphorical explanations intrinsically problematic, as Camus seems to suggest? Metaphorical explanations are problematic when the metaphor that is offered to clarify the target concept is itself unclear or insufficiently understood. If the physics and nature of the solar system are well understood, why would appealing to the metaphor of the solar system be problematic? Perhaps Plato is here reminding us that we have agreed to forgo the 'longer and fuller road' that leads to 'precise answer[s]' (4.435c) in favor of a less demanding path that leads to a vantage point from which we see the same truths as we would from the more demanding path, but we see them less clearly and distinctly, from a distance. Walking the longer road of dialectic requires doing without hypotheses and metaphors, Socrates tells us later (6.511ae, 7.533c), but we will find them helpful while walking the less demanding trail we are on.

Interestingly enough, Socrates does not exactly go in for personification of the soul's parts in a metaphor he explicitly endorses later in the *Republic*. In the 'image of the soul in words' (9.588b) he offers in Book IX, the appetitive part is not a person but rather 'a multicolored beast with a ring of many heads that it can grow and change at will' (9.488c). While we might worry about the capacity of such a creature to form beliefs and agreements, remember that in distinguishing political courage from its natural analogue, which resembles but strictly speaking is not courage, Socrates notes that 'animals and slaves' can possess 'correct belief' about what is appropriately feared, however such beliefs are 'not the result of education [... nor] inculcated by law' (4.430b) and thus they cannot possess courage proper but only its natural facsimile. While the hydra-headed beast representing the appetites can come to *obey* the commands issued by the rational part, as a dog can come to

---

2   Albert Camus, *The Myth of Sisyphus*, trans. by Justin O'Brien (New York: Vintage International, 2018), p. 20.

obey its master's commands, it is a stretch to think the beast or the dog *agrees* in the robust cognitive sense required.

So it seems there is a glitch in the city-soul analogy, but perhaps such glitches are to be expected on the less precise path we are treading, since an analogy need not be perfect for it to be correct and helpful.

Personal Justice: Intrapersonal Being versus Interpersonal Doing (4.443c–444e)

Finally, we get Plato's answer to the *Republic's* first question. Just as a city is just when each class does its own work, a person is just when each part of the soul does its own work. A person who possesses a just soul will do their own work: bakers will bake, cobblers will cobble, auxiliaries will defend, guardians will rule, etc. But the essence of justice is the harmony of the soul's parts, not the individual's acting in certain ways.

Socrates' definition of justice is strikingly different from the definitions Polemarchus and Cephalus offered in Book I. To think of justice as telling the truth and paying one's debts or to think of it as benefiting one's friends and harming one's enemies is to think of justice primarily in terms of how one acts toward others. While Socrates thinks that the just person will treat others in certain ways, he does not think of justice primarily in terms of action: 'Justice [...] is not concerned with someone doing his own externally, but with what is inside him, with what is truly himself and his own' (4.443c). So where Cephalus and Polemarchus, both spokesmen for the commonsense morality of the day, think of justice as a matter of what one does, Socrates thinks of it as primarily a matter of how one is, of what one is like, internally. The essence of justice is not to be found in external, interpersonal doing, but rather in internal, intrapersonal being.

That is quite a shift—so much so that some philosophers think that Socrates has changed the subject and indeed has committed the fallacy of irrelevance.[3] Although I understand the point of this objection, I cannot say that I find it compelling. Socrates has not really changed the subject

---

3   David Sachs, 'A Fallacy in Plato's *Republic*', *Philosophical Review,* 72 (1963), 141–58. The first of many responses is Raphael Demos, 'A Fallacy in Plato's *Republic?*', *Philosophical Review,* 73 (1964), 395–98.

so much as deepened it. Polemarchus is thinking of justice in terms of action, but Socrates argues that it is something more fundamental than that, that Polemarchus' thinking is literally too superficial: it is looking at the surface manifestations of justice without understanding its underlying essence, just as someone who thinks of water in terms of clarity and wetness is missing its molecular essence. It is not that Socrates is unconcerned with just actions, but rather than he thinks they are really merely expressions of the underlying virtue, to be explained in terms of inner character: 'the action is just and fine that preserves this inner harmony and helps achieve it' (4.443e).

As we noted earlier, Plato is offering what is nowadays called a *virtue ethics*, which takes the virtues to be morally fundamental. Consequentialist moral philosophers like John Stuart Mill think that good outcomes are morally basic, explaining right action and virtuous character in terms of those outcomes: an action is right if and only if it produces the best possible (or a sufficiently good) outcome, and a virtue is a reliable disposition to bring about good outcomes. Deontological moral philosophers such as Immanuel Kant deny that right action is to be explained in terms of good consequences, thinking that certain kinds of action are right in themselves; for deontologists like Kant, virtues are dispositions to do one's duty.

Although this is a bit of a simplification, moral theories can be distinguished by which family of moral concepts—virtues, outcomes, duties—they take to be explanatorily basic in the sense of explaining or defining the other moral concepts. Although deontology and consequentialism have dominated modern moral philosophizing in the English-speaking world for several centuries, virtue ethics has enjoyed a revival in recent decades. The basic idea, really, is that *being* a certain kind of person is morally more fundamental that *doing* certain kinds of actions. While the consequentialists and deontologists focus on actions—although they differ strenuously in what explains why right actions are right—virtue ethicists focus on persons and their characters, thinking that someone in whom the virtues have been cultivated (by upbringing, education, and individual effort) can be trusted to figure out what action to perform in whatever circumstances they find themselves.

So, for a virtue ethicist such as Plato, an action is just because it is the sort of action a just person would perform in the circumstances. Now, merely doing *what* the just person does is not enough to make one just: there is a distinction between *doing a just* act and *being just.* If I am doing what the just person would do, then I am acting justly, but I might not yet possess the virtue of justice. Plato's student Aristotle insisted that to *act* justly, I must do what the just person does; but to *be* just, to possess the virtue of justice, I must perform just acts *as* the just person performs them. I must be properly motivated, which requires at a minimum that I be motivated by what is fine or noble (what is *kalon,* that crucial concept we encountered in Books II and III) rather than by self-interest, and that, with a few exceptions we enjoy or at least are not internally resistant to performing the action.

Socrates puts his definition to the test by asking Glaucon what kind of acts the just person, as they have defined her or him, will and will not perform. Socrates is asking Glaucon whether the proposed definition of personal justice squares with commonsense. If the just person, as conceived of by Socrates, would rob temples, steal, betray friends, or break contracts (4.443a)—a list of unjust actions which Thrasymachus earlier specified as parts of injustice (1.344a) and which will be noted later as typical of people with tyrannical souls (9.575b)—then the definition must be rejected, just as Cephalus' and Polemarchus' definitions were rejected for having implications that they themselves could not accept. If Socrates' definition implied that a just person would perform such actions, it would theoretically be open to Glaucon to still accept the definition and change his mind about the moral status of thievery, temple robbery, betrayal, etc. But that would sound the death-knell for Socrates' moral theory and would be rhetorically disastrous. Glaucon agrees that the just person would not perform these kinds of actions, the kinds of actions we can expect of someone wearing Gyges' ring, of someone who thinks they can 'do injustice with impunity' (2.360c). Socrates thinks his just person *is* incorruptible: they are ἀδαμάντινος (*adamantinos*) (1.360b): adamantine, made of steel, unshakably committed to justice and disgusted by injustice.

As Socrates has defined it, justice (which, we should remember, is best thought of as virtue generally) is a kind of inner, psychic health: 'Virtue seems, then, to be a kind of health, fine condition, and wellbeing of the soul' (4.444d). This is unsurprising, given Socrates' moral realism. There are facts about what health is and what contributes to it, and we are likely to roll our eyes at someone who says, 'Who's to say that a diet of potato chips and ice cream is unhealthy?' 'Experts and indeed anyone who understands nutrition is to say', we want to respond. As a kind of inner health and harmony, virtue is similarly susceptible to this same kind of realism. If Socrates is right, there turn out to be moral facts, just as there are dietary facts—and what those facts are is not up to us in any meaningful way. We may be unaware of these facts, but we *discover* them, we do not *invent* them.

There is an objection we should address before closing. The objection turns on Socrates' emphasis on inner harmony in his account of justice. For example, he says that the just person 'harmonizes the three parts of himself like three limiting notes in a musical scale—high, low, and middle' (4.443d), that 'he becomes entirely one, moderate and harmonious' (4.443e); moreover, 'the action is just [...] that preserves this inner harmony and helps achieve it' (4.443e). The objection is that inner harmony is compatible with injustice. Consider a harmonious psychopath in whom reason, with the aid of spirit, rules the appetites. The psychopath does not really want to kill and eat other human beings, but believes that reason commands him to do so. So, the objection goes, if a harmonious soul is a just soul, it follows that a Socratically just person *could* do these awful things. But clearly a just person would not murder and cannibalize (let alone rob temples and break promises), so Socrates' account must be rejected.

Given what he says in Book IX, we can imagine that Socrates might respond by insisting that our harmonious psychopath has a tyrannical soul, which is highly disordered and unharmonious—that our imagined counter-example is not really conceivable. But this seems to simply beg the question, to assume the truth of the very thing Socrates is supposed to be arguing for. A better response would be to point out that while harmony is a necessary condition of a soul's being just (that is, a soul cannot be just without also being harmonious), it is not by itself sufficient (that is, it is false that any soul that is harmonious is thereby just). It is not that a harmonious soul is a just soul, as the objection assumes, but rather that a just soul is a harmonious soul. It is not enough that the rational part governs, Socrates should reply; it must get things right: wisdom is a kind of knowledge and knowledge requires truth—we can only know what is true, and it is not true that murder and cannibalism are morally permissible, other things being equal. We can probably imagine circumstances in which they might be, but the remorseless, harmonious psychopath we have imagined is not in such a situation.

It should not be surprising that Socrates' response presupposes moral realism. He thinks that moral knowledge, which presupposes moral truth, is possible. Such knowledge is rare and limited to philosopher-queens and -kings, but it is possible. Readers who are more skeptical will take this as a point of weakness—not because they themselves reject moral realism (though some surely will) but rather because Socrates' response presupposes moral realism without ever arguing for it. Even if we share his belief that there are genuine moral truths, we might find ourselves in a situation analogous to the situation Glaucon and Adeimantus found themselves in in Book II, agreeing with Socrates but seeing that our belief in moral realism is not justified. Of course, that does not make it false, but it leaves us in an epistemically perilous state. Socrates, we should remember, does not claim to *know* that moral realism is true; he is working with what his interlocutors believe, so his assuming the truth of moral realism is not problematic from within the framework of the *Republic.* But from outside that framework, as critical readers and thinkers, we should find it problematic, if we agree with him but can offer no arguments that would justify that agreement.

Many readers will find this account of justice intuitively appealing, especially as it places reason at the center—or, perhaps better, at the helm—of a well-lived life. Socrates will discuss the varieties of unjust souls in Books VIII and IX, but it will be helpful to trace one out here, if only briefly, in order to give us a richer sense of this account of justice. A clear, illustrative contrast is with a soul (and city) he deems oligarchic, one which takes amassing wealth to be life's ultimate purpose. While the just person loves virtue, the oligarch loves wealth. As Socrates describes the oligarch, they are still more or less conventionally decent, though they are likely to cheat a bit if they can do so with impunity. In terms of their soul's structure, the most distinctive contrast is that while reason governs the just person's soul, appetite—in particular the desire for money—governs the money-loving oligarch's. For Plato, in a well-ordered and thus just soul, reason determines which ends and goals one ought to pursue. This is its task, a task that requires the personal virtue of wisdom in order to be done well. But the oligarchic money-lover has appetite setting their ends: 'He makes the rational and spirited parts sit on the ground beneath appetite, one on either side, reducing them to slaves' (8.553c). In contemporary philosophical lingo, the money-lover reduces reason to the purely instrumental role of determining the best means to achieve the ends set by appetite. It is not that figuring out the most effective means to a given end is not a task for reason; it surely is. But that is not all reason is good for, and indeed, important as such reasoning is, it is decidedly secondary in importance, in Plato's view, to determining what is good in itself, what is worth pursuing as an end. The problem, Plato thinks, is that reason has *only* this instrumental role in the money-lover's soul and that in determining what ends and goals to pursue, appetite is taking over a task that does not properly belong to it. Appetite is meddling and not doing its own work, as the Specialization Principle and justice require. Reason, not appetite, is supposed to determine which things are good, so a soul in which appetite is doing reason's work is unjust. If we are reluctant to label as unjust souls whose possessors adhere to conventional morality despite being governed by appetite rather than reason—the example of Cephalus immediately comes to mind— we can at least regard them as non-just, reserving 'unjust' for more obviously bad folk.

Though many of us are no doubt inclined to agree with Plato about the centrality of reason to a well-lived life, we would do well to remember that great eighteenth-century Scottish philosopher David Hume disagrees strenuously with Plato about the role reason should (and indeed can) play in a well-lived life. Hume famously says, 'Reason is and ought only to be the slave of the passions',[4] but Hume is emphatically not suggesting that we should give ourselves over to a passion for money; instead, he is making a point about human psychology that plays up the affective, emotional side of our nature and downplays the rational. We regularly mistake the 'calm passions'—such as benevolence, kindness to children, and the general appetite for good—for reason, since they lack the force of 'violent passions' such as anger and romantic love. We will

---

4   Hume, *Treatise*, p. 415 (II.iii.3).

not settle Hume's disagreement with Plato here, but I raise it to remind readers that, despite the prominence of reason in the history of Western philosophy, the issue is, like most fundamental philosophical issues, not settled.

Hopefully this brief foray into the oligarchic soul helps to illustrate Plato's definition of justice.

Some Suggestions for Further Reading

Readers interested in a philosophically astute discussion of the three-part soul will want to read Chapter 13 ('*Republic* IV: The Division of the Soul') of Terence Irwin, *Plato's Ethics* (New York: Oxford University Press, 1995), pp. 203–22, which has informed my understanding of Plato's psychology. Irwin is a leading scholar of ancient philosophy and the book as a whole is extraordinarily good, covering not just the *Republic* but many other dialogues as well. *Plato and the Divided Self,* ed. by Rachel Barney, Tad Brennan, and Charles Brittain (New York: Cambridge University Press, 2012), https://doi.org/10.1017/cbo9780511977831, contains excellent essays on Plato's division of the soul in the *Republic* and elsewhere.

For an excellent discussion of the concept of virtue, both epistemic and moral, interested readers should see Heather Battaly, *Virtue* (Malden, MA: Polity Press, 2015).

Readers interested in exploring the biological, social, and philosophical nature of disgust should see William Ian Miller's *The Anatomy of Disgust* (Cambridge, MA: Harvard University Press, 1998), along with a helpful review: Martha Nussbaum, 'Foul Play', *The New Republic,* 217.20 (1997), 32–38.

Readers interested in metaphor will find Zoltán Kövecses, *Metaphor: A Practical Introduction,* 2nd ed. (New York: Oxford University Press, 2010) well worth their attention.

Readers interested in Hume's view that sentiment, not reason, is the basis of morality, should see the first two sections of Book III of his classic *A Treatise of Human Nature,* 'Moral Distinctions Not Deriv'd From Reason' and 'Moral Distinctions Deriv'd From a Moral Sense.' The

Treatise is available in many editions and readers will find a modernized version of the *Treatise* (and most significant philosophical texts of the early modern period) at Jonathan Bennett's wonderfully helpful *Early Modern Texts* (http://www.earlymoderntexts.com/).

Readers interested in parallels between Plato and Freud might start with A.W. Price, 'Plato and Freud', in *The Person and the Human Mind: Issues in Ancient and Modern Philosophy,* ed. by Christopher Gill (Oxford: Clarendon Press, 1990). For an engaging account of Freud's philosophical significance, see Jonathan Lear, *Freud,* 2nd ed. (New York: Routledge, 2015), https://doi.org/10.4324/9781315771915, part of the excellent *Routledge Philosophers* series.

Readers curious about the potential permissibility of cannibalism will find a fascinating discussion in Peter Suber, *The Case of the Speluncean Explorers: Nine New Opinions* (New York: Routledge, 1998), which includes and expands on Lon Fuller, 'The Case of the Speluncean Explorers', *Harvard Law Review,* 62 (1949), 616–45, on the occasion of its 50th anniversary.

For an excellent exploration of the relations between virtue and health, interested readers should see Paul Bloomfield, *Moral Reality* (New York: Oxford University Press, 2001), https://doi.org/10.1093/0195137132.00 1.0001.

Ernst Herter, *Amazonenkampf* (1891). Photograph by Mutter
Erde (2017), Wikimedia, Public Domain, https://upload.
wikimedia.org/wikipedia/commons/6/65/Ernst_Herter_-_
Amazonenkampf%2C_c._1891.jpg

7. Questions about the Ideal *Polis*
The Three Waves
Book V

Having answered the *Republic*'s first question, Plato has Socrates immediately start in on its second: 'whether it is more profitable to act justly, live in a fine way, and be just, whether one is known to be so or not' (4.445a). Since his method is to work with claims that his interlocutors believe, we might have expected Socrates to pause and ask if anyone has any questions about the definition of justice they have arrived at, but instead he immediately starts in on the *Republic*'s second question on the final page of Book IV. But as Book V begins, Polemarchus, who has been silent since Book I, jumps back into the fray, piping up with some questions which will lead to a 'digression' (8.543c), as Socrates later puts it, that comprises Books V, VI, and VII, taking up about one hundred pages of the Greek text.

Literary Artistry as a Way of Doing Philosophy
(5.449b–d)

The opening of Book V is subtly but strikingly similar to the opening of Book I, and it is worth pausing to consider Plato's literary way of making a philosophical point. Book I, readers will remember, begins with Socrates and Glaucon returning to Athens proper from its port, the Piraeus. Polemarchus' unnamed slave bids them to wait for his master, after the slave 'caught hold of [Socrates'] cloak' (1.327b). In

https://doi.org/10.11647/OBP.0229.07

the banter that follows, Socrates playfully asks if Polemarchus will let them go (1.327c). It is striking and clearly no accident that this scene is more or less repeated with the same vocabulary at the beginning of Book V: Polemarchus 'took hold of [Adeimantus'] cloak' asking, 'Shall we let it go?'. When Adeimantus replies in the negative, Socrates asks, 'What is it that you will not let go?', to which Adeimantus replies, 'You' (5.449b). What is Plato up to here? Why does he reprise the beginning of Book I here at the outset of Book V, with the same vocabulary? Although it may be just pleasing literary symmetry enjoyable for its own sake, I suspect there is more to it than that. I think that Plato is using literary form to make a substantive point about the nature of philosophy: philosophy is always starting over, always examining its foundations. Though we have travelled quite a distance from the opening scene, the conclusions it ultimately led to, especially the account of justice as each part of the soul doing its own work, need to be scrutinized. Doing so is important given the method Socrates and company have adopted, which relies on shared agreement about premises to derive conclusions. Plato might have made this point more directly, but making the point so subtly as almost certainly to be missed the first time around seems not just a more elegant but a more effective way of making the point that doing philosophy well invariably involves examining one's conclusions and starting points. It is more effective, I think, since he lets his readers make this point for themselves, by prompting us to ask why he rhymes the beginnings of Books I and V. And indeed the conclusion I have drawn, that he is making a point about the nature of philosophy, is one that should itself be revisited, as there may be more going on than that—or he might be making a different point altogether. We will not pursue it any further, but I hope at least that this discussion helps readers to appreciate not just the literary quality of the *Republic* but also the way in which Plato seamlessly joins literary form and philosophical content. It is one of the reasons that the *Republic* is a treasure that bears repeated re-reading.

The Three Waves (5.450a–451c)

Adeimantus and Polemarchus are prompted by the implications of a nugget of commonsense Greek wisdom that Socrates utters in Book IV after giving the rulers of the ideal city their charge to guard above everything else the program of education and upbringing they worked out in Books II and III: 'all the other things we are omitting, for example, that marriage, the having of wives and the procreation of children must be governed as far as possible by the old proverb: Friends possess everything in common' (4.424a). While Socrates wants to avoid exploring such details, Adeimantus and Polemarchus insist that he do so. It is not that they disagree with the proverb Socrates has appealed to, but rather that it 'requires an explanation (λόγος [*logos*])' (5.449c): they want its implications explained and justified, since they run so contrary to Athenian social arrangements and customs. When even Thrasymachus agrees, Socrates has little choice but to accede to their wishes, even though he would prefer to avoid this 'swarm of arguments' his friends have stirred up. As at the beginning of Book II, Glaucon and Adeimantus agree with Socrates, but they are sufficiently self-aware to see that their belief is unjustified; hence their insistence that Socrates provide an explanation—a *logos*.

The social arrangements proposed or implied in the design of the ideal city will be scrutinized by two questions: 'Is it possible?' and 'Is it optimal?' The kind of possibility in question here is not *logical* possibility but rather something more along the lines of practicality: could this arrangement be realized in an actual city? If the answer is 'yes', they turn to the second question, which asks whether this arrangement would be optimal or at least beneficial. In a nutshell, the questions can be collapsed into one: *Could* we really live this way, and if so, *should* we—would it be good for us if we did?

In one of his not infrequent confessions of pessimism or trepidation, Socrates is leery of the line of inquiry Adeimantus and company are insisting on, since mistakes about what is the best way for humans to live—and here it is good to remember that their discussion 'concerns no ordinary topic but the way we ought to live' (1.352d)—can be disastrous. A mistake here will likely lead to a true falsehood, the very worst thing to believe. But Socrates fares forward, facing each of the Three Waves. The metaphor of the wave is a powerful one for the residents of a sea-faring *polis*, especially as the discussion that constitutes the *Republic* takes place in the Piraeus, the port of Athens. The waves come in order of increasing severity: the first concerns whether women can be guardians; the second concerns the abolition or de-privatization of the traditional family; the third concerns the ideal city itself. We will look at the first two in this chapter and explore the third in the next, since Socrates takes the end of Book V and the whole of Books VI and VII to address it.

The First Wave: Can Women Be Guardians? (5.451c–457c)

Since friends have all things in common and the citizens of the ideal *polis* are friends—bringing about this friendship should be one of the fruits of the Noble Falsehood—the citizens will share the same upbringing and education, as well as the same jobs. There is no reason, Socrates thinks, why being female is by itself a disqualifier. Like the people listening to Socrates, many readers will be surprised by this, though probably for different reasons. Indeed, Glaucon and company find the very idea 'ridiculous', a complaint one encounters at least half a dozen times in one page of the Greek text (5.452). Physical education is an important part of the would-be guardians' education, and by Athenian custom much of this, especially wrestling, occurs when the participants are naked. Thus they find it difficult to take Socrates' proposal seriously.

As is often the case in the *Republic*, in addition to the issue immediately at hand—here, whether women can participate in the education required of would-be guardians—there are deeper issues which transcend the boundaries of the *Republic* and which should be of interest even to those who regard the ideal *polis* as decidedly dystopic. One, of course, is the status of women; another is the status of societal norms. As Socrates diagnoses Glaucon's reasoning, the idea of women wrestling naked is ridiculous because 'it is contrary to custom (παρὰ τὸ ἔθος [*para to ethos*])' (5.452a). But why, Socrates asks, adhere to local custom? After all, at one point it was contrary to custom for *men* to wrestle naked, and that probably incited ridicule then, too. Since customs can change over time, perhaps we will give up the custom barring women from wrestling naked, too.

But Socrates has a deeper point to make than that, one that challenges the normative force of cultural customs, and one that should not surprise us, given his commitment to philosophical reflection. A cultural relativist holds that an action is right (and, alternatively, wrong) if and only if one's culture approves (or, alternatively, disapproves) of it. That is all there is to rightness and wrongness; there is no culture-transcending standard by which to assess the norms of one's own culture or those of another. One problematic consequence of cultural relativism—and remember that one way to test a claim is to consider its implications— is that it makes the idea of moral progress nonsensical. Sure, we now disapprove of slavery and thus regard it as wrong, but that is not an *improvement* on the earlier standard; it is just a different standard. And what goes for one culture viewed over time goes for different cultures viewed at the same time: your culture holds that women should not vote, mine holds that they should. One is not better than another, on the relativist's view: they are different, not better or worse—because to hold that anti-slavery or pro-female suffrage norms are better than their opposites requires a higher, culture-transcending standard by which to assess those cultural standards, and these are the very things denied by the cultural relativist. The argument pattern here should be familiar: *A* implies *B,* and *B* is false—or, at least, the person we are talking with regards it as false—so *A* must also be false. Consider this argument:

P1   If (*A*) cultural relativism is true then (*B*) the idea of moral progress is incoherent.

P2   (*not-B*) The idea of moral progress is *not* incoherent.

C   Therefore, (*not-A*) cultural relativism is not true.

The argument is logically valid, so a die-hard relativist wishing to deny its conclusion must either reject P1, holding that cultural relativism does not imply that moral progress is incoherent, or reject P2, conceding that the idea of moral progress is not coherent, after all. These are both tall orders, for relativism, holding that what one's culture approves of is right, implies that there is no standard by which to judge one culture's standards to be better than another culture's— and there is no standard by which to assess my culture's former standards and its current standards. No standard is better; they are just different. Since progress means change for the better, it is difficult to see how a cultural relativist could regard moral progress as coherent, given their insistence that there are no standards by which to assess a culture's standards.

Socrates does not make the moral progress argument, but it is presumably something he would endorse, since he rejects the cultural relativism that takes one's culture's standards as sound just because they are one's culture's standards. 'It is foolish', he thinks, turning Glaucon's objection back on him by employing the same word (γέλοιος [*geloios*]), 'to think that anything besides the bad is ridiculous [...] and it is foolish to take seriously any standard of what is fine and beautiful other than the good' (5.452de). Socrates is not a nihilist or anarchist; he is not opposed to cultural norms and standards *per se*—it would be odd if he were, given the amount of time he has so far devoted in the *Republic* to an educational program designed to cultivate the right ones. What he is opposed to is uncritical acceptance of one's culture's norms, to regarding them as correct or beyond question merely because they are the norms of one's culture. That fact that one's culture approves of *x* and *y* and disapproves of *z* is one thing; whether one's culture *ought* to do so is a different matter entirely. The subsequent books in the *Republic* will reveal something of what Socrates takes the good to be, but even if we find ourselves disagreeing down the road with his particular version of moral realism, we can agree with him about the role that critical reflection and reasoned argument ought to play in determining which norms a culture ought to possess. 'What was ridiculous to the eyes', Socrates says, 'faded away in the face of what argument showed to be the best' (5.452d). Women wrestling naked seems ridiculous to Glaucon and his friends, but until one has scrutinized one's culture's standards, it is not clear that it really *is* ridiculous.

Socrates' critique of Glaucon's appeal to what seems ridiculous echoes his earlier remarks on disgust and cultivating the right distastes. Finding something ridiculous differs from finding it disgusting: laughing at something is a much weaker form of disapproval than being nauseated by it. But they are both modes of disapproval, ways of registering *that* something is improper. These modes of disapproval are typically not rational: we are raised to find certain things ridiculous and certain things disgusting while we are 'young and unable to grasp the reason' (3.401a). Socrates calls on reason to help determine whether what *seems* absurd or disgusting really *is* absurd or disgusting, and if so, why. If we cannot justify our tastes and distastes, perhaps we ought to give them up. In his ideal *polis*, no one needs to give up the norms they have absorbed from their culture, because the educational system is supposed to guarantee that the only norms and values available for absorption are correct. But those of us not raised in utopias will need to scrutinize our culture's norms and values, since we cannot be sure those norms and values are correct. To my mind, the value of liberal education, and especially philosophical education, is to be found in their enabling us to better scrutinize and evaluate the norms, values, and beliefs we were raised to have, so that we are in a position to endorse some and reject others, thereby making our norms, beliefs, and values truly our own. Without critical scrutiny, these norms, values, and beliefs are not really our own, and we are not fully free: we might be free of interference, but we lack the freedom that comes from genuine, deep self-direction. (We will return to this distinction between negative and positive freedom below, in Chapter Twelve.)

Having made his general point about cultural norms, Socrates brings the argument back to the question of whether having women as guardians is possible. In a move that is a model of intellectual fairness, Socrates decides to 'give the argument against ourselves' (5.453a). That is, he articulates what he takes to be the best argument against the view he holds. It is worth pausing to admire this kind of intellectual fairness, especially as it seems in such short supply these days. How many of us, after all, are willing or able to give a fair hearing to political and moral arguments we disagree with, let alone give them a reasonable reconstruction? As we noted earlier, much political and moral debate traffics in the production and consumption of strawmen: we caricature the views of our opponents and then think we have refuted our opponents by knocking down these caricatures. A quick glance at the 'comments' section of most online newspapers should provide ample evidence for the prevalence of strawmen.

The argument Socrates considers is a powerful one, since it appeals to the Specialization Principle, which structures the economic life in the ideal *polis* and indeed is the basis of the definition of justice, in arguing against the view that women can be guardians. The Specialization

Principle implies that 'each must do his own work in accordance with his nature' (5.453b). But of course, 'the natures of men and women are different' (5.453e), so how can Socrates hold that men and women may perform the same tasks? Socrates' position is self-contradictory, argues the imagined opponent: he can't endorse the Specialization Principle *and* hold that women can be guardians, since the former implies that the latter is false.

It is a powerful argument, of just the sort that Socrates regularly gives against others. Although he acknowledges the argument's rhetorical force, he finds it philosophically unsatisfying, since it is an example of *eristic,* which was discussed briefly in Chapter Two. The opponent, perhaps unwittingly, is quarrelling or wrangling (ἐρίζειν [*erizein*]), aiming to win the argument, rather than to get at the truth of the matter. The argument's main fault is that it fails to make a relevant distinction and so arrives at its conclusion illegitimately. Although it gets the Separation Principle right, it fails to distinguish different kinds of nature and employ the one that is relevant to the argument. Consider bald and long-haired men, for example *Seinfeld*'s George Costanza and the supermodel Fabio. Clearly their natures are different, but from that it does not follow that George cannot be a cobbler if Fabio is, because whether one is bald or has a full head of lustrous hair is irrelevant to the craft of cobbling. It is not that the bald and the tricho-luscious are not different, but rather that the difference between them—between their natures—is not relevant to the issue at hand. Thinking otherwise, Socrates says, is 'ridiculous' (5.454d).

What is distinctive of a guardian-ruler is the kind of soul they have, a soul capable of wisdom, of knowledge of what is best for the city as a whole. The primary difference between men and women is biological or physical ('somatic' might be more precise): 'they differ only in this respect, that the females bear children while the males beget them' (5.454d). There is no reason to think, Socrates insists, that this physical difference must make for a psychic difference. Consider a female doctor, a male doctor, and a male cobbler. If asked, 'Which two are more similar to each other than to the other?', you would rightly respond that you cannot answer the question until you know the relevant parameter of comparison. *Physically,* the male doctor and male cobbler are more similar to each other than either is to the female doctor. *Psychologically*, the male doctor and female doctor are more similar to each other than either is to the male cobbler. The souls of cobblers differ in nature from the souls of doctors, being susceptible of acquiring a different kind of skill—perhaps this is a difference between iron and bronze souls. But as naturally different as cobblers' and doctors' souls are from each other, they are more like each other than they are like the souls of guardians, who, rather than possessing a skill or craft, possess a virtue. All three possess knowledge, but the objects of knowledge—how to make shoes, how to cure the sick, what is best for the city as a whole—are strikingly different, and, as we saw earlier, skills are fundamentally different from virtues, insofar as skills are morally neutral while virtues are not.

The upshot of all this is that men and women having all tasks in common, and especially the task of guardianship, is possible: it is not contrary to nature. While men may on average be physically stronger than women, this difference in physical strength is not relevant to ruling or soldiering, since it may well not hold in particular cases. As I write this, the world record for the marathon for men is roughly twelve and a half minutes faster than the world record for women (2:01:39 versus 2:14:04), but the fastest women's time is *really* fast, and is much, much faster than the overwhelming majority of men can run. It was the twenty-third fastest time run that day (13 October 2019) in the Chicago Marathon, faster than 24,604 of the men who completed the race. That men on average run or swim faster or lift more weight than women is irrelevant to what this particular woman and that particular man can do, and it is the particular person's qualifications that are relevant, not the average qualifications of groups they belong to.

Having shown that it is possible for women to be guardians and to receive the same education as their male counterparts, Socrates makes short work of the other question, whether it is optimal. Given that the only thing standing in its way is unreasoned cultural prejudice, it is no wonder that Socrates regards this arrangement as for the best. After all, he reasons, why would you not have golden-souled guardians in charge, whatever their sex, given that physical difference is irrelevant to the task of ruling?

Is Plato a Feminist?

Plato's perhaps surprising insistence that women can be guardians prompts us to ask, 'Is Plato a feminist?' To answer this question, we need to know what it is to be a feminist, a thornier task than it might at first seem. The Stanford Encyclopedia of Philosophy (an excellent, free, online resource) has half a dozen entries for different kinds of feminism and half a dozen again for feminist approaches to various philosophical topics such as knowledge, the self, science, ethics, etc. I am going to make the simplifying assumption—hopefully not an over-simplifying one—that at feminism's root is a belief in and commitment to gender equality. The idea here is that men and woman are morally equal, that being a woman is never in itself a reason to give a woman's interests less weight. We know that Plato is not an egalitarian, but importing a contemporary moral principle (one animating the work of Peter Singer, among others) can shed helpful light on this section's question.

The Principle of Equal Consideration of Interests (PECI, for short) holds that the interests of all parties affected by an action or decision ought to be given equal consideration *unless* there is a morally relevant fact or difference that justifies *un*equal consideration. The first thing to notice about the PECI is that it is a moral principle; it is not attempting to describe how people actually act and decide; rather, it is a principle about how we *ought* to act. A second thing to notice is that its currency is *consideration*, which is different than treatment. A teacher who gives every student the same grade treats the students equally, but this is not what the PECI demands. Instead, it demands that the teacher give equal consideration to all: they use the same standards to evaluate their work, do not play favorites, etc. There is a clear sense in which such a teacher is also treating their students equally, but it is worth noting how *consideration* and *treatment* differ. If there are 200 applicants for a job, the only way to treat all applicants equally in the strict sense is to hire all of them or none of them. What the PECI requires is that the prospective employer use fair standards and apply those standards equally. That is what I take a commitment to equal consideration to require.

A third point worth mentioning is that the PECI mandates presumptive rather than absolute equality of consideration. It recognizes that there may be times when *un*equal consideration is called for—but as the fourth point makes clear, unequal consideration is permissible only if there is a *morally relevant* difference between parties or a *morally relevant* fact that would justify unequal consideration. Psychologists are adept at discovering the factors that decision-makers take to be *psychologically relevant* and which *explain* why we often do not give equal consideration to all parties affected by our actions. But the PECI is a normative principle, not a descriptive one: it requires a morally relevant fact that justifies unequal consideration, not a psychologically relevant fact that explains it.

A racist violates the PECI by taking racial difference to justify giving unequal consideration to the interests of those affected by their actions. They violate the PECI because, with very few exceptions, racial difference is not a morally relevant difference. Racial difference is clearly—and sadly—psychologically relevant to racists, since it helps to explain why they act and think as they do. But it is rarely morally relevant: other things being equal it does not *justify* giving unequal consideration based on race. In parallel fashion, a sexist takes sex-difference to be a morally relevant difference when it presumptively is not. This is not to say that race- and sex-differences are never relevant. If Brad Pitt complains to *Variety* that the director of an upcoming film about the life of Martin Luther King, Jr. is racist because they would not even consider him for the part, we might think he is joking, since in this instance racial identity seems quite morally relevant, not least because it would be offensive to have a white actor appear in blackface to play Dr King. More seriously, this is not to say that race- and sex-based affirmative action policies cannot be justified, but rather that they stand in need of justification: since the presumption is that race and sex are not morally relevant, the burden of justification falls on the person or policy appealing to them.

Although Plato is no egalitarian, there is a sense in which he accepts the PECI. He takes the kind of soul one has—gold, silver, bronze, iron—to be relevant to whether one is eligible to participate in governing the *polis* and indeed whether one's thoughts about governing the city should be given any consideration. Readers who are egalitarian democrats—and that is 'democrat' with a small d, implying not party affiliation but rather a view about who is entitled to have a say in how one's community is governed—will think that Plato is mistaken about this: every competent adult should have equal rights to political participation. But that point aside, it is clear, I think, that Plato certainly accepts the PECI with respect to sex-difference: 'there is no way of life concerned with the management of the city that belongs to a woman because she is a woman or to a man because he is a man, but the various natures are distributed in the same way in both creatures. Women share by nature in every way of life just as men do' (5.455d). In the lingo of the PECI, for Plato sex-difference is not a morally relevant difference that would justify giving unequal consideration to the interests of men and women.

We should note that the attitude that Plato has Socrates express here is deeply at odds with Athenian attitudes of their day. Women played no role in governing Athens, and well-to-do women would never be seen by themselves outside the home. His attitude would have seemed less radical in Sparta, where women were sufficiently engaged in public life for Plutarch to be able to compile a volume entitled *Sayings of Spartan Women*.

That certainly inclines us toward a 'yes' answer to the question of whether Plato is a feminist. Affirmative support can also be found in the Second Wave, which we will get to shortly. Put briefly, Plato de-privatizes and indeed abolishes the traditional nuclear family, doing away with traditional marriage and child-rearing, and instead having children raised communally by people with a natural aptitude for it. To the extent that the traditional family can be a site of patriarchal oppression, limiting which roles and opportunities are available to women, Plato's doing away with it lends support to the judgment that he is a feminist.

But this very same point also provides a reason to doubt that Plato is a feminist. In addition to its commitment to gender-equality, feminism is plausibly characterized as committed to recognizing and overcoming gender-based oppression, where oppression is the systematic disadvantaging of one group for the benefit of another. Although Plato has Socrates argue that it is both possible and optimal for suitable women to be guardians in the ideal *polis*, there is no hint that he recognizes that his culture oppresses women; nor does he aim to liberate the women of the ideal *polis* from oppression: his motivation in advocating gender equality is that it benefits the *polis*, not that doing so is a matter of social justice or fairness. If women are liberated from oppression, it is accidental rather than intentional, which is a point in favor of a negative answer to the question of whether Plato is a feminist.

Another Second Wave issue that counts against Plato's being a feminist is what we can call *the asymmetry of possession*. Possession is an asymmetrical relation: except in a metaphorical sense, I possess my possessions: they belong to me, I do not belong to them. Some relations, such as *being siblings*, are symmetrical: if Mary is my sibling, I am her sibling. But other relations, such as *being a sister of*, are asymmetrical: if Mary is my sister, it does not necessarily follow that I am Mary's sister. Given that possession is asymmetrical, Socrates' saying that 'all these women are to belong in common to all the men' (5.457c [literally, they are to be κοινάς (*koinas*): shared in common]) is problematic for thinking him a feminist. If Plato really were committed to gender equality, we would expect Socrates to then say something like, 'and of course all the men belong in common to all the women.' But he does not, which suggests that women are *not* after all to be thought of as fully equal to men.

The last reason against thinking that Plato (or at least Socrates, if I can depart for a moment from my practice of not worrying about distinguishing them) is not a feminist is one that many readers will already have noticed for themselves: the *Republic* is sprinkled with misogynistic remarks. For example, when discussing the irrational, appetitive part of the soul, Socrates says, 'one finds all kinds of diverse desires, pleasures, and pains, mostly in children, women, household slaves, and in those of the inferior majority who are called free' (4.431c). Later in Book V he will characterize stripping corpses on the battlefield as 'small minded and womanish' (5.469d). In both cases (and many others) he seems to be operating with a male-female binary in which the female pole is decidedly negative. This is perhaps the kicker: in Book VIII when disparaging democracy he bemoans 'the extent of the legal equality of men and women and of the freedom in the relations between them' (8.563b). Could a real feminist regard equality before the law as a *bad* thing? It is hard to see how this could be the case.

The conclusion, I think, is that although there are good points to be made on the other side, Plato is not, all things considered, a feminist. Given his time and place, his insistence that there can be philosopher-queens as well as philosopher-kings (7.540c) is surprising and laudatory, even if it falls short of what those of us today who are committed to gender equality and equity would hope for.

The Second Wave: Extending the Household to the *Polis* (5.457c–471b)

When discussing whether Plato was a feminist, I described the Second Wave as the abolition of the family. This is not quite accurate, since the operative notion for Plato is the notion of the household (οἰκία [*oikia*]), a wider notion than our notion of the family, though they are clearly related. Plato's plan is to obliterate the boundaries between households so that the *polis* becomes one large *oikia* or household. There is some scholarly controversy about whether the extension of the household applies to everyone in the *polis* or just the auxiliaries and guardians. Much of what Socrates says suggests the latter, but since bronze and iron parents can have gold or silver children, it is hard to see how de-privatizing the family could work unless the city is one large household. Similarly, the seriousness with which he takes the city-soul analogy, when coupled with his view that the best city is most like a single person (5.462c), suggests the ideal of the *polis* as one big household. This is an interesting question, though perhaps of interest mainly to specialists, so, having raised it, I will set it to one side.

We saw above that the women are 'to belong in common to all the men' and, a related point which we did not mention above, 'none are to live privately with any man' (5.457c). We met this absence of privacy earlier, when toward the very end of Book III Socrates described what life is like for guardians and auxiliaries in the ideal *polis*: they live a barracks life, 'like soldiers in a camp' (3.416d), having no private property 'beyond what is wholly necessary' (a qualification that allows a guardian to say things like, 'hey, that's *my* toothbrush') and no private dwellings. The end is nigh when guardians possess 'private land, houses, and currency' (3.417a), since this will distract their focus away from what is good for the community and toward what is good for them individually. The Greek phrase being translated as 'private' is a form of ἴδιος (*idios*), from which the English word 'idiot' derives. But the implication is individuality in opposition to what is common or shared (κοινός [*koinos*]) or public, rather than some sort of mental thickness or incapacity, though even our word retains a bit of this when we think of an idiot as 'living in his own world.' We should try to avoid reading our modern notion of privacy into the text here; 'individual property' would do just as well as a translation, especially as *idios* often means simply 'individual' elsewhere in the *Republic* (e.g., Thrasymachus argues that injustice is beneficial to the individual (ἰδίᾳ [*idia(i)*] (1.344a)) or 'unique or peculiar' (e.g., Socrates insists that 'each craft benefits us in its own peculiar (ἰδίαν [*idian*]) way' (1.346a), though 'peculiar' has its own misdirecting connotations).

The children too will be 'possessed in common' (5.457c), though here the rationale is quite surprising: they are possessed in common 'so that no parent will know his own offspring or any child his parent' (5.457d). Socrates thinks that it is obvious that de-privatizing the family would be beneficial, thinking he need only address whether it is possible to put this arrangement into practice. In an all-too-rare expression of disagreement, Glaucon thinks that Socrates is mistaken on this score and insists that he justify his claim that doing away with the family is a good thing.

Given the centrality of *family* to everyday, commonsense, moral thinking and to many readers' conceptions of what a happy, well-lived life centers on, Socrates faces an uphill battle. Few readers, I suspect, will find what he says fully convincing and follow him all the way to the *community* pole of the individual-community duality we have seen at play in the *Republic,* but many will be willing to move the arrow a bit more in that direction if they give Socrates a fair hearing. There is a lot to dislike in what Socrates says here. Talk of eugenics and racial purity (5.460c) is beyond being merely creepy in a post-Holocaust world, and raising children in rearing pens (5.460c) seems to fail to do justice to human dignity, just as reducing marriage to state-sanctioned sexual hook-ups for the purposes of producing citizens fails to do justice to the dignity of marriage. The amount of deception guardians will use to rig the procreation lotteries (which determine who will have sex with whom, and when) will probably seem to most readers to be not merely innocuous verbal falsehoods, but rather indicative of governmental moral depravity. One need not think lying is absolutely forbidden—few of us do, really—to be troubled by lies that might even be beneficial. And many readers will doubt that the guardians' lies will be beneficial, even if they are efficient.

But there are also things to like in what Socrates says. He is concerned with civic unity, with the integrity of the ideal *polis.* The worst thing that can happen to a city, he argues, is for it to be divided rather than united; whatever divides and dis-integrates a city is the greatest evil, he says at 5.462a, reprising and modifying a point he made when he defined political justice (4.434bc). We might disagree that this is the *worst* thing that can happen while conceding that Socrates has a point, that a fragmented, divided city or nation is in bad shape, not functioning well, not politically healthy. His concern with faction and internal strife was certainly shared by America's founders, as for example one finds in *Federalist* #10, by James Madison (though readers familiar with the history of the early United States know how strife- and faction-ridden political life then was). A *polis* in which citizens say 'mine' about the same things is a *polis* that is unified: if all the children are *my* children, I am unlikely to favor some over others; I will want all of the city's children to flourish and succeed, since I think of all of them as *mine*.

It is because Socrates thinks that 'the best-governed city is one in which most people say 'mine' and 'not mine' about the same things in the same way' (5.462c) that he thinks that an arrangement in which 'no mother [or father] knows her own child' (5.460c) is optimal: it unifies the city, making it 'most like a single person' (5.462c). In my state of Wisconsin, about 15% of the children live in poverty (there are disputes about the correct number, since there are disputes about the proper way to measure poverty). If everyone in Wisconsin thought of these children as their children, I doubt that we would find it tolerable. We would be less likely to think it is someone else's problem to solve or to donate a few canned goods to the local food pantry and be done with it. This, it seems to me, is the viable, contemporary take-way from Socrates' communitarianism. Many readers will look upon the familial arrangements in the ideal *polis* with horror, regarding them as dystopic rather than utopic. But one can be a bit more community-minded and a bit less individualistic without following Socrates all the way. If thinking about the Second Wave leads readers to reflect on where they land on the *community–individual* spectrum, and if that landing spot is where they think they *ought* to be landing, then we are doing what Plato really wants us to be doing: thinking for ourselves. We might find ourselves agreeing with Socrates that a life or culture too far to the *individual* side of the spectrum embodies 'a silly, adolescent idea of happiness' (5.466b).

Having argued that converting the *polis* into one large household is beneficial, Socrates then starts to argue for its possibility. He focuses on warfare, which we will discuss briefly in a moment, but we might hope for more argument about whether dissolving the private family or household is psychologically possible for creatures like us. The worry is that Plato's plan assumes that the intense affection parents typically feel for their children can be spread to all the children of the community. If this affection and instinct to protect one's offspring is a matter of biology, a cultural arrangement that does away with it might have trouble gaining traction. From a certain evolutionary perspective, parents love their children and seek to protect them because those children carry their DNA; we might well wonder whether this strong parental love can be extended to those with a different genetic make-up. While this is a question that Plato cannot be faulted for not answering, it is a question *we* might want an answer to as we reflect upon the meaning Plato's proposal might have *for us*. Though Plato stressed human malleability in his account of education and enculturation, it is doubtful that humans are infinitely malleable, and our biology might put the brakes on his plan to household the *polis*, so to speak. There is more to be said about this, but for now we will just note it and move on to Socrates' remarks on the ethics of warfare.

Crucial to this discussion is a distinction between war (πόλεμός [*polemos*]) and civil war or faction (στάσις [*stasis*]). War occurs between parties that are naturally enemies, while faction occurs between natural friends. Greeks and non-Greeks—barbarians—are natural enemies; non-Greeks are fundamentally different and other, being 'foreign and strange' (5.470b). Greeks, by contrast, are 'one's own and akin' (5.470b) and thus natural friends. Greekness does not seem to be a racial notion in the modern sense; Greeks are united by a shared language, cosmological mythology, and poetic tradition rather than biology. When Greek city-states fight each other, Socrates thinks, they should do so knowing that they will one day be reconciled. They should not, for example, burn houses or ravage fields. The trouble, as Plato sees it, is that Greeks fail to distinguish between Greeks and non-Greeks in warfare, fighting against each other the way they should fight only against non-Greeks. There is a moral distinction they need to make: 'they must treat barbarians the way [they] currently treat each other' (5.471b), and stop treating other Greeks as they currently do.

We saw in the First Wave that, in the language of the PECI, sex was not a morally relevant difference that would justify giving unequal weights to the interests of men and women. Here, in the Second Wave, however, Socrates insists that race or ethnicity *is* morally relevant to the weighting of interests while engaging in warfare. The trouble, Socrates argues, is that Greeks are acting as though Greekness is not a morally relevant difference. They weigh the interests of Greeks and non-Greeks equally, but they should not be doing this: Greeks should give Greek interests greater weight than non-Greek interests, and thus change the ways in which they conduct the warfare that seems so inevitable in their world.

It would be interesting to explore why for Plato race or ethnicity is a morally relevant difference while gender is not, but in the interest of moving forward we will set that issue aside and move on to the Third Wave.

Some Suggestions for Further Reading

Readers interested in the status of women and the nature of the family in classical Athens should see Sarah Pomeroy, *Godesses, Whores, Wives, and Slaves: Women in Classical Antiquity* (New York: Schocken Books, 1975) and Pomeroy, *Families in Classical and Hellenistic Greece* (New York: Oxford University Press, 1997). Plutarch's *Sayings of Spartan Women* can be found in Plutarch, *Moralia*, vol. 3, trans. by Frank Cole Babbitt (Cambridge, MA: Harvard University Press [Loeb Classical Library], 1931), pp. 453–69.

There has been much discussion of the question of Plato and feminism. Interested readers might start with Julia Annas, 'Plato's *Republic* and Feminism', *Philosophy*, 51 (1976), 307–21 (reprinted in *Plato: Ethics, Politics, Religion, and the Soul*, ed. by Gail Fine (New York: Oxford University Press, 1999) and C.D.C Reeve, 'The Naked Old Women in the Palaestra', in *Plato's Republic: Critical Essays*, ed. by Richard Kraut (Lanham, MD: Rowman & Littlefield, 1997), pp. 129–41, which is written as a dialogue.

Readers interested in the ethics of war might start with the Stanford Encyclopedia of Philosophy article by Seth Lazar (https://plato. stanford.edu/entries/war/), which gives an excellent overview and a full bibliography. Michael Walzer, *Just and Unjust Wars: A Moral Argument with Historical Illustrations*, 5th ed. (New York: Basic Books, 2015), is a contemporary classic.

The philosophical literature on equality is vast, but Peter Singer's *Practical Ethics* (New York: Cambridge University Press, 2011), https:// doi.org/10.1017/cbo9780511975950, is an excellent starting place. Though some of Singer's views are controversial, he is philosophically astute and a very clear writer.

John La Farge, *The Relation of the Individual to the State: Socrates and His Friends Discuss 'The Republic', as in Plato's Account*; color study for mural (1903). Photograph by Pharos (2017), Wikimedia, Public Domain, https://commons.wikimedia.org/wiki/ File:The_Relation_of_the_Individual_to_the_State-_Socrates_and_ His_Friends_Discuss_%22The_Republic,%22_as_in_Plato%27s_ Account;_Color_Study_for_Mural,_Supreme_Court_Room,_Saint_ Paul,_Minnesota_State_Capitol,_Saint_Paul_MET_187194.jpg

8. Surfing the Third Wave
Plato's Metaphysical Elevator, the Powers Argument, and the Infallibility of Knowledge
Book V

Socrates regards the last of the Three Waves, 'whether it is possible for this constitution to come into being' (5.471c), as 'the biggest and most difficult one' (5.472a). The constitution he refers to is not a written document as in the US or even a collection of documents as in the UK; it is the conceptual organization of the ideal city itself. 'Constitution' translates the Greek word πολιτεία (*politeia*, whence the English word 'politics'), which is in fact the Greek title of the *Republic*. Socrates thinks that the ideal *polis* is indeed possible, but the condition of its being made real is as bold as it is famous and controversial:

> Until philosophers rule as kings or those who are now called kings and leading men genuinely and adequately philosophize, that is, until political power and philosophy entirely coincide, while the many natures who at present pursue either one exclusively are forcibly prevented from doing so, cities will have no rest from evils, Glaucon, nor, I think, will the human race. And, until this happens, the constitution we have been describing in theory will never be born to the fullest extent possible or see the light of the sun. It is because I saw how very paradoxical this statement would be that I hesitated to make it for so long, for it is hard

   https://doi.org/10.11647/OBP.0229.08

to face up to the fact that there can be no happiness, either public, or private, in any other city. (5.473c–e)

Glaucon's reaction to Socrates' inspirational little speech might not be what Socrates was hoping for: he thinks people will think that Socrates is either crazy or dangerous. So Socrates has his work cut out for him.

Philosopher-Kings and Political Animals (5.471c–474c)

There is a lot going on in this famous paragraph. One crucial point is that political power and political wisdom are not merely separated in the non-ideal city that Socrates and company inhabit but are in fact at odds with each other. If those with political power lack political wisdom, they will lack the virtue necessary to perform well their function, governing. Even if those in power reject Thrasymachus' self-interested conception of ruling and aim to act for the city's benefit rather than their own, they are likely to get things wrong as often as they get them right if they merely have beliefs about what is best for the city; what they need is knowledge. And those who possess this knowledge—true philosophers—have little interest in getting their hands dirty in politics, preferring a life of intellectual inquiry over political activity. Socrates thinks that this division between political power and political wisdom must be overcome, perhaps even by force, if the ideal city is to be made real. But the force in question will turn out to be the force of rational persuasion, rather than physical compulsion (thus reprising the force–persuasion theme raised in the *Republic*'s opening scene.)

Socrates doubles down on the importance of marrying political power and philosophy. Not only is their union the necessary condition for realizing this 'theoretical model of a good city' (5.472e), but it is also required for human happiness itself: 'there can be no happiness, either public, or private, in any other city.' It is this claim, Glaucon thinks, that people will find ridiculous or worse. But Socrates' claim has more going for it than Glaucon first thinks. Socrates is suggesting that humans, being essentially social creatures, cannot fully flourish in defective cities or when living in Thoreau-like solitude. When Aristotle says early in his *Politics* that 'a human is by nature a political animal',[1] he is not saying

---

1   Aristotle, *Politics*, I.2 1253a2–3.

that humans love to argue about politics or anything like that but rather that we are the kind of animal that lives in a *polis*, a view that Socrates surely agrees with. And many readers who are uncomfortable with Plato's community-first ethos might find that their own conceptions of a good human life involve active engagement in a community, even if only one made up of their family and friends. Socrates will have something to say in Book VI about how one can live reasonably happily in an unjust and thus unhappy city, but only in a just city can a person fully flourish and be as happy as it is possible for a human being to be.

Socrates' solution to the Third Wave prompts the issue which will organize the remainder of Book V as well as Books VI and VII: 'we need to define [...] who the philosophers are that we dare to say must rule' (5.474b). This project of distinguishing philosopher from non-philosopher will take us into the deep end of the philosophical pool, so to speak, since the distinction will be twofold, drawing on Plato's metaphysics (his account of the ultimate nature, structure, and constituents of reality, which will involve the famous theory of the Forms) and epistemology (his theory of knowledge). Metaphysics and epistemology are intimately related in Plato's thought, as we will soon see when we examine the marquee argument of Book V, the Powers Argument. It is fair to say that this is the most intellectually challenging part of the *Republic*, but also the most intellectually rewarding, I think.

Philosophers and Non-Philosophers

The epistemological distinction between philosophers, who should govern, and non-philosophers, who should not, is that philosophers have knowledge of what is best for the city, while non-philosophers have belief or opinion (δόξα [*doxa*, whence our word 'orthodoxy': correct belief]). Indeed, at the end of Book V, Socrates distinguishes between φιλόσοφος (*philosophoi*), lovers of wisdom, and φιλόδοξοι (*philodoxai*), lovers of belief. We met the distinction between knowledge and belief back in Book IV, where it was put to use in explaining the cardinal virtues of wisdom and courage. The distinctive virtue of the guardian-rulers is wisdom, which is *knowledge* of what is best for the city as a whole. Courage, the distinctive virtue of the auxiliaries, is a matter not of knowledge but of *belief*—unshakably true *belief* about what is appropriately feared, but something falling short of knowledge. An auxiliary will believe without doubt *that* dishonor and enslavement are worse than death, but they need not know *why* this is the case in order to perform their function well (although they may have true beliefs about why). Plato will have more to say about how knowledge differs from belief in Books VI and VII, especially in the analogies of the Divided Line and the Cave. For now, it is enough to note that the distinction is at the heart of Socrates' response to the Third Wave: philosophers have knowledge while non-philosophers only have belief.

The metaphysical distinction between philosopher and non-philosopher will turn out to be intimately related to this first, epistemological distinction, since it is a distinction between the objects of knowledge and belief. The word 'metaphysics' often conjures up thoughts of crystals, incense, New Age healing, etc., but this is not the philosophical sense. Philosophically speaking, metaphysics concerns the ultimate nature, structure, and constituents of reality. Where natural scientists try to discover and explain causal connections between events, metaphysically minded philosophers want to understand what causation itself is. They want to know what kinds of things exist: is everything that exists physical, or do non-physical things exist? For example, is the human mind something fully physical, reducible without remainder to the brain? Or is it something non-physical? If minds are non-physical, how do they interact with the body, which is decidedly physical? These are not the kinds of metaphysical questions that Plato asks; they assumed a central place in Western metaphysics with the thought of René Descartes (1596–1650). But hopefully they give the reader a sense of what sorts of concerns are addressed by metaphysics.

We have beliefs about the particular things that make up our everyday world, on Plato's view, but we have knowledge of the Forms— the timeless essences of the particulars.[2]

A brief jump ahead to the beginning of Book X will be helpful in getting clearer about what the Forms are. There, Socrates reminds Glaucon that their 'usual procedure [...] [is to] hypothesize a single Form in connection with each of the many things to which we apply the same name' (10.596a). There must be something, Plato thinks, that all just

---

2   As is often done, I will use 'Form' with a capital F when talking of these distinctively
    Platonic entities.

actions have in common, that all courageous actions have in common, that all red things have in common. Grasping this common feature—the essence or the Form, the real definition—is the task of philosophy, for Plato. His example in Book X is rather mundane: beds. 'The form', he says, 'is our term for the being of a bed' (10.597a), where 'being' means what the thing *is:* its essence, what it is to be a bed. So far, assuming a common feature seems like a reasonable, innocuous assumption. While there are many particular beds and many particular just actions, there is a single, unifying Form or essence of bedness and one of justice. So where particulars are *many*, Forms are *one.*

Another crucial difference between Forms and particulars is that particulars are ever-changing. 'Of all the many beautiful things', Socrates asks, 'is there one that will not also appear ugly? Or is there any one of those just things that will not also appear unjust? Or one of those pious things that will not also appear impious?' (5.479a) Although Plato does not share the subjectivist view that beauty is in the eye of the beholder, the beauty example is a helpful one. The sky to the west is beautiful right now, but in an hour, after the sun has set, it no longer is. Nor is it beautiful to my color-blind friend. The bouquet of flowers on the dining room table will not evoke 'oohs' and 'ahs' in two weeks. Thus, beauty seems both temporal and perspectival. As we saw in Book I, returning the weapon you have borrowed is usually just, but in a particular set of circumstances (say, its owner is deranged) it is not. Telling the truth is usually the right thing to do but sometimes the demands of kindness trump the demands of honesty. That fox seems big when standing next to the squirrel, but small when standing next to the bear. And so on. Being ever-changing and unstable are hallmarks of concrete particulars. Bob Dylan captures something of Plato's point when he sings, 'He not busy born is busy dying.' I hope my non-existence is a long way off in the future, but every day I live I am one day closer to my death—hence, I seem to be both living and dying, just as every beautiful thing seems both beautiful and not beautiful.

The Forms are altogether different, on Plato's view. Unlike the many particular beautiful things, the Form of beauty is permanent, stable, unchanging: 'the beautiful itself', Socrates says, 'remains always the same in all respects' (5.479a). It is the only thing that is always and everywhere beautiful. The same goes for the Forms of justice, piety, redness, bigness, whatever. While the world of particulars is in constant flux, the world of the Forms is stable and unchanging. We experience particular things and events via our senses, but the Forms 'are intelligible but not visible' (6.507b): we perceive them with our minds, not our senses.

One of Plato's ways of referring to the Form of something drives this point home: the Form of a thing is the ἰδέα—literally, the *idea*—of the thing. We cannot see or taste or touch or smell or hear ideas; we can only think them. But the word 'idea' can be misleading, since for Plato the Forms are not psychological entities like thoughts or feelings, which depend for their existence on someone having them, as 'idea' might suggest. Unlike ordinary thoughts and ideas, which cannot exist without thinkers thinking and having them, Plato's Forms are mind-independently real, not depending for their existence upon thinkers thinking them. This is one of the most distinctive features of the Forms. It is one thing to claim that there is a common essence shared by particular things; it is another to claim that these common essences or Forms are not dependent, psychological entities but are instead mind-independently real. While the shadow my hand casts is real, it seems somehow less real than my hand, since its existence depends on the presence of the hand. Ideas and thoughts and feelings and moods seem similar to shadows in this regard: they are dependent entities, depending on conscious subjects for their existence. Plato does not deny this. But the Forms are not dependent psychological entities. It turns out that the Forms depend upon the Form of the good—goodness itself—but they are decisively unlike our ordinary ideas and thoughts. If this all sounds a bit weird, thinking about numbers can be helpful. Although the two coffee cups on the table are concrete particular objects, the number two is an abstract object, capable of being instantiated in space and time by infinitely many pairs of concrete particular objects but it is not itself a concrete particular—at least on a plausible philosophy of mathematics known, perhaps unsurprisingly, as Platonism. One reason for thinking of mathematical objects as mind-independently real is that doing so helps us make sense of other beliefs many of us have about these objects. It will seem to many readers, for example, that the Pythagorean Theorem is timelessly true and would still be true even if no person ever thought of it. We should resist the temptation to say that numbers and the Forms have always existed, because 'always existed' is a temporal notion, and the idea here is that such entities are outside of time.

Plato's Metaphysical Elevator

We can think of Plato's metaphysics via the metaphor of an elevator, as in this diagram.

Level 4
The Form of F is more real than the many particular Fs.

Level 3
The Form of F is real: it is a non-spatiotemporal, mind-independent entity.

Level 2
There is a form of F (the real definition of F), which all particular F things have in common.

Level 1
The many particular F things are real: they are spatiotemporal, mind-independent entities.

At Level One we find the everyday objects making up the world we experience through our five senses: trees, squirrels, rocks, picnic tables, etc. Most readers, I assume, think these objects are metaphysically real, existing independently of our minds and still there when we close our eyes or when we no longer exist. This is a plausible, commonsense philosophical view, though of course not all philosophers hold it. The great Irish philosopher George Berkeley (1685–1753), for one, thought that what we ordinarily take to be mind-independently real things are in reality mind-dependent ideas. We are tempted to think of them as mind-independently real because they seem to persist in our absence, but, he thought, this is only because *God* continues to think them when we do not. Berkeley's motto was *esse est percipi*: to exist is to be perceived. This seems right for headaches, for example, which require someone to perceive them; they are not floating around in space, waiting to land on an unfortunate victim. So while some philosophers will not even get on Plato's elevator at the first floor, most of us will.

At Level Two we find those real definitions or essences that Socrates is forever seeking, the trait or property that all *F* things have in common: chairness, justice itself, etc. Most readers, I suspect, will take Plato's elevator to Level Two. We think that the many particular things we experience through our senses come in clusters unified by common properties: there are red things, round things, beautiful things, just and unjust actions and social arrangements, etc. Ascending to Level Two results from agreeing with Socrates that there is 'a single form in connection with each of the many things to which we apply the same name' (10.596a). Indeed, the *Republic* is the search for the Form of justice, as many of Plato's dialogues are searches for the Forms or essences of various virtues such as piety, courage, temperance, etc. But at level two, we find forms, rather than Forms, since they are not mind-independently real, existing in their own right.

Not everyone will follow Plato to Level Two, however. The great twentieth-century philosopher Ludwig Wittgenstein (1889–1951), for one, declined the invitation, thinking that the search for *one* commonality was misguided and inevitably futile. If we consider the wide variety of games—card games, board games, ball games, party games, computer games, etc.—we will see, Wittgenstein thought, that there need not be features common to everything we call a game:

> Or is there always winning and losing, or competition between players? Think of solitaire. In ball games there is winning and losing; but when a child throws his ball at the wall and catches it again, this feature has disappeared [...] Think now of games like ring-a-ring-a-roses; here is the element of amusement, but how many other characteristic features have

disappeared! And we can go through the many, many other groups of games in the same way; can see how similarities crop up and disappear.[3]

Instead of an essence shared by all games, Wittgenstein finds 'a complicated network of similarities overlapping and crisscrossing', which he dubs a family resemblance. Not everyone accepts Wittgenstein's view; Bernard Suits, for one, thought he had found the essence of *game*. But it is worth noting that contemporary psychology and cognitive science seem to side with Wittgenstein over Plato. According to *prototype theory*, first articulated by the cognitive psychologist Eleanor Rosch in the early 1970s, our concept of, say, *bird*, involves a cluster of features, some more important than others, with certain examples serving as prototypes.[4] If you want to give someone an example of a bird, you are likelier to offer a robin or cardinal as an example than you are to offer a penguin, because penguins lack one of the prototypical—but not necessary—traits of we associate with birds, namely the ability to fly.

Even though Wittgenstein would not ascend to Level Two, preferring *family resemblances* to *essences*, many readers will follow Socrates there. It is at Level Three, though, where Platonism really starts to kick in, for Level Three involves a commitment to the real, mind-independent existence of these Forms or common properties. At Level Three, we discover essences and Forms; we do not invent them. It is one thing to regard the Form or essence of justice or kindness or chairness as a *psychological* entity, a conceptual construct having no mind-independent existence in its own right. It is another thing entirely to regard the Form as mind-independently real, something that is to be discovered rather than invented. You can ascend to Level Two while thinking that the Forms are like ordinary ideas and thoughts, not real in themselves but rather depending for their existence on thinkers thinking them. But ascending from Level Two to Level Three requires a considerable jump in what philosophers call 'ontological commitment', a fancy-sounding but precise phrase indicating which kinds of things one is prepared to say exist in their own right. Few people, for example, are ontologically committed to unicorns or the tooth fairy: most of us do not regard

---

3   Ludwig Wittgenstein, *Philosophical Investigations*, 3rd. ed., trans. by G. E. M. Anscombe (Oxford: Basil Blackwell, 1973), §66, p. 32.
4   Eleanor Rosch, 'Natural categories', *Cognitive Psychology*, 4 (1973), 328–50.

them as mind-independently real. And while most of us think that our thoughts and feelings are 'real' in an everyday sense—the sense which contrasts 'real' with 'imaginary' or 'hallucinatory'—we do not regard them as real in the sense of existing in their own right, mind-independently. Many people who find the ascent to Level Two unproblematic and obvious will balk at ascending to Level Three. Why go there, after all? It seems needlessly complicated or metaphysically profligate to posit the real, mind-independent existence of Socrates' real definitions.

Many readers are familiar with Ockham's Razor, which in one formulation tells us that the simplest explanation of a phenomenon is usually correct. Perhaps less familiar is the *ontological* formulation of the Razor, which bids us not to multiply entities beyond necessity: *non sunt multiplicanda entia sine necessitate.* In short, if you do not need to posit the existence of certain things or kinds to make sense of your experience, then don't; be metaphysically frugal and parsimonious. No doubt this metaphysical or ontological simplicity is related to explanatory simplicity: explanations involving fewer kinds of entities will probably be simpler. It is as though there is an ontology tax that philosophers are keen to avoid paying. Most of us find ontological commitment to ships and shoes and sealing wax unproblematic because it is difficult to make sense of our everyday experiences without a commitment to the real existence of the spatiotemporal objects that we sit on, stub our toes on, eat, etc. But many readers will resist ontological realism about Plato's Forms, feeling they can understand and explain their experiences without appeal to them.

The journalist Hunter S. Thompson once wrote, 'When the going gets weird, the weird turn pro'.[5] If so, then Level Four is where one loses one's amateur standing. For those ascending to Level Four go beyond ontological commitment to the real, mind-independent existence of the Forms that typified Level Three. On Level Four, the Forms are not merely mind-independently real but are *more real* than the spatiotemporal particulars that are instances of them. The idea that the essence of chairness is more real than the chair one is sitting on is, well, pretty weird. Many people will get off the Platonic elevator at Level Two, being

---

5   Hunter S. Thompson, *The Great Shark Hunt: Strange Tales from a Strange Time* (New York: Simon & Schuster, 1979), p. 36.

philosophically unwilling, perhaps for Ockham-inspired reasons, to ascend to Level Three. But of those who go to Level Three, few, I suspect, will be willing to go all the way to Level Four, and readers might be forgiven for thinking that Socrates has gotten into the drugs reserved for the rulers of the city (5.459c). But—bad jokes aside: the drugs are not *those* kinds of drugs, anyway—his reasons for ascending to Levels Three and Four are philosophical rather than psychedelic, and it is to those philosophical reasons that we now turn.

Marrying Metaphysics and Epistemology: The Powers Argument (5.476d–480a)

The metaphysical and epistemological distinctions are intimately related, for Plato. In what I call the Powers Argument, he starts with epistemology and ends up at metaphysics, arguing that the distinction between knowledge and belief requires allegiance to the Forms, since knowledge and belief, being different powers, must have distinct kinds of objects. The Powers Argument is crucial to addressing the Third Wave, since it will help 'define […] who the philosophers are that we dare to say must rule' (5.474b), but its implications go beyond this, as it attempts to give good reasons to ride the Metaphysical Elevator all the way up.

The epistemological and metaphysical distinctions fit together this way: concrete particular things are the objects of belief, while the Forms are the objects of knowledge. A non-philosopher has beliefs about the many particular things and activities that make up the furniture of our everyday world: chairs, just actions, cats, sunsets. They 'believe[] in beautiful things, but do[] not believe in the beautiful itself' (5.476c). The philosopher, by contrast, is 'able to see and embrace the nature of the beautiful itself' (5.476b), the Form or essence in virtue of which all particular beautiful things are beautiful. A non-philosopher can have a true belief that a sunset is beautiful but never knowledge of this. Indeed, 'there is no knowledge of such things' (7.529b), as the Forms and not particulars are the proper objects of knowledge, on Plato's view. But perhaps something that falls short of knowledge but is more than true belief—knowledge with an asterisk—is possible where particulars are concerned. If so, a philosopher might know* that this particular sunset or that particular painting is beautiful by grasping the Form of beauty and seeing that the painting or sunset is an instance of—participates in, as Plato often puts it—the Form, if only temporarily. Such a philosopher would know *why* the sunset is beautiful, which is beyond the cognitive capacities of a non-philosopher, who lacks access to the Form of beauty and thus never ascends above true belief.

The Powers Argument's crucial concept, which gives it its name, is the concept of a power (δύναμις [*dunamis*, whence the word 'dynamic']). Sight, hearing, touch, taste, and smell are ordinary examples of powers, which we might also call 'capacities' or 'faculties'. Animals typically have the power of sight; rocks do not. Even though powers are what enable us to see, hear, touch, taste, and smell the world, powers themselves are not the kinds of things we can see, hear, touch, taste, and smell. We distinguish them, Socrates says, by what they do and what they are 'set over' (5.477d)—by their functions and their objects: 'What is set over the same things and does the same I call the same power; what is set over something different and does something different I call a different one' (5.477d). Talk of knowledge and belief as *powers*, analogous to sight and hearing, might make this first premise sound odd to modern ears, but this is how Socrates conceives of them. The second premise is the claim that knowledge and belief are different powers, which Glaucon regards as obviously true to 'a person with any understanding' (5.477e). From these two premises Socrates concludes that knowledge and belief must have different objects. This conclusion seems innocuous enough, but we will soon see that it is anything but.

Having established, he thinks, that knowledge and belief must have different objects, Socrates then tries to determine what these different objects are. Knowledge's object, Glaucon agrees, is 'what is' (5.478a). There is a trifold ambiguity here that we should be aware of. In the existential sense, 'what is' means *what exists, what is real*. Someone who asks, 'Is there a god?', is using 'is' in the existential sense. In the epistemic sense, 'what is' means *what is true, what is the case*. News anchor Walter Cronkite's signature sign-off, 'And that's the way it is', employed 'is' in the epistemic sense. In the predicative sense, 'is' serves to link subject and predicate: the sky is blue, Jonas Starker is a great cellist, etc. So 'what is' means *what is* ..., where the dots are filled in with some predicate: *what is red, what is beautiful, what is just,* etc.

Plato does not make explicit which sense of 'is' Glaucon has in mind when he says that knowledge's object is 'what is.' To get a sense of the argument without becoming ensnared in scholarly controversy, I propose that we read 'what is' in the existential sense, given the metaphysical implications of the argument. Taken this way, when Socrates says that 'knowledge is set over what is' (5.478a), he is saying that the objects of knowledge—what we know when we know something—exist: they are real. And the Forms exist, so they are objects of knowledge. Ignorance, by contrast, has as its object 'what is not' (5.477a, 478c): what does not exist. (It is odd to think of ignorance as a power or capacity, since it does not enable its possessor to do anything, as powers usually do, but let us set aside this minor point.) Since belief is in between knowledge and ignorance, 'darker than knowledge but clearer than ignorance' (5.478c), its objects will be intermediate between *what is* and *what is not*. Thus the objects of belief 'participate in both being and not-being' (5.478e): they straddle both existence and nonexistence, not fully real but not unreal, either. In short, the objects of belief are the particulars of everyday experience.

To summarize: knowledge and belief, being different powers, must have different objects. Indeed, they have very different kinds of objects: knowledge's objects are the timeless Forms, while belief's objects are the spatiotemporal particulars that make up our everyday world. So there are two metaphysically different worlds: the world of the Forms and the world of particulars. The world of the Forms is the world of reality while the world of particulars is the world of appearance—but not, I hasten to add, a world of illusion. Plato is very careful with his language here, emphasizing that those things we think of as *being* beautiful really only *appear* beautiful, since they also *appear* ugly. 'Is there any one of those just things', Socrates asks, 'that will not also appear unjust? Or one of those pious things that will not also appear impious?' (5.479a) Plato is *not* claiming that our everyday world is illusory in the sense of not being real. It is just not *as* real as the world of the Forms. It is smack dab in the middle, metaphysically, more real than complete non-existence, but less real than complete existence.

Problems with the Powers Argument

That is a lot to take in, so let us pause and restate the argument in premise-conclusion form, in order to grasp its structure more clearly, which should help us analyze it:

P1 x and y are the same power IF AND ONLY IF

(a) x and y have the same objects AND

(b) x and y have the same function. (5.477d)

P2   Knowledge and belief are different powers. (5.477b,e)

C1   So, knowledge and belief have different objects AND different functions. (5.478a)

C2   So, knowledge and belief have different objects.

P3   Knowledge's object is what is. (5.478a,c)

P4   Belief is intermediate between knowledge and ignorance. (5.478d)

P5   Ignorance's object is what is not. (5.478c)

C3   So, belief's object is what is AND what is not. (5.478d)

(A minor detail regarding C1: Grube's translation does not quite square with the Greek text here, which is better captured by C2—which logically follows from C1. I do not think anything rides on Grube's addition, but some readers, especially brave souls wrestling with the Greek text, will want to know this.) Let us work backwards, starting with C3. We have already noted that for Plato particular things are bundles of opposites, simultaneously beautiful and not beautiful, just and not just, etc.: 'each of them always participates in both opposites' (5.479b). But Socrates now takes this to imply that these particular things are 'intermediates between what is not and what purely is' (5.479d). This is something new. It is one thing to claim that predicates like '...is beautiful' both apply and do not apply to one and the same particular object—that the particular thing participates in both beauty and non-beauty. But why would this imply that any particular 'participates in both being and non-being' (5.478d), that it somehow both exists and does not exist? There seems to be something a little fishy here. Socrates seems to slide from the predicative sense of 'is', where it links subjects and predicates, to its existential, existence-asserting sense. That is, he seems to slide from

(Predicative)   Any particular thing both is beautiful and is not beautiful

to

(Existential)   Any particular thing both is and is not,

as if he simply crossed out the occurrences of 'beautiful' in (Predicative).

Bertrand Russell once wrote that employing the same word to express such different senses was 'a disgrace to the human race'.[6] Russell's hyperbole is no doubt tongue-in-cheek, but there is a serious point in the background: philosophy often requires attention to linguistic subtleties like the distinction between the senses of 'is'. In this portion of the argument, Socrates seems to elide the distinction between the predicative and existential senses, drawing a conclusion employing the latter from a premise employing the former. I stress that he *seems* to me to be doing this; I am not insisting that he actually does so. Such insistence would violate the principle of charity, which requires us to interpret texts and utterances in ways that maximize their truth and reasonableness and logical validity. But sometimes even very smart people make logical blunders, and the principle of charity does not require us to pretend otherwise. If this were a different book, aimed at a different audience, we would explore this question in depth and detail. Some people are sufficiently fascinated by issues like this as to become Plato scholars, and no doubt some of those scholars are rolling their eyes or at least arching their eyebrows at what I have said here. But—and here I am on firm logical ground—this is not a different book than it is, so I tentatively suggest that we view this apparent equivocation between senses of 'is' as a heuristic device to help us think critically about the argument and move on.

These concerns about whether Socrates makes this predicative-to-existential slide fade into the background when we see how problematic the first part of the argument is, the derivation of C1 from P1 and P2. Glaucon thinks that C1 'necessarily' (5.478a) follows from P1 and P2,

---

6   Bertrand Russell, *Introduction to Mathematical Philosophy* (New York: MacMillan, 1919), p. 172.

but his confidence is misplaced, since the conclusion does not follow necessarily at all. Since the conclusion could still be false even if we assume that the premises are true, the argument is invalid. To see this, consider a parallel example. Two Constitutional conditions of eligibility to be President of the United States are (*a*) that one be at least thirty-five years old and (*b*) that one be a natural-born citizen. From the fact that my friend Geoff is not eligible to be President, it does *not* follow that he is not at least thirty-five *and* that he is not a natural born citizen; what follows is that either Geoff is not at least thirty-five years old OR Geoff is not a natural-born citizen. Both negative conclusions might follow, as they do in the case for my cat Frobisher, who, despite having been born here, is not a citizen of the US and is well shy of thirty-five. But all we— and Socrates—are entitled to is the *or*. If I know that Geoff is well past thirty-five, I can then conclude that he is not a natural-born citizen (he is, in fact, Canadian). But until I know that, I am jumping to a conclusion I am not entitled to draw. What Socrates should conclude from P1 and P2 is that EITHER knowledge and belief have different objects OR they have different tasks. It might be that both their objects and tasks differ, but Socrates is not entitled to conclude that. To get to C2, the conclusion that knowledge and belief have different objects, from C1, which now functions as the premise that they either have different tasks or different objects, he has to show that knowledge and belief do not have different tasks. But without doing this, he is jumping to a conclusion—C2—that he is not entitled to.

So Plato, in the person of Socrates, has committed one of the gravest of philosophical sins: he has given a logically invalid argument. But even if we could fix the logical invalidity, switching the 'AND' in C1 to an 'OR', it is difficult to see how Socrates can get to C2. Powers differ more often by having different tasks or functions than by having different objects. Shepherds and butchers, for example, share a common object, sheep, but they have different tasks in relation to that object: shepherds seek to nurture sheep while butchers seek to turn them into lamb chops. On a common conception of education (though one we will see Plato calling into question in Book VII), teaching and learning have the same object, knowledge, but have different tasks or functions with respect to that object: teaching seeks to impart or instill knowledge while learning seeks to acquire it. And so on.

Perhaps the trouble is thinking of knowledge and belief as *powers* or capacities. Plato thinks that each of the senses has a distinct object: sight's object is color, hearing's is sound, etc. In the *Theaetetus,* a dialogue roughly contemporary with the *Republic,* Socrates says, 'what you perceive through one power, you cannot perceive through another' (185a). Cases of synesthesia aside, this has the ring of truth, though it seems to have the odd implication that we cannot see and smell and taste the same object, when it seems clear that we can: I see the coffee, smell it, taste it, etc. But Socrates could respond that we see the coffee's color, smell its aroma, feel its heat, etc. These various sensations are synthesized or integrated into a unified sensory impression, but the various senses are modular, operating independently. We perceive the coffee by or through perceiving its sensible qualities. But, a critic might insist, it is not the case that these powers ultimately have different objects; instead, they have a common object: the coffee. It is true that their intermediary objects are different properties or qualities of that object—we see color, smell aroma, etc.—but there is a common object that those various sensory qualities belong to. So we have reason to be skeptical of the first premise of the Powers Argument. And even if we give Socrates the benefit of the doubt and take him to be talking of the various intermediate objects of these powers, not the ultimate object, we might wonder what reason we have to think of knowledge and belief as analogous to powers in having unique objects.

Most contemporary philosophers would agree with the spirit of P2, since they think that knowledge and belief are different cognitive or epistemic states, though they would be unlikely to think of them as 'powers'. Few, though, would agree with Plato's conclusion that knowledge and belief have different kinds of objects. As discussed earlier, on the JTB (Justified True Belief) conception of knowledge, to know something is to have a belief that is not only true but is also justified, which (on a plausible account of what it is to be justified in believing something) requires good reasons for having the belief. Most contemporary philosophers would regard C2 as false, since knowledge and belief, though different, have the same objects: propositions. In the first sentence of the Gettysburg Address, Lincoln speaks of the Founders' dedication to 'the proposition that all men are created equal.' If he had said it in French (*'la proposition que tous les hommes sont créés égaux'*) he would have expressed the same proposition. Even though we express propositions in language, at heart propositions are conceptual entities rather than linguistic ones, and the same proposition can be expressed in different languages. Lincoln believed in the proposition of fundamental human equality, while Plato, we have seen, did not. Both Anna, who grew up in Wisconsin and has looked at her share of roadmaps and atlases, and Bryce, a 'Coastie' with a vague picture of the geography of North America who has trouble locating Wisconsin on a map (for him the Midwest is a vague 'blobject'), believe the proposition that Wisconsin is east of the Mississippi River. On the JTB conception, Anna knows this while Bryce does not. Though Bryce's belief is true, he does not have good reasons for it, since when pressed the only reason he offers is, 'I just think it is'. Though Anna and Bryce are in different cognitive and epistemic states, their objects are the same, the proposition that Wisconsin is east of the Mississippi River.

Or so say most contemporary epistemologists. That most contemporary philosophers think C2 is false does not make it false, of course, but in the next section we will see reason to think they are probably right about this.

Plato's Fallible Conception of Infallibility

So why does Plato have someone as smart as Socrates make such a logically flawed argument? It may be that the argument accurately reflects Socrates' reasoning, which Plato faithfully reproduces, though that seems unlikely. Perhaps this is one of those instances of Plato's intentionally having Socrates make a bad argument in hopes of engaging the reader in philosophical dialogue, since the yes-men Socrates is talking with do not seem up to the task. That is certainly possible, but here it does not ring true—at least to me. In those instances in Book I when the bad arguments seem intentional—e.g., in Socrates' first refutation of Polemarchus—there was a substantive philosophical point that Plato seemed to want his readers to work out for themselves (that virtues are not crafts or skills). But given how much is at stake here—reasons for believing in Plato's Forms, for taking Plato's Elevator to the Third and Fourth Levels—it is an odd time for such a lesson. Perhaps Plato has independent reasons for believing C2, that knowledge and belief have different objects, and this makes him less attentive than he should be to the quality of the reasons he offers here in support of this belief. It is a common enough human failing, but it *is* surprising to see Plato falling victim to it here.

Those independent reasons for thinking C2 is true can be found in the discussion Socrates and Glaucon have about P2. Glaucon agrees—as we all should—that knowledge and belief are different. 'How could a person with any understanding', he asks, 'think that a fallible power is the same as an infallible one?' (5.477e) The idea that belief is fallible should ring true: we regularly believe things that are not true. We *think* they are true, of course, and sometimes insist that they are. After all, we probably would not believe them if we knew they were false, since to believe something is, at least in part, to take it to be true. But while I can believe things that are false, I cannot know things that are false. I might believe that Orson Welles directed *The Third Man* or that Edward Albee wrote *Desert Solitaire,* but I cannot know these things, since they are false. On the JTB conception, remember, my beliefs count as knowledge only if they are true (though being true is not enough: those true beliefs also have to be justified). For contemporary philosophers, that is the sense in which knowledge is infallible and belief is fallible: I can believe things that are false but I cannot know things that are false.

Plato seems to have a different understanding of the infallibility of knowledge, one that goes beyond the view that we cannot know things that are false and holds that we cannot know things that *could* be false. In other words, the objects of knowledge must not only be true, they must be necessarily true. While a contingent truth could be false, a necessary truth cannot possibly be false: it *must* be true. The candidates for such things are few, but the truths of mathematics offer the most intuitively plausible examples of necessary truths. Although it is not completely uncontroversial, I think that the Pythagorean Theorem is necessarily true, that it was true even before anyone thought of it and would be true even if no one ever thought of it, even if no creatures capable of understanding geometry had ever existed. That the square of the hypotenuse of a right triangle is equal to the sum of the squares of the other two sides is not merely a mind-independent truth, it is a mind-independent truth that could not be false. Given the nature of right triangles, there is no way the square of the hypotenuse could not equal the sum of the squares of the other two sides. If there are two mittens and one stocking cap on the table, it is mind-independently true there are three things on the table: it does not matter whether I am looking at them or not; there are three things on the table. But it is merely a contingent truth that there are three things on the table; I could have just as easily kept my stocking cap on (it is cold in here!), in which case there would only be *two* items on the table. So while it is true that there are three items on the table, it is a contingent truth. But that three is the sum of one and two is a necessary truth: it cannot be otherwise. And here it is important not to confuse numbers with numerals, which are our names for numbers. We could use the word 'two' to name the number three and the word 'three' to name the number two—heck, we could call two 'Ethel' and three 'Fred'. The English sentence 'two plus one is three' is only contingently true, since which words attach to which objects is a contingent fact of English. But the proposition it expresses, that the sum of two and one is three, is necessarily true, regardless of which names or numerals we use to designate the numbers.

The crucial difference between these two conceptions of the infallibility of knowledge is that the contemporary conception of infallibility is a claim about the nature of knowledge, while for Plato it is a claim about the objects of knowledge:

Contemporary: Necessarily, if someone knows that p, then p is true.

Plato: If someone knows that p, then p is necessarily true.

A lot rides on where 'necessarily' appears—or as linguists and philosophers would say, on its scope. There is a world of difference between

Not Trying   I am not trying to hear what they are saying

and

Trying Not   I am trying not to hear what they are saying.

Not Trying is true so long as I am not making an effort to hear what they are saying (e.g., I am not leaning in, putting my ear to the wall, etc.); if I hear what they are saying, perhaps the fault is theirs and not mine, since I was not eavesdropping. But *Trying Not* requires that I make an effort to not hear them (e.g., I cover my ears, change locations, etc.).;

if I hear what they are saying, I have failed in my attempt to not hear them—perhaps I should have tried harder. Similarly, the difference between the contemporary and Platonic conceptions of the infallibility of knowledge is a difference in the scope of the adverb 'necessarily'. On the contemporary account, what is necessarily true is a claim about the nature of knowledge, that if I know that p, then p is true—so I can have knowledge only of things that are true. On the account I am attributing to Plato, it is the proposition known that is necessarily true: if I know that p, then p is necessarily true—so I can have knowledge only of necessary truths, never of merely contingent truths.

If Plato understands the infallibility of knowledge as I have suggested, it is no wonder that he thinks that knowledge and belief must have different objects. Only the Forms, Plato thinks, have the necessity required of objects of knowledge, since only the Form of beauty is completely beautiful; particular beautiful things are too awash in contingency and opposition to make the grade. (The self-predication of the Forms—the view that the Form of beauty is beautiful, the Form of justice is just—is of great interest to Plato scholars, but it is an issue we need not tangle with here. Suffice it to say that there are problems with this view: if the Forms are self-predicating, then the Form of beauty is beautiful and the Form of justice is just. That might seem just fine, but then the Form of bigness is big and the Form of smallness is small, the Form of redness is red and the Form of squareness is square—all of which are odd implications for entities that are not spatiotemporal.)

Most of the truths of our everyday lives—our names, where we parked the car, our favorite flavor of ice cream, how many (if any) children we have—are contingent truths, not necessary truths: they could have been otherwise. My parents could have named me Ivan instead of Sean; I parked the car in the street but I could have parked it in the driveway or in the garage, etc. Things could be different than they are. On the ordinary conception of knowledge, I know that my name is Sean and that I have two cats. But on the stronger understanding of the infallibility of knowledge that Plato seems to have, I *do not* know these things, since they are only contingently and not necessarily true and thus not proper objects of knowledge. This will strike many readers as quite counter-intuitive; most of us feel quite confident that we know our names (though where we parked the car might be a different matter entirely, especially for garageless city-dwellers).

So it is plausible that Plato's view about the infallibility of knowledge is what accounts for his belief that knowledge and belief must have different objects. And it might help explain why he does not seem aware of the weaknesses of the actual argument he gives to support that belief. But there are still the facts that the Powers Argument is logically invalid and its key first premise is false. It is certainly the marquee argument of Book V, intended to provide good reasons to accept Plato's distinctive metaphysics. Of course, Plato's metaphysics might still be correct: the conclusion of an invalid argument can still be true. But as things stand, there is a gaping hole in the middle of the *Republic*.

Some Suggestions for Further Reading

Readers looking for an excellent introduction to metaphysics by one of the best contemporary philosophers will find it in Peter Van Inwagen, *Metaphysics* (4th ed.) (Boulder: Westview Press, 2014).

Readers interested in a good, brief introduction to epistemology should see Jennifer Nagel, *Knowledge: A Very Short Introduction* (New York: Oxford University Press, 2014), https://doi.org/10.1093/actrade/9780199661268.001.0001.

For an overview of Plato's metaphysics and epistemology, interested readers should see Allan Silverman, 'Plato's Middle Period Metaphysics and Epistemology', in the ever-helpful Stanford Encyclopedia of Philosophy (https://plato.stanford.edu/entries/plato-metaphysics/).

For an advanced discussion of some of the issues treated in this chapter, interested readers might start with Gail Fine, 'Knowledge and Belief in *Republic* V', in *Plato 1: Metaphysics and Epistemology*, ed. by Gail Fine (New York: Oxford University Press, 2000), pp. 215–46. Gregory Vlastos, 'A Metaphysical Paradox', in *Plato's Republic: Critical Essays*, ed. by Richard Kraut (Lanham, MD: Rowman & Littlefield, 1997), pp. 181–95, is an accessible discussion of Plato's two-worlds metaphysics by one of the twentieth century's leading Plato scholars.

For readers interested in Wittgenstein's philosophy, his *Philosophical Investigations*, 3rd ed., trans. by G. E. M. Anscombe (Oxford: Basil Blackwell, 1973) is a good place to start. Bernard Suits, *The Grasshopper: Games, Life, and Utopia*, 3rd ed. (Peterborough, ON: Broadview Press, 2014) is of great interest in itself and also for its anti-Wittgensteinian analysis of the concept of a game.

Readers interested in Berkeley's philosophy might start with George Berkeley, *Principles of Human Knowledge and Three Dialogues Between Hylas and Philonous*, ed. by Roger Woolhouse (Harmondsworth: Penguin Classics, 1988). Jonathan Bennett's helpful modernization can be found at *Early Modern Texts* (http://www.earlymoderntexts.com/).

Readers interested in the philosophy of mathematics might start with Stewart Shapiro, *Thinking about Mathematics: The Philosophy of Mathematics* (New York: Oxford University Press, 2000). *Philosophy of Mathematics: Selected Readings,* ed. by Paul Benacerraf and Hilary Putnam, 2nd ed. (Princeton: Princeton University Press, 1983) is a classic collection of essays on this fascinating and difficult area of philosophy.

Plato's *Theaetetus* is a Socratic dialogue especially focused on epistemology. The *Parmenides* explores the complexities of the theory of the Forms, among other things. There are excellent translations of both in *Plato: Complete Works*, ed. by John Cooper (Indianapolis: Hackett Publishing, 1997). Hackett also offers stand-alone translations along with informative, detailed introductions.

B-side of bell krater with scene of three young men with himatia in an arena. Photograph by Ángel M. Felicísimo (2016), Wikimedia, Public Domain, https://commons.wikimedia.org/wiki/File:Cr%C3%A1tera_(38877852382).jpg

9. The Philosopher's Virtues
Book VI

Although there are serious problems with the Powers Argument, its invalidity and unsoundness do not entail that the ideal city will get washed away by the Third Wave. For even if we reject the mind-independent reality of the Forms or, more cautiously, regard belief in their mind-independence as unjustified, we can still agree with Plato that ideal rulers will possess knowledge of what is best for the city. Although the distinction between knowledge and belief is crucial to Plato's distinction between philosopher and non-philosopher, knowledge and belief can be different epistemic states even if they do not have different objects. So the distinction between knowledge and belief, and the distinction between philosopher and non-philosopher that it underlies, can survive the failures of the Powers Argument, since the distinction itself does not depend on Plato's particular way of making it.

In this chapter, we will look at another way in which Plato tries to distinguish between 'a true philosopher and [...] a counterfeit one' (6.485d). He is especially keen to distinguish genuine philosophers from sophists, the professional teachers of rhetoric whom the public mistakenly takes to be philosophers. In doing so, Plato will not only shore up his response to the Third Wave by further 'defin[ing] who the philosophers are that we dare to say must rule' (5.474b), but he will also exonerate Socrates, who, as many readers know, was tried and convicted of impiety and corrupting the youth of Athens and put to death for those alleged crimes in BCE 399. Sophists, and not philosophers, Plato insists, are guilty of corrupting the youth (6.492a). In a phrase that will recall

https://doi.org/10.11647/OBP.0229.09

his Book I exchange with Thrasymachus, Socrates wants to discover who the philosophers are 'in the most exact sense of the term' (6.503b).

In asking 'whether a soul is philosophic or not' (6.486b), Plato indicates that being a philosopher is a matter of nature as well as nurture. All the education and nurture in the world will not produce a philosopher if the underlying philosophic nature is not present, and improperly educating someone with a philosophic nature will not just fail to produce a philosopher, it is likely to produce moral depravity: 'the best natures become outstandingly bad when they receive a bad upbringing' (6.491e). Those who naturally possess the intellectual wherewithal to be philosophers but who do not receive the right kind of education can do far more harm than their less intellectually endowed fellows. Plato seems to have in mind here the historical Alcibiades, a beautiful, brilliant young Athenian who proved a traitor, switching sides to Sparta in the Peloponnesian War. Fans of the television drama *Breaking Bad* will not be far off the mark in taking Walter White as an example of Plato's point, since his intellectual prowess makes him far worse, morally, than his partner and former student, Jesse.

Socrates' task is to describe the philosophic nature, to show what philosophers are like in contrast with non-philosophers. In Book VII he will discuss their nurture, expanding on the program of education already spelled out in Books II and III. In Book V the distinction between philosopher and non-philosopher rested on the distinction between knowledge and belief, which led us to the metaphysical distinction between Forms and particulars. Here the focus is on the virtues that true philosophers can and do possess.

Loving the Truth

The most important of these virtues is love for the truth. Not only must philosophers 'be without falsehood, they must refuse to accept what is false, hate it, and have a love for the truth' (6.485c). This will strike many readers as surprising in light of Socrates' earlier insistence that the rulers will have to employ falsehood in governing, for example in rigging the lotteries determining the 'sacred marriages.' In addressing the Second Wave, Socrates conceded that 'our rulers will have to make considerable use of falsehood and deception for the benefit of those they rule' (5.459c). Is Plato being inconsistent here? It may look that way at first, but on closer examination it seems not. After all, rulers can *employ* falsehoods even though they *hate* them and reluctantly use them only when something important is at stake, when the falsehood is beneficial to those it is being told to, and when it is the only or perhaps the most effective means to bringing about the benefit. And the distinction between true or genuine falsehoods and merely verbal falsehoods, which we met toward the end of Book II, blunts the charge of inconsistency as well. While rulers will find employing verbal falsehoods useful, presumably they will never employ the radically false and soul-distorting true or genuine falsehoods. The rulers can hate what is most truly or genuinely false but reluctantly employ mere verbal falsehoods, which are 'useful and so not deserving of hatred' (2.382c). Verbal falsehoods are like medicine (2.382c, 3.389b), after all, and medical treatment is one of Glaucon's main examples of goods that are 'onerous but beneficial' (2.357c), not intrinsically desirable (and perhaps intrinsically *un*desirable) but useful. While there may be a tension in Plato's view, upon reflection it seems to fall far short of inconsistency.

That this crucial philosophical virtue involves love should not be surprising, given the centrality of truth to the philosophical enterprise and indeed that philosophy is, etymologically, the love (*philein*) of wisdom (*sophia*). Love of truth pairs well with the role played by the guardian-rulers' love for the city back in Book III, which Socrates reminds us of here in Book VI: the rulers must be 'lovers of their city (φιλόπολις [*philopolis*])' (6.503a). We noted earlier Plato's playing up the *cognitive* dimension of love, focusing on the lover's belief that their beloved's flourishing is an essential part of their own flourishing. This is not to say that their love is *merely* cognitive, involving no feelings for the beloved or commitment to it. Perhaps Plato focuses on love's cognitive dimension because its affective dimension—how it feels—is so obvious and potent that it is likely to lead us to think of love as exclusively a matter of feeling. Plato, committed as he is to the centrality of reason in a well-lived life, wishes to remedy this by highlighting love's rational, cognitive side. Back in Book III Socrates claimed that 'the right kind of love (ὁ ὀρθὸς ἔρως [*ho orthos erôs*]) has nothing mad or licentious about it' and instead is 'the love of order and beauty that has been moderated by education' (3.403a). Although we tend to think of *erôs*—erotic or romantic love—in terms of sexual passion, Plato argues in the *Symposium* that its proper object is the Form of or essence of beauty. The goal of the musical education, after all, is 'love of the fine and beautiful' (3.403c).

The love philosophers have and feel for the truth is στέργειν (*stergein*) rather than ἔρως or φιλία, but perhaps we should not read too much into this, as Plato does not here draw hard-and-fast distinctions between kinds of love as later authors are wont to do, e.g., between *philia, eros,* and *agapê* (friendly love, erotic or romantic love, and neighborly love). But it is telling that *stergein* typically refers to parental love, which clearly involves the parent's identifying their child's wellbeing with their own, and which involves a distinctive kind of affection.

Love of truth may well be the Socratic virtue par excellence, though when we first meet Thrasymachus, he insists that Socrates is φιλότιμος (*philotimos*), a lover of honor and victory (rather than truth) who just wants to win arguments. This seems an ironic projection on Thrasymachus' part, since he aims to persuade his audience of a pre-determined conclusion by the power of his rhetorical skill, rather than to investigate the matter and accept whatever conclusions reason leads us to. Knowing how to win arguments is the skill the sophist teaches, and it is the skill most at home in the law-court. Philosophical investigation also requires skill, and we have attended to some places where logical skill is not as developed as it should be. But philosophy requires more than skill, Plato suggests. It requires the virtue of loving the truth, which in turn implies a respect for rigor well expressed by Socrates' dictum that 'whatever direction the argument blows us, that is where we must go' (3.394d).

In addition to respect for rigor, another sub-virtue is open-mindedness, which we might think of as openness to rational persuasion. We noted earlier how the *Republic*'s opening exchange raises the opposition between force and persuasion. When Polemarchus jokingly asks, 'But could you persuade us, if we will not listen?' (1.327c), he is making the serious point that philosophical inquiry requires that we do not have a pre-determined outcome, as a lawyer trying a case might, or at least that we are open to countervailing reasons and evidence.

Intellectual Virtues and Character Virtues

An interesting feature of this leading philosophical virtue is that loving the truth seems to straddle two distinct kinds of virtues, intellectual virtue and character virtue. Perhaps because he was by nature less taxonomically inclined than his student Aristotle (whose inclinations in this regard were no doubt shaped by his biological investigations), Plato does not explicitly distinguish between these kinds of virtue, as Aristotle does in his seminal work in moral philosophy, the *Nicomachean Ethics*. Readers will recall that a virtue is the state or condition that enables its possessor to perform its function well, where its function is its purpose or characteristic activity. A knife's function is to cut, so sharpness is its virtue, since a knife must be sharp if it is to cut well. Where character virtues such as moderation and courage enable morally correct behavior, intellectual virtues such as wisdom are traits that enable their possessors to gain knowledge. The function or goal they enable is knowledge. So genuine philosophers, Socrates tells us, must possess intellectual virtues such as quickness or ease in learning (6.486c, 6.487a, 6.490c, 6.494b, 6.503c) and a good memory (6.490c, 6.494b, 6.503c). The absence of the latter trait allows Plato a few jokes along the way: Glaucon, in admitting that he has forgotten that they aim to make the city as a whole happy and just (7.519e), thereby implicitly concedes that he lacks a philosophical nature, at least to some degree. Even Socrates himself admits that he cannot remember whose question prompted his articulating this principle (5.465e). And clearly a good memory will be important to the agreement-based, question-and-answer method they have adopted to investigate the *Republic*'s two main questions.

Loving truth enables knowledge, since loving wealth or honor more than or instead of truth will hamper rather than enable learning. Thus love of truth seems, like being a quick learner or having a good memory, to be an intellectual virtue. But love of truth tells us not just about a person's intellect but also about their character, since it tells us about what they value. Thus it seems as much a virtue of character as an intellectual virtue. The person who loves the truth can be counted on to act well and rightly when for example truth and self-interest conflict. Moreover, some intellectual virtues such as quickness and ease in learning are like skills in so far as they are morally neutral, depending for their moral status on the subjects learned and the end to which the knowledge gained is put. A quick learner with a good memory will master the mechanics of terrorism more quickly than a forgetful, slow learner will. Love of truth, by contrast, seems to lack this moral neutrality, as does wisdom—at least on Plato's conception of moral knowledge. If one really *knows* what is good, Plato has Socrates argue in the *Protagoras*, one would act on that knowledge if one were able to. The idea of knowing what is good or right but not acting on that knowledge—the problem of weakness of will—is not a genuine possibility. Exploring whether Plato was right about this will take us too far afield, and unsurprisingly there is much scholarly debate on the topic. But this melding of moral knowledge and moral conduct helps us see why *love of truth* has a foot on each side of the divide between intellectual and character virtues.

Another philosophic virtue worthy of our attention is high-mindedness (μεγαλοπρέπεια [*megaloprepeia*], which is sometimes translated as 'magnificence'). Like many of the virtues discussed in Book VI, we first met high-mindedness in Book III (e.g., 3.402c), where it was implicit in the musical-poetic cultivation of courage: 'a decent man does not think that death is a terrible thing for someone to suffer' (3.387d) and thus must be 'told stories that will make them least afraid of death' (3.386a). High-mindedness is a virtue of knowing what really matters, what is worth taking seriously. Socrates suggests that a high-minded person will not 'consider human life to be something important' (6.486a), but this is best taken as a point about life's *relative* importance. It is not valueless, something to be thrown away on a whim, but it is not as important as the good of the city. Living is not itself an intrinsic good, though living well is. And if living well, which for Plato requires living justly, requires sacrificing one's life for the good of one's city, then the high-minded person will (ideally) have no hesitation in doing so. High-mindedness looms in the background of Plato's deepest criticisms of poetry in Book X. 'Human affairs are not worth taking very seriously', Socrates insists in Book X (10.604b), and poetry is dangerously corrupting because it leads us to 'take [our] sufferings seriously' (10.605d). Readers familiar with Stoicism will see its Socratic roots in the virtue of high-mindedness.

Virtues of Personal Style

In addition to virtues of character and intellect, Socrates proposes another family of virtues as distinctive of the philosophical nature. Gracefulness, which we met back in Book III when discussing poetic meter or rhythm (e.g., 3.400c, 3.400d, 3.401a, 3.401d), is not a matter of character or intellect so much as a matter of personal, aesthetic style. Would-be philosopher-kings must be graceful (εὔχαρις [*eucharis*]) (5.487a), and indeed they approach the divine as they absorb gracefulness from studying the Forms (6.500c).

We meet a similar group of personal-aesthetic virtues in Aristotle's *Nicomachean Ethics,* where traits such as *wit* and *sociability* are on Aristotle's official list of virtues, on a par with canonical, cardinal virtues such as courage and moderation. The way Plato and Aristotle treat such traits suggests that they did not draw a sharp line between character and personality, between moral and non-moral traits, as we moderns tend to do. Their attitudes toward the personal-aesthetic virtues suggests a more holistic, integrated picture of human goodness on which calling someone 'a good person' is not an exclusively moral evaluation. There is a lively scholarly debate about whether our modern notion of morality is even to be found in ancient Greek philosophical thought. At the very least, it seems safe to say that beauty and goodness are more intimately connected for Plato and Aristotle than they are for us. Proper aesthetic sensibility is the basis for morality; and the crucial notion of what is *kalon*—fine or noble or beautiful—is inescapably aesthetic.

A Game of Checkers (6.487b–d)

It is perhaps surprising that a willingness to speak up and challenge assertions that others accept does not make Socrates' list of philosophical virtues. It is certainly an admirable trait, and one that Adeimantus displays with some frequency throughout the *Republic.* In Book II, after Glaucon raises the issues he want Socrates to address, Adeimantus insists that 'the most important thing' (which he takes to be the hypocritical way Athenian culture praises justice) 'has not been said yet' (2.362d). Book IV begins with Adeimantus questioning how ideal the ideal *polis* can be, given that the guardian-rulers' austere lifestyle will leave them unhappy (4.419a). And Book V begins with Adeimantus (prompted by Polemarchus) interrupting Socrates' immediately moving to consider the *Republic's* second question, when he still has questions about the way Socrates has answered the first, which prompts the Three Waves. Adeimantus shows that interrupting a speaker is not always rude, and he models a willingness to not be cowed by an intellectual superior.

Here in Book VI Adeimantus jumps in to answer a question Socrates has posed to Glaucon—not the first such interruption in the *Republic*—about whether he would be willing to 'entrust the city' to the philosopher-kings whose nature he has been describing (6.487a). Adeimantus does not object to particular claims Socrates has made; he does not deny that philosophers must be courageous or quick learners, nor does he challenge the status of the personal-aesthetic virtues. Instead, he offers a broader objection, suggesting that Socrates' whole procedure is unlikely to persuade anyone to 'entrust the city to [philosophers] and to them alone' (6.487a). He articulates the perspective of people who are not convinced by the Socratic chain or reasoning, feeling merely outmaneuvered and not persuaded:

> Just as inexperienced checkers players are trapped by the experts in the end and cannot make a move, so too they [i.e., your vanquished interlocutors] are trapped in the end and have nothing to say in this different kind of checkers, which is played not with disks but with words. Yet the truth is not affected by this outcome. I say this with a view to the present case, for someone might well say that he is unable to oppose you as you ask each of your questions, yet he sees that of all those who take up philosophy [...] the greatest number become cranks, not to say completely vicious, while those who seem completely decent are rendered useless to the city because of the studies you recommend. (6.487b–d)

Polemarchus, for one, knows whereof Adeimantus speaks: Socrates argued in Book I that defining justice as benefiting friends and harming enemies led to the conclusion that the just person is a kind of thief and justice itself is a craft of stealing. When asked if this is what he meant, Polemarchus insists, 'No, by god, it is not. I do not know any more what I did mean, but I still believe that to benefit one's friends and harm one's enemies is justice' (1.334b). There were good reasons for him to resist the conclusion Socrates has led him to, but even though he did not see what these reasons were and thus how he could resist the conclusion, Polemarchus hung on to his definition of justice, feeling outmaneuvered by Socrates rather than persuaded by him.

Adeimantus is not accusing Socrates of acting in bad faith but rather is pointing out that Socrates is perceived by many of his fellow citizens not as better at arriving at moral truth but simply better at intellectual checkers than they are. They can and will persist in believing their seemingly refuted views, since Socrates' philosophical argumentation seems to be nothing more than 'a kind of game of contradiction' (7.539b). In short, to Socrates' question about entrusting the city to philosopher-kings, the solution to the Third Wave—Adeimantus seems to be saying, 'Well, *I* might entrust the city to them, Socrates, but most people will not. Why would they, when they think of philosophers as useless at best and vicious at worse? They will nod in seeming agreement with you, but nothing you have said so far will change their minds: they think you are just playing word-games.'

It is no accident that it is Adeimantus who in Book II insists—twice (2.367b–e)—that Socrates not merely give yet another 'theoretical argument' that the just life is happier. Here he is doing much the same thing, asking not for a reworked version of the Powers Argument but for something less abstract and more accessible. Socrates obliged Adeimantus' request in Book II by offering the city-soul analogy, which of course structures the rest of the *Republic,* and here in Book VI he responds in a similar but even more procedurally transparent vein: 'The question you ask needs to be answered by means of an image or simile' (6.487e). So Socrates will meet Adeimantus' checkers metaphor with one of his own, meant to show why his fellow citizens regard philosophers as useless.

Analogical thinking is at the heart of the *Republic.* Its very method is analogical, asking us to think about the nature and value of justice as a virtue of persons by first thinking about it as a virtue of city-states. Here in Book VI, Socrates explicitly appeals to similes (6.487e, 6.488a, 6.489a) and analogies (the Greek terms are εἰκών [*eikôn:* likeness, image, reflection], from which we get the English word 'icon', and ἀνάλογον [*analogon:* proportionate to, resembling], from which we get the English word 'analogy'). Socrates, who describes himself as 'greedy for images' (6.488a), is forgoing the 'longer and fuller road' that leads to 'precise answer[s]' (4.435c) in favor of a less demanding path that offers a view of the same truths the more demanding path leads to, but the view is less clear and distinct. The road of dialectic, which requires doing without hypotheses and metaphors (6.511ae, 7.533c), is not just longer; it is a 'rough, steep path' (7.515e) that only those few who are blessed with a philosophical nature are capable of following. The rest of us—most of us, given that 'the majority cannot be philosophic' (6.494a)—will have to be content with an easier, less rigorous path. In the next chapter we will explore the major metaphors of Books VI and VII—the analogies of the Sun, Line, and Cave. Here we will look briefly at Socrates' analogical response to Adeimantus' challenge. Given the critique of painting, poetry, and the other imitative arts that awaits us in Book X, it is striking that here Socrates embraces the role of painter (γραφῆς [*graphês*] (6.488a)) as he constructs his analogies.

The Ship of State Sails the Third Wave (6.487e–490e)

Socrates' surprising response to Adeimantus' suggestion that most people think that philosophers are useless at best and vicious at worst is that 'they seem to me to speak the truth' (6.487d). The 'seem' will turn out to be important: Socrates does not think genuine philosophers really *are* useless or vicious, but he understands that people who do not distinguish the genuine philosophers from the pretenders will think they are. It is in this spirit that he offers the Ship of State analogy, hoping to explain 'what the most decent people experience in relation to their city' (6.488a) and why they think philosophers are useless.

Think of the city as a ship, he suggests. Whom should the owner select as its captain? Obviously, the owner *should* select the person who possesses 'the art of navigation' (6.488b), since only a person possessing the relevant nautical skills has sufficient knowledge to chart the appropriate course to get the ship safely to its destination. But the owner, who knows nothing of navigation and is near-sighted and hard of hearing, to boot, will not choose 'the true captain' (6.488e), alas. The sailors clamor for the job, but while each of them understands his particular role on the ship and can follow the captain's orders, none of them is qualified to give such orders, despite thinking they are. (This is an early instance of the Dunning-Kruger Effect, a cognitive bias leading people to overestimate their abilities and fail to recognize their lack of competence in certain areas.) The owner chooses not the person skilled in navigation but rather 'the person who is clever at persuading or forcing the shipowner' (6.488d), with predictably bad results. And analogously the citizens choose for their ruler not the person who possesses wisdom and knows what is best for the city as a whole, but rather someone who charms and flatters them. 'But why blame the philosophers and regard them as useless?', Socrates seems to ask. That they are not in fact chosen for the job for which they are qualified tells us more about their fellow citizens than it does about them. Just as genuine captains do not beg ship owners for jobs or doctors do not beg the sick to be allowed to treat them, 'it is not for the ruler, if he is truly any use, to beg the others to accept his rule' (6.489c).

Rulers, doctors, and captains are entitled to maintain their self-respect, which presumably entitles them to refuse to sing along to the Temptations' 'Ain't Too Proud to Beg' as they go about their business. But given that what is at stake is the wellbeing of the city, perhaps this seemingly legitimate pride is a vice, not a virtue. We will see in Book VII that Socrates thinks that possessing political wisdom does not in itself entail an obligation to seek to govern; only a philosopher-king or -queen raised by the ideal city would be under such an obligation. One might think that those who possess political wisdom should be sufficiently interested in the wellbeing of their city for a bit of begging to be in order. This might seem to go against Plato's dictum that 'it is those who are not lovers of ruling who must rule' (7.521b), but one can be willing to rule without loving ruling, if only to avoid the punishment of being 'ruled by someone worse than oneself' (1.347c). The historian Gordon Wood remarks that at least early in American political life, 'Gentlemen generally stood, not ran, for election, and canvassing for an office, as [Aaron] Burr was said to have done for the vice-presidency in 1792, was widely thought to be improper'.[1] Perhaps Socrates shares something like this view and thus regards actively seeking office as unseemly.

---

1   Gordon S. Wood, *Empire of Liberty: A History of the Early Republic, 1789–1815* (New York: Oxford University Press, 2011), p. 160.

Tending the Beast (6.490e–495a)

Against those genuine, wisdom-possessing philosophers are people who *seem* to possess wisdom but actually do not: sophists. If we think of the citizens of Athens as 'a huge, strong beast' (6.493a), these sophists have a knack for learning how best to placate the beast, how to take advantage of its moods and satisfy its appetites. But the pseudo-philosophical sophist 'knows nothing about which of [the beast's] convictions is fine or shameful, good or bad, just or unjust, but he applies all these names in accordance with how the beast reacts—calling what it enjoys good, and what angers it bad. He has no other account to give of these terms' (6.493b). The sophist's 'wisdom' consists in telling the beast what it wants to hear, which echoes a point Socrates made earlier: 'The person who is honored and considered clever and wise in importance matters by such badly governed cities is the one who serves them most pleasantly, indulges them, flatters them, anticipates their wishes, and is clever at fulfilling them' (4.426c). Sophists, mere pretenders to wisdom, are adept at 'tending the beast' (6.493b), but their skill lies in persuasion, not truth-seeking. (In the dialogue the *Gorgias*, Plato has Socrates suggest that the sophists fall short of possessing skill or craft (τέχνη [*technê*]) and instead merely have a 'knack' (ἐμπειρία [*empeiria*], whence the word 'empirical') but we can safely ignore that interesting issue here.) What they possess is not wisdom, but it is not really surprising that it passes for wisdom. After all, most of us are prey to flattery, and for Socrates and Plato, 'the majority cannot be philosophic' (6.494a)—hence the anti-democratic nature of the ideal *polis*. For Plato, it is not merely the case that most of us *do not* possess wisdom, but rather that most of us *cannot* possess it. Given his conception of knowledge, we can see why he holds this strongly anti-democratic view. Wisdom is knowledge of what is best for the city as a whole, and to possess such knowledge one must grasp the Form of the good. Only someone with this stable, true model of goodness will be able to 'establish here on earth conventions of what is fine or just or good' (6.484d). Readers who do not share Socrates' austere conception of knowledge will likely think that genuine wisdom, while still rare and very different from the focus-group politicking of modern sophists, is more common than Socrates allows.

Shelter from the Storm (6.496a–497c)

Suppose that Socrates is right that no one can be happy in a *polis* not governed by philosophers. Given 'the madness of the majority' and the fact that 'hardly anyone acts sanely in public affairs' (6.496c), a person trying to live well—which requires living justly—is 'like a man who has fallen among wild animals and is neither willing to join them in doing injustice nor sufficiently strong to oppose the general savagery alone' (6.496d). What should such a person do? I suspect that many readers will be disappointed by Socrates' answer. For rather than urging political engagement to reform and improve a *polis* that falls short of their ideals of justice or advocating revolution to overthrow a *polis* that is not merely non-just but is positively unjust, Socrates instead counsels withdrawal from public affairs, urging those who want to live justly in unjust city-states to 'lead a quiet life and do their own work [...] like someone who takes refuge under a little wall from a storm [...] [and] is satisfied if he can somehow lead his present life free from injustice and impious acts and depart from it with good hope, blameless and content' (6.496d).

Many politically inclined readers will reject this approach, seeing it as acquiescent to injustice, but the fair-minded among them should be able to appreciate why some will find it attractive. While Socrates' preferred path seems apolitical, its defenders might reply that he is actually offering a different kind of politics, one that is interior rather than exterior: keep the constitution of the ideal city firmly in mind and 'make oneself its citizen' (9.592b). As with the virtue of high-mindedness discussed earlier, we can see here the seeds of the stoic idea of cosmopolitanism: one is not primarily a citizen of the city-state one inhabits in space and time but rather a universal *polis*. And surely high-mindedness is at work as one seeks shelter from the storm: if indeed 'Human affairs are not worth taking very seriously' (10.604b), why not tend to one's inner *polis* rather than muck about in the outer one, especially since that outer *polis* will be genuinely habitable only by a remarkable stroke of luck or by divine intervention:

> no city, constitution, or individual man will ever become perfect until either some chance event compels those few philosophers who are not vicious (the ones who are now called useless) to take charge of a city,

whether they want to or not, and compels the city to obey them, or until
a god inspires the present rulers and kings or their offspring with a true
erotic love for true philosophy. (6.499b)

Many readers will share Socrates' pessimism about the likelihood that
the—or an—ideal *polis* can be realized in the actual world, but many will
be troubled at his seeming to reject political action as well as what seems
to be his focus on the ideal world rather than the admittedly imperfect
actual world.

Looking at how Socrates himself lived in Athens, a *polis* that fell
far short of the ideal that Plato sketches in the *Republic*, might be
instructive here. Did Socrates follow his own advice? He did *not* pack
up and leave, even after being convicted of impiety and corrupting the
youth in a trial that, however procedurally fair it was, yielded what
seems a substantively unjust verdict. He refuses to leave, because the
best arguments lead him to conclude that leaving would be unjust.
Socrates did not 'lead a quiet life'; if he had, it is unlikely that we
would ever have heard of him or that Athens would have treated him
as it did. But he 'did his own work', as he conceived of it. His God-
given work, he tells us in the *Apology*, was to be a gadfly, questioning
and exhorting Athenians to virtue (30e). In his final words to the
jurors, he asks them to do for his sons what he tried to do for them:
to correct them 'if they seem to care about riches, or anything, more
than about virtue' (41e).

So it seems that Socrates did not live the quiet life he counsels. But
when the so-called Thirty Tyrants, installed by Sparta to govern Athens
after the end of the Peloponnesian War, demanded that Socrates bring
them Leon of Salamis for execution, he refused, regarding the act as
unjust and impious. So his eschewing politics did not entail complicity
in injustice or collaboration with the unjust. Alas, though, he did not
try to prevent others from doing so, nor did he try to warn Leon. While
the others went to Salamis to fetch Leon, Socrates 'went quietly home'
(32d).

Some Suggestions for Further Reading

For an excellent discussion of virtue and the virtues, interested readers should see Heather Battaly, *Virtue* (Malden, MA: Polity Press, 2015).

The philosophical literature on truth is vast. A good place to start is Michael P. Lynch, *True to Life: Why Truth Matters* (Cambridge, MA: MIT Press, 2004), https://doi.org/10.7551/mitpress/6919.001.0001

Readers interested in the question of morality and the ancient Greeks will benefit from Richard Kraut, 'Doing without Morality', *Oxford Studies in Ancient Philosophy*, 30 (2006), 159–200, although his focus is explicitly on Aristotle. Bernard Williams famously claims that 'Greek ethical thought [...] basically lacks the concept of *morality* altogether', in the chapter 'Philosophy', in *The Legacy of Greece: A New Appraisal*, ed. by M.I. Finley (Oxford: Clarendon Press, 1981), pp. 202–55.

Readers interested in the personal-aesthetic virtues will find much of interest in Aristotle's *Nicomachean Ethics*, excellently translated by Terence Irwin (2nd ed., Indianapolis: Hackett Publishing, 1999), especially Book IV, which discusses virtues such as friendliness, wit, and magnificence.

Readers interested in the trial and death of Socrates will want to read at least the *Apology* and *Crito*, available (among other places) in *Five Dialogues: Euthyphro, Apology, Crito, Meno, Phaedo*, trans. by G. M. A. Grube, ed. by John Cooper (Indianapolis: Hackett Publishing, 2002), which contains other dialogues of great interest. Thomas Brickhouse and Nicholas Smith, *Socrates on Trial* (Princeton: Princeton University Press, 1990) is an excellent discussion, and I.F. Stone, *The Trial of Socrates* (New York: Anchor Books, 1989) offers an interesting and very unsympathetic take on Socrates. Xenophon, *Conversations of Socrates*, trans. by Robin Waterfield (New York: Penguin Books, 1990), presents an interestingly different picture of Socrates than Plato does, though both are Socrates' contemporaries.

Achilles and Ajax playing a board game overseen by Athena (c. 510 BCE). Photograph by Aisha Abdel (2018), Wikimedia, Public Domain, https://commons.wikimedia.org/wiki/Category:Black-figure_pottery#/media/File:Attic_Black-Figure_Neck_Amphora_-_Achilles_and_Ajax_playing_a_board_game_overseen_by_Athena.jpg

10. Metaphors to Think by
The Sun and Divided Line Analogies
Book VI

The analogies we looked at in the last chapter are interesting, but they are merely appetizers to the metaphorical feast Socrates soon serves, which features the Sun, Line, and Cave analogies (the last of which we will cover in the next chapter). It is philosophical fare of the highest order, since the topic is 'the most important subject' which is 'even more important than justice and the other virtues' (6.504d)—the Form of goodness itself: 'the form of the good is the most important thing to learn about [... since] it is by their relation to it that just things and the others become useful and beneficial [...] [but] we have no adequate knowledge of it' (6.505a).

The Greek rendered by 'the form of the good' is ἡ τοῦ ἀγαθοῦ ἰδέα (*hê tou agatou idea*)—literally, the idea of the good. As noted earlier, for Plato an ἰδέα is not an idea in our ordinary sense but rather something that is not only mind-independently real but is actually more real than the many particular instances of it. The metaphysical elevator goes all the way up to Level Four, though here Plato implies that there is yet another floor, where a very special Form, the Form of the good, resides.

To get a sense of the importance of the Form of the good, consider first the distinctive virtue of the philosopher-rulers, political wisdom. Political wisdom is knowledge of what is best for the city, but one cannot *know* what is superlatively good for the city without understanding what goodness itself is: 'I do not suppose that just and fine things will

   https://doi.org/10.11647/OBP.0229.10

have acquired much of a guardian in someone who does not even know in what way they are good. And I divine that no one will have adequate knowledge of them until he knows this' (6.506a).

Although one can *believe* that something is good without grasping why it is, one cannot *know* that something is good without knowing why that thing is good—and one cannot know this, Socrates thinks, without knowing what goodness itself is. A ruler who does not understand what goodness itself is will at best have true beliefs about what is good for the city, but that falls far short of the knowledge required for genuine wisdom.

So what is the Form of the good, goodness itself?

What the Good Is Not (6.505a-d)

Socrates does not claim to know what the good is, but he does think he knows what it is not. Narrowing the field by excluding unworkable options is a kind of intellectual progress, and so he begins with two untenable accounts of the nature of the good. The first view, held by 'the majority' is the view that 'pleasure is the good' (6.505b). This is hedonism, the view that pleasure is the only thing that is good in itself. Any other thing that is good is good extrinsically, by being a means to the one intrinsically good thing, pleasure. Although they often run in the same harness, hedonism is distinct from egoism, the view that one's interests count for more than the interests of others (perhaps because others' interests do not count at all). Classical utilitarians such as Jeremy Bentham and John Stuart Mill were hedonists but not egoists. They regarded *total* net pleasure, the result of subtracting the pain an action produces from the pleasure it produces, as the standard of right action, where the interests of all parties affected by the action are given equal weight.

Socrates immediately locates a problem for hedonism: 'there are bad pleasures' (6.505c), which even hedonism's advocates will concede. Although he does not give any examples, they are not hard to come by. Imagine a peeping Tom who is very careful not to be seen; he derives a great deal of pleasure from spying on his neighbors through his high-powered (and well-hidden) telescope, and they are none wiser, so there is no pain he is inflicting to offset the pleasure he produces for himself.

But his action still seems wrong, and his pleasure is an evil pleasure, as almost anyone would think. Even though philosophical questions are not best settled by majority vote, anyone who concedes that the peeping Tom's pleasure is bad should reject hedonism, for how can pleasure be what is good in itself if there are pleasures that are bad in themselves?

The second view Socrates considers has a bit more going for it than hedonism; if nothing else, it is held by 'more sophisticated' folks. It is the view that 'the good [...] is knowledge' (6.505b), which we might awkwardly dub 'Epistemicism' (from the Greek word for knowledge, *epistemê*). This seems like a view that Socrates would find attractive, given the centrality of knowledge to philosophy, but he quickly dismisses it—not, as with hedonism, because there are instances of bad knowledge (though presumably there are) but because Epistemicism leads to an infinite regress (or, more properly, an infinite *progress*). Knowledge always has an object, he reminds Glaucon. If I have knowledge, I have knowledge *of* or *about* something; there is no such thing as mere, objectless knowledge. The various crafts are similar in being knowledge of *how* to do certain things, but they are distinguished by their objects: farmers know how to farm, doctors know how to heal, etc. Similarly, the grammarian and mathematician both possess the same kind of knowledge—theoretical or propositional knowledge *that* certain propositions are true, as opposed to knowledge of *how* to do things—but they too are distinguished by their objects. If we ask the sophisticates who hold that the good is knowledge what that knowledge's object is, they will reply, Socrates thinks, that 'it is knowledge of the good' (6.505b). This is highly problematic, and not just because it is circular. If the good is identical to knowledge, then for every occurrence of 'the good' we can substitute 'knowledge', just as we can substitute '2+1' for any instance of '3' in a mathematical formula (e.g., since $3^2 = 9$, it follows that $(2+1)^2 = 9$). But if the knowledge in question is knowledge of the good, then the Epistemicist's core claim,

(E)   The good = knowledge.

becomes

(E*)   The good = knowledge of the good.

But by substituting 'knowledge of the good' for 'the good', (E*) generates

(E**)   The good = knowledge of ~~the good~~ knowledge of the good,

which in turn generates

(E***)   The good = knowledge of knowledge of knowledge of the good,

and so on, with no end in sight!

Clearly, Socrates thinks knowledge is good. But it is *a* good, not *the* good. It is one of philosophy's distinctive goods, but knowledge is not *the* good—it is not what goodness is. But even if we do not know what the good is, Socrates thinks we know two things it is not, and that is at least a start. So what does Socrates think the good is?

The Analogy of the Sun (6.506d–509d)

Socrates does not answer this question directly, but not because he is being cagey, as Thrasymachus might suggest. And not (at least not explicitly) because he thinks the good cannot be defined in any non-circular way. The eighteenth-century philosopher Joseph Butler remarked that 'Everything is what it is, and not another thing', which the twentieth-century philosopher G.E. Moore quoted at the outset of his *Principia Ethica* before arguing that any attempt to give a real definition of goodness was doomed to fail. Cinema lovers may recall a memorable exchange in the film *The Deer Hunter* between Mike (Robert De Niro) and Stanley (John Cazale), in which Mike, holding up a bullet, says, 'Stanley, see this? This is this. This ain't something else. This is this'.[1] Stanley does not understand the lesson, but I suspect Socrates, Butler, and Moore would all be sympathetic to Mike's point, since the good is what it is and not some other thing.

So why does Socrates not provide a value for *x* in the philosophical equation *the good = x*? Why does he choose to 'abandon the quest for what the good itself is for the time being' (6.506d)? Although antagonists like Thrasymachus will scoff, I believe it is because Socrates possesses the virtue of epistemic humility: he claims not to know what the good is and insists that one should not 'talk about things one does not know as if one does know them' (6.506c), which is what he'd be

---

1   *The Deer Hunter*, dir. by Michael Cimino (Universal Pictures, 1978).

doing if he responded directly to Adeimantus' request for an account of the good. But while he cannot say what the good is, he thinks he can say something about what it is like, which brings us to the Sun Analogy. In Book VII Socrates will suggest that dialectic—rigorous, Forms-based philosophical reflection—is the only avenue to genuine knowledge. As he did earlier in Book VI, he reminds Glaucon and company that they will be avoiding this 'longer road' (6.504c) and proceeding in a less exact, hypothetical way which will give them a sense of what the good is, but which will fall well short of full-blown philosophical knowledge of it.

Socrates' plan is to explain the Form of the good in terms of something more readily understandable: the sun. He suggests that the good—the Form or essence of goodness itself—plays the same role in the intelligible realm that the sun plays in the visible realm. Strictly speaking, the focus is the sun's role in the *sensible* realm, the world of sense-experience, but we will follow Socrates in using 'visible' to designate this realm, which also includes what he can hear, touch, taste, and smell as well as what we can see. While he cannot say what the good *is*, he can say what he thinks the good *does*. His idea is that the sun: the visible world :: the good: the intelligible world—the roles the sun and the good play in their respective worlds are analogous. In the visible world, the sun by its light enables us to see the many particular things—and also enables their existence. In the intelligible world, the good by its truth enables us to know the Forms—and also enables the existence of the Forms. Seeing something requires both a visible object *and* the power of sight. But it also requires 'a third kind of thing' (6.507d)—light. Without light to illuminate the object, the power of sight will not reveal that object to us. The sun is the main and most obvious source of light, so the sun enables us see visible objects. But it does more than enable their being seen, Socrates thinks; it enables their very existence. This is certainly true of living things, which depend for their existence on the light of the sun. (It is less clear that this is true of rocks, but we need not be sticklers about this.) The same goes for the Form of the good:

> what gives truth to the things known and the power to know to the knower is the form of the good. And though it is the cause of knowledge and truth, it is also an object of knowledge [...] not only do the objects

of knowledge owe their being known to the good, but their being is also
due to it. (6.508e–9b)

So, just as the sun provides the light that enables us to see visible
objects, the Form of the good provides the truth that enables us to know
intelligible objects, which of course are the forms: 'the many beautiful
things and the rest are visible but not intelligible, while the [F]orms are
intelligible but not visible' (6.507b). Beautiful things owe not only their
being seen but also their very existence to the sun. Similarly, the Form
of beauty depends for both its knowability and its very existence on the
Form of the good.

Thus the Form of the good plays a foundational role in Plato's
epistemology, since it is the condition of all knowledge, and also in
his metaphysics, since it is the condition of the existence of the other
Forms and in turn the existence of concrete particular objects. Particular
beautiful things are beautiful because they partake, if only temporarily,
in the Form of beauty; they are temporary, spatiotemporal images or
copies of the Form of beauty itself. Similarly, a particular just action or
soul is just because it participates in the Form of justice, and so on. And
since beautiful things and just actions are good and useful, they must
also participate in the Form of the good: 'it is by their relation to [the
Form of the good] that just things and the others become useful and
beneficial' (6.505a). Thus the Form of the good subsumes the Forms of
justice, wisdom, courage, etc.; not only would they not be good without
it, they would not exist without it. So goodness is at the core of Plato's
conception of the universe, both epistemologically and metaphysically.

The Divided Line (6.509e–511e)

Socrates follows the Sun Analogy with a linear perspective on how
the visible and intelligible worlds differ. His focus here is largely
epistemological, though as we might expect metaphysics looms in the
background. Having already said a bit about how knowledge and belief
differ, here Plato goes into more detail, saying more about their distinct
objects (thus drawing on the ill-fated Powers Argument) and also
making distinctions between different kinds of knowledge and belief.
We can think of the line as a sort of epistemological companion to the
Metaphysical Elevator, in which one ascends epistemologically from

belief to knowledge and metaphysically from concrete particular objects to the Form of the good.

Start a line segment and divide it unevenly, as below, into two sub-segments. Let one segment represent the visible world and the other the intelligible world:

Intelligible

Visible

Fig. 1. The Visible World and the Intelligible World

Belief is the epistemic state (or, as Socrates would have it, the power) that operates in the visible world, while knowledge governs the intelligible world. Since length corresponds to 'relative clarity and opacity' (6.509d), the line segment representing the intelligible realm will be longer than the segment representing the visible realm. This should make sense, given Plato's view that the Forms, which are at home in the intelligible realm, are both more real than the particulars and are epistemically clearer: the Forms are objects of knowledge, while the particulars are objects of belief. Belief, while clearer than ignorance, is darker and opaquer than knowledge, as Socrates claimed earlier (5.478c). So, even though there are more objects in the visible world than in the intelligible world, since the relation between particulars and their Forms is a relation of many to one, the segment representing the intelligible realm is longer than the segment representing the visible realm.

Now here comes a slightly tricky part: divide each sub-segment again by the same ratio as the entire line was divided:

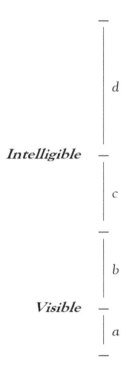

Fig. 2. The Visible World (*a* and *b*) and the Intelligible World (*c* and *d*)

So now the visible world comprises sub-segments *a* and *b* and the intelligible world comprises *c* and *d*, and with the ratios of both *a* to *b* and *c* to *d* identical to the original ratio of *Visible* to *Intelligible*. An obvious consequence of this is that *a*:*b* :: *c*:*d*. A less obvious consequence, which Socrates either does not notice or notices but does not mention, is that *b* and *c* turn out to be the same length. Given that the line is arranged in terms of 'relative clarity and opacity' (6.509d), the equality of *b* and *c* suggests an epistemic and metaphysical parity between the highest visible and lowest intelligible sub-sections of the line, and it is hard to see Socrates endorsing such a view. This is at least a wrinkle in the Divided Line analogy, but let us assume that it is a wrinkle that can be ironed out and move on.

Now we will see the parallel between metaphysics and epistemology. Plato further divides the main epistemic states or powers, *Belief* and *Knowledge*, which appear on the line's right side in Fig. 3:

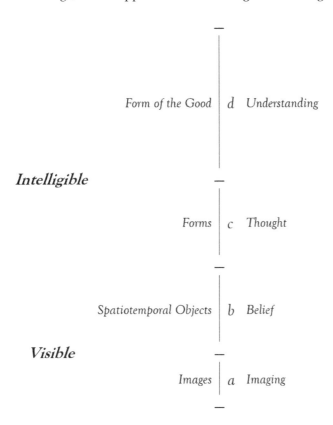

Fig. 3. The Visible World and the Intelligible World: Belief and Knowledge

The two bottom sub-segments of the line, *a* and *b*, which together make up the visible realm, have different objects. The lowest level, *a*, has images (εἰκόνες [*eikones*]) for its objects—shadows and reflections and, presumably, the analogies and metaphors of the sort that Socrates is so 'greedy for' in Book VI, as well as the paintings, sculptures, and poems that he will criticize in Book X. The second lowest level, *b*, comprises the original items of which those images are copies. The bed in which Van Gogh slept in his room at Arles, which served as the model for his famous paintings of it, would be an object appropriate to *b*, while the paintings of the bed, being copies of that spatiotemporal object, belong in *a*. In addition, we might think the second-hand opinions that many of us have, opinions we merely parrot from our favorite news source, belong here in *a*. Many readers active on Facebook or Twitter will be familiar with someone whose social media mission seems to be reposting or re-tweeting stories and memes that express the views they have gotten from others. (When someone says, 'I have thought about this a lot', one hopes they mean this literally, where 'thought' is a verb, and they have scrutinized and analyzed and seen implications of the point in question. What we are often saying, alas, is 'I have a thought about this, and I think that thought a lot', where 'thought' is a noun, and thinking that thought does not require critical examination of the idea's merits and demerits, etc.) In addition to their different objects, *a* and *b* also differ in terms of the epistemic or cognitive states operating in them. While Plato generally talks of belief (δόξα [*doxa*]) as operating in the visible realm, here he distinguishes between εἰκασία [*eikasia*], imagining (or merely imaging) and πίστις [*pistis*], which is translatable as 'belief' but which suggests credence, trust, and sincerity as well.

The intelligible realm is where the Forms live. While the sub-segments of *Visible* had different kinds of objects, here the objects are the same: Forms (although the Form of the good operates in *d*, the highest level). Segments *c* and *d*—Thought (διάνοια [*dianoia*]) and Understanding (νόησις [*noêsis*]), respectively—are distinguished by how knowers are related to the Forms that populate the intelligible world.

Hypotheses and First Principles in the Divided Line

A crucial difference between Thought (*c*) and Understanding (*d*) is the role that hypothesis (ὑπόθεσις [*hypothesis*], literally, what is placed or set under something) plays. Mathematicians, who occupy themselves in Thought, employ hypotheses in their thinking: they 'hypothesize the odd and the even, the various figures, the three kinds of angles' (6.510c), etc. But, Socrates thinks, they 'do not think it is necessary to give any account (λόγος [*logos*]) of them' (6.510c), presumably because these hypotheses seem so obviously true that no justification is needed. Just as mathematicians take it for granted that there are numbers and triangles, physicists assume the existence of an external world of spatiotemporal objects, whose properties and behavior they study without feeling the need to justify this assumption. They treat their hypotheses as 'first principles (ἀρχή [*archê*]))' (6.510d)—as foundations—and draw conclusions from them. The mathematicians' conclusions are not about the particular triangle or circle drawn on the blackboard; the physicists' are not about the particular electrons in this particular cloud chamber; rather, they are about triangles and circles in themselves, or about electrons in themselves. Both try to prove things about the Forms, on the model of inquiry depicted by the Divided Line.

By contrast, the philosopher, who roams the realm of Understanding, recognizes hypotheses *as* hypotheses; they do not think of their hypotheses and assumptions as self-evidently true first principles requiring no justification. Unlike their mathematical and scientific cousins, the philosopher does not treat a hypothesis as an unassailable foundation or 'first principle' but rather as something that stands in need of a *logos,* a justification or rationale. The hardest part of philosophy, Socrates says, 'has to do with giving a rational account' (6.498a). It is not that mathematicians and scientists are too lazy to justify their hypotheses, but rather that they do not feel the need to do so, since their assumptions seem so obviously true. But so long as the foundational hypothesis is unaccounted for, what follows cannot fully count as *knowledge*, on Socrates' view, even though it involves grasping mathematical Forms: 'What mechanism could possibly turn any agreement into knowledge when it begins with something unknown and puts together the conclusion and steps in between from what is unknown?' (7.533c)

Socrates implies here that mathematicians can give valid arguments (arguments whose conclusions must be true *if* their premises are true), but that the conclusions of their arguments are merely conditionally and not absolutely true. That is a far cry from giving an argument whose conclusion must be true, period, which would require showing that the hypotheses in question *are* true and do not merely *seem* to be true. While the mathematician's valid arguments might be sound, the mathematician is never in a position to know whether their arguments are sound or not until they justify the hypothesis—the *if*—on which the conclusion ultimately rests.

To get a sense of what is at stake, consider a hypothesis that many readers encountered in high school geometry class, Euclid's parallel postulate. That parallel lines extended indefinitely in space will never meet seems so intuitively obvious as to be axiomatic. No wonder geometers do not try to 'give an account' of this hypothesis. Doing so seems a waste of time, and developing a geometry that rejects that postulate seems a fool's errand. But, as many readers know, the geometry required for Einstein's general theory of relativity is non-Euclidean, geometry that rejects the parallel postulate. Space, on Einstein's view, is curved, so Euclidean geometry misdescribes it. The assumption that parallel lines indefinitely extended in space would never touch seemed too obvious to need a justification, but it turns out to be false. That is the kind of worry Socrates has about the realm of Thought.

Dialectic and Understanding

It is not that hypotheses are dispensed with in the realm of Understanding. Instead, they are treated as hypotheses, as needing justification, rather than as first principles requiring no justification:

> It does not consider these hypotheses as first principles but truly as hypotheses—stepping stones to take off from, enabling it to reach the unhypothetical first principle of everything. Having grasped this principle, it reverses itself, and, keeping hold of what follows from it, comes down to conclusion without making use of anything visible at all, but only of forms themselves, moving on from forms to forms, and ending in forms. (6.511b)

Understanding is the result of what Socrates calls 'dialectic'—that is what the initial 'it' in the quotation just above refers to. Dialectic is the longer, harder road that Socrates chooses not to travel in the *Republic*, opting instead for a discussion relying on analogies and metaphors. Dialectic is like mathematical thinking in having the Forms for its objects, but, as we just noted, dialectic treats hypotheses and assumptions differently than mathematical thinking. Here are some of dialectic's distinctive features, which ground ways in which Understanding differs from Thought:

1. *Giving an account.* The dialectician—i.e., the genuine philosopher—'is able to give an account of the being of each thing' (7.534b). In addition to being able to *grasp* the essence of the thing under discussion, the philosopher is also able to *explain* that essence, to give an account of it. 'Someone who is able to give an account of the being of each thing [is] dialectical', Socrates says. 'But insofar as he is unable to give an account of something, either to himself or to another [...] he has [no] understanding of it' (7.534b). Book V's lovers of sights and sounds may have many true beliefs about which objects are beautiful, but being unable to grasp the Form of beauty, they are unable to explain why a beautiful thing is beautiful, and thus lack knowledge. Similarly, the geometer who assumes that the parallel postulate is true but who is unable to justify that assumption lacks Understanding: they think with concepts they do not fully understand.

2. *Integrated knowledge.* Presumably, the mathematician is able to give an account of the various mathematical objects she concerns herself with. But the dialectician is also able to see connections between the individual Forms: she sees 'their association and relationship with one another' (7.531c) and so achieves a unified intellectual vision. 'Anyone who can achieve a unified vision is dialectical', Socrates says, 'and anyone who cannot is not' (7.537c). A geometer is probably able to achieve a unified grasp of the various geometric Forms; it is hard to imagine someone specializing in, say, rectangles who knows nothing about circles or spheres or trapezoids. But the philosopher—the dialectician—is able to unify different domains of study, understanding not just geometry and physics or game theory and biology in themselves, but grasping how these disciplines and the Forms they study are interrelated. In short, the philosopher sees and makes connections between disparate domains.

3. *Purely formal reasoning.* Thought relies on visual aids: the geometer's object in trying to prove a theorem about the nature of triangles is the Form of triangularity, but they draw particular triangles on particular chalkboards as an aid for grasping the triangle's essence. Those drawings are aids borrowed from the visible realm. Understanding, by contrast, proceeds 'without making use of anything visible at all, but

only of Forms themselves, moving on from forms to forms, and ending in forms' (6.511b). The dialectician is able to think with the Forms alone: her seeing is purely intellectual, and does not involve any objects from the visible realm at all, or the kinds of metaphors Socrates employs to make sense of the Form of the good. Dialectic 'tries through argument and apart from all sense perceptions to find the being of things and does not give up until he grasps the good itself with understanding itself' (7.532a).

4. *The Form of the good.* Perhaps dialectic's most distinctive feature, and thus the most important difference between Understanding and Thought, is that dialectic involves seeing how the various Forms are related to the Form of the good. Thus dialectic requires the most complete kind of intellectual integration possible. This integration is both horizontal, so to speak, understanding how Forms are related to each other, and also vertical, understanding how these Forms are related the Form of the good, which, as the condition of both the knowability and existence of the Forms, is at a level higher than them—Level Five, so to speak, on Plato's Metaphysical Elevator. Plato's universe is fundamentally ordained toward the good: the Form of the good is 'the unhypothetical first principle of everything' (6.511b), and one does not fully grasp a thing's essence until one grasps the end it aims at, as well. Dialectical understanding is thus a very tall order.

5. *Foundationalism.* The contemporary epistemological distinction between foundationalism and coherentism sheds light on the difference between Thought and Understanding. Even though Plato does not think of knowledge as justified true belief, his concern with *giving an account* implies that a discussion of justification is not completely out of order. A coherentist holds that a belief's being justified is a matter of its being properly related to other beliefs: one's beliefs hang together in a coherent way, with minimal inconsistency between beliefs. Presumably *some* inconsistency has to be allowed; otherwise no one's beliefs would be justified, since we all unknowingly have beliefs that are at odds with each other. The foundationalist, by contrast, thinks that at least one belief must be justified in a non-inferential way, not getting its justification from another belief. Such a belief is the foundation—the *archê*—of the justification of all other beliefs.

The realm of Thought is coherentist: the mathematician's conclusions are 'in full agreement' with the hypotheses they treat as first principles. The realm of Understanding, by contrast, is foundationalist: it rests ultimately on the Form of the good, which is the source of the intelligibility (and indeed the existence) of the other Forms. Ironically, the procedure for determining whether one grasps this foundation seems itself coherentist: 'Unless someone can distinguish in an account the form of the good from everything else, can survive all refutation, as if in a battle [...] and can come through all of this with his account still intact, you'll say that he does not know the good itself' (7.534bc). We have witnessed this procedure, *elenchus*, throughout the *Republic*, starting with Cephalus' and Polemarchus' and Thrasymachus' accounts of justice. We saw it most recently in the two accounts of the good that Socrates rejected earlier in Book VI. Socrates *seems* to suggest that what makes an account of x true is that it can survive the sort of cross-examination we have seen so far in the *Republic*. But his actual view, I think, is not that coherence *constitutes* the correctness of an account, but rather that coherence is the best *criterion* of correctness: an account is not made true by its having no internal inconsistencies and no false implications or entailments; instead, its consistency and coherence are good evidence—and perhaps the best evidence—that it is true.

Readers familiar with Plato's *Euthyphro* will find there a helpful example of this distinction between constitution and criterion. One of the *Euthyphro*'s main questions is whether the gods love holiness because it is holy or whether holiness is holy because the gods love it. That is, do the gods' loving x make x holy or constitute x's holiness, so x's holiness is due to the external fact that the gods love it rather than some of its internal features? Or is the gods' loving x simply good evidence that x is holy, their love for x being a criterion of x's being holy, but not what constitutes x's holiness? In short, is x loved because it is holy, or holy because it is loved?

That an account of the good or any important concept is maximally coherent suggests that it is correct, but coherence is criterial rather than constitutive of its being true. What makes an account true is its connection to the Form of the good.

Socrates' Hypothetical Method

Before moving on, we should note how transparent Socrates has been in employing hypotheses in the *Republic*, reminding Glaucon and company of the conditional nature of any conclusions they draw from their hypotheses. For example, when offering the Opposition Principle as the basis for dividing the soul (4.436b), he remarks, 'let us hypothesize (ὑποθέμενοι [*hypothemenoi*) that this is correct and carry on. But if we agree that it should ever be shown to be incorrect, all the consequences we have drawn from it will also be lost' (4.437a). Socrates is reminding us that by employing hypotheses and analogies we are travelling on a less rigorous path, one that will give us a sense of what the good is but will not let us look on it directly. This should make sense, for even if Socrates is a genuine philosopher-king (though he claims otherwise), the rest of us—Glaucon, Polemarchus, you, me—are not, and we would be blinded by trying to look directly at the good, just as we would be blinded if we looked directly at the sun. So Socrates opts for the hypothetical, analogical method, which allows us to *think* about the good without *understanding* it. For that, dialectic is needed.

Dialectic: It's No Game

Socrates appeals to dialectic to distinguish genuine from counterfeit philosophers, as his response to the Third Wave requires of him. It also enriches his explanation of the negative view of philosophers so many Athenians have. The trouble is that 'a great evil comes from dialectic as it is currently practiced' (7.537e), since the young people who practice it imitate Socrates' method of intellectual cross-examination but 'misuse it by treating it as a kind of game of contradiction' (7.539b). A genuine philosopher, who loves and reveres the truth, regards dialectic as the best means of getting at the truth and employs it in that spirit. But without reverence for the truth, dialectic becomes merely a game aimed at humiliating the bloviating pretender to knowledge and thus showing how clever its practitioner is. It is no wonder, then, that his fellow citizens regard Socrates as a bad influence on the young people who flock to him.

Unsurprisingly, Socrates employs yet another metaphor to address the dangers of dialectic when it is not practiced with the love of truth. Imagine a bright young person 'brought up surrounded by much wealth and many flatterers [...] who finds out, when he has become a man, that he is not the child of his professed parents and that he cannot discover his real ones' (7.538a). This turns the young person's world upside down: core beliefs about who they are turn out to be false, they regard their adoptive parents as liars and no longer live as they were raised to do. This is what it is like to be a young person whose core moral beliefs are challenged. A person who is properly raised will, like Glaucon and Adeimantus, believe that the just life is happier, that they ought to be motivated by what is fine and noble rather than by narrow self-interest, but they do not know why the just life is happier or what the fine and noble really is. Dialectic as practiced by counterfeit philosophers 'shakes him from his convictions, and makes him believe that the fine is no more fine than shameful, and the same with the just, the good, and the things he honored most' (7.538d). It induces a kind of intellectual and moral vertigo: values and ways of life that seemed so certain now seem flimsy and evanescent. Improperly deployed, dialectic turns young people into relativists or nihilists who think of traditional moral virtues such as justice as shams in much the same way Thrasymachus did back in Book I: as tools clever people use to dupe simpletons like the unknowing orphan until the scales fall from their eyes. That so many of Plato's dialogues end without discovering the nature of the virtue in question—that is, in *aporia*: difficulty or befuddlement—probably does not help, either. Rather than thinking that eliminating wrong accounts is a kind of progress, the clever game-player thinks he is shown that there *is* no answer.

Socrates thinks that few young people are sufficiently 'orderly and steady by nature' (7.539d) to practice dialectic properly; instead of being 'willing to engage in discussion in order to look for the truth', the bright young person 'plays at contradiction for sport.' (7.539c) They will imitate and thus internalize the wrong models (7.539bc), which echoes the concerns Socrates raised when discussing how and why 'the storytellers' needed to be 'supervised.' Thus in the advanced education for would-be philosopher-queens and -kings that we will look at after discussing the Cave Analogy, students are not trained in dialectic until they reach the age of thirty (7.537d).

So dialectic is no game. It is dangerous if practiced without a love of truth, capable of doing real damage to both its practitioner and its victims. But it also promises great cognitive benefit, as it is the genuine philosopher's tool par excellence, a tool enabling full understanding. This understanding goes far beyond the kind of understanding Socrates' analogies can yield, which Glaucon claims at the close of Book VI. He understands (μανθάνω) Understanding (νόησις), but he does not Understand it.

Some Suggestions for Further Reading

Readers interested in exploring the Sun and Line analogies in greater depth and detail might try Nicholas Denyer, 'Sun and Line: The Role of the Good', in *The Cambridge Companion to Plato's Republic,* ed. by G. R. F. Ferrari (New York: Cambridge University Press, 2007), https://doi. org/10.1017/ccol0521839637, pp. 284–309, or Chapter 10 ('Understanding the Good: Sun, Line, and Cave') of Julia Annas, *An Introduction to Plato's Republic* (New York: Oxford University Press, 1981), pp. 242–71, which is reprinted in *Plato's Republic: Critical Essays,* ed. by R. Kraut (Lanham, MD: Rowman & Littlefield, 1997), pp. 143–68.

Readers interested in the 'wrinkle' in the Line (that segments *b* and *c* have the same length) might first see Chapter 9 (esp. pp. 203–4) of R. C. Cross and A. D. Woozley, *Plato's Republic: A Philosophical Commentary* (New York: St. Martin's Press, 1964), pp. 196–230.

Readers interested in exploring the distinction between coherentism and foundationalism might start with the first section of Erik Olsson's 'Coherentist Theories of Epistemic Justification', in the *Stanford Encyclopedia of Philosophy* (https://plato.stanford.edu/entries/justep-coherence/). Susan Haack, *Evidence and Inquiry: A Pragmatist Reconstruction of Epistemology,* 2nd ed. (Amherst, NY: Prometheus Books, 2009) seeks a middle ground between the two, which she dubs 'Foundherentism.' William Alston, *Epistemic Justification: Essays in the Theory of Knowledge* (Ithaca: Cornell University Press, 1989) contains excellent essays on justification by one of the leading epistemologists of the last century.

Markus Maurer, drawing of Plato's 'Allegory of the Cave' with
Wikipedia's logo as the sun (2015). Photograph by Crystallizedcarbon
(2015), Wikimedia, CC BY-SA 3.0, https://commons.wikimedia.
org/wiki/File:Plato_Cave_Wikipedia.gif#/media/File:Plato_Cave_
Wikipedia.gif

11. The Allegory of the Cave
Book VII

The Allegory of the Cave is arguably the most famous part of the *Republic*. Although it is clearly related to the Sun and Divided Line analogies (indeed, Socrates explicitly connects the Cave and the Sun at 7.517bc), Plato marks its special status by opening Book VII with it, emphasizing its importance typographically, so to speak (he will do much the same thing in Book IX with the discussion of the tyrannical soul). Although an allegory is sometimes defined as a symbolic narrative that can be interpreted as having a hidden meaning, Plato is not cagey about the Cave Allegory's meaning: it is about 'the effect of education (παιδεία [*paideia*]) and the lack of it on our nature' (7.514a). Given how visual the allegory is, many readers will find it helpful to draw themselves a diagram of it.

Education, the Allegory's topic, is not what most people think it is, says Plato: it is not 'putting knowledge into souls that lack it' (7.518b). Though education sometimes requires that kind of transmission of knowledge from teacher to student, this is not its essence, which instead is 'turning the whole soul' (7.518d)—turning it around, ultimately toward the Form of the good. *Education as turning around* is a powerful metaphor, capturing the way in which learning involves gaining new perspectives, seeing everyday things and events from new points of view. Everyone, Plato insists, is capable of education in this sense (7.518c). But not everyone is capable of making it out of the Cave into the intelligible world of the Forms, just as not everyone is capable of winning a Nobel Prize in Physics or an Olympic medal in Figure Skating. Nonetheless,

 https://doi.org/10.11647/OBP.0229.11

everyone has the capacity to be educated, to turn their soul from what is less real toward what is more real.

Stages in the Cave Allegory

I count six distinct stages in the Cave Allegory. While such divisions are always prey to arbitrariness and subjective preference, I hope that the division I offer sheds light on what Plato is up to here.

In the first stage, the cave's residents are prisoners, chained to their seats and unable to move not only their bodies but—crucially—their heads. They can only look straight ahead, and thus have only one perspective on what they see on the cave's wall. What they see are the shadows of a sort of puppet show taking place behind them, with shadows cast by the light of a fire. The puppets are various artifacts: 'statues of people and other animals, made out of stone, wood, and every material' (7.514b). The prisoners watch the shadow-play, ignorant of the true nature of what they see: they 'believe that the truth is nothing other than the shadows of those artifacts' (7.515c). They take for reality what is a mere image of it. Some readers will have already noticed that Stage One is parallel to the lowest section of the Divided Line (segment a), the objects of which are images and shadows.

In the second stage, one of the prisoners is freed from their bonds. Plato does not tell us by whom or how; we are left to wonder whether the prisoner was saved by human agency or by the natural decay of their fetters. There is reason to think it is the former, since the freed prisoner is 'suddenly compelled to stand up, turn his head, walk, and look up toward the light' (7.515c), and somebody else seems to be doing the compelling. This is not the only time Plato connects education with compulsion, with being forced to turn one's head and gain a new perspective. Nor is it the only time when the head-turning that constitutes education will be painful. When the freed prisoner is forced to look at the shadow-casting fire that until this moment they were unaware of, they will be 'pained and dazzled and unable to see the things whose shadows they had seen before' (7.515c). They will probably not like the experience at all, even though in being freed from their fetters they are thereby 'cured of [their] ignorance' (7.515c)—not merely freed but cured, as if ignorance is a disease. It is a comfortable disease, to borrow a phrase from e. e. cummings, for it is a world the cave-dweller is familiar with and comfortable in. Turned around and out of their comfort zone, they are unable to recognize the shadow-casting puppets, despite their skill at recognizing the shadows the puppets cast on the wall. Although the artifacts are, like any sensible particulars, not fully real, they are *more* real than the shadows they cast. Thus in looking at the shadow-casting artifacts the freed prisoner is 'a bit closer to the things that are and is turned towards things that are more' (7.515d); this is the *existential* sense of the verb 'to be' that we distinguished earlier: the prisoner is closer to the things that are real—that exist—and indeed is coming closer to the things that are fully real: the Forms. While not everyone is capable of making it out of the Cave, Plato thinks that everyone is capable of being turned from the shadows to the shadow-casting artifacts—of moving from the lowest segment (segment a) of the Divided Line to the next highest (segment b), the realm of belief proper.

Screens—television screens, phone screens, computer screens—are the Cave walls of today. When we uncritically accept the words and images we see there, we are like the chained prisoners. But if we turn and look at the sources of the information flickering before us, we might recognize that the information is distorted by bias and ulterior motive. Unlike the Cave's puppeteers, who do not seem to derive any benefit from their shadow-casting, the shadow-casters of our age typically *do* derive some benefit, and frequently their power depends upon our remaining chained, accepting the images they project before us, and believing that 'the truth is nothing other than the shadows' (7.515e). While being turned around is good for us, we often do not initially like it. But there is also a danger that in being turned around we will reject information we disagree with and take its source to be biased. Clearly, many sources *are* biased, but if we reject every artifact that comes from a puppeteer we do not like, it is not clear that we are any better off than we were before we turned to look. In fact, we might be worse off if we fall prey to the belief that critical thinking involves (merely) rejecting—perhaps as 'fake news'—anything emanating from sources we identify as 'liberal' or 'conservative' or whatever. Education, in the end, is not just any kind of turning around; it requires that the student be 'turned the right way' (7.518).

In the third stage we again see the role that compulsion plays in the Cave Allegory, for an unnamed, unidentified someone will 'drag [the freed prisoner] away from there by force, up the rough, steep path' (7.515e). Although Socrates devotes just one sentence to the third stage, what he says later in Book VII indicates that this rough, steep path symbolizes the formal education that potential philosopher-rulers receive. This four-subject education is the basis of the *quadrivium* of classical liberal education, the sort of education suitable to a free person. It is education centered on number: arithmetic (number itself), geometry (number in space), harmonics or music theory (number in time), and physics or astronomy (number in space and time). All these number-based subjects 'lead the soul and turn it around towards the study of that which is' (7.524e), which ultimately is the Form of the good. While there are certainly practical applications of these subjects, the would-be philosopher-queens and -kings study them 'not like tradesmen and retailers [... but] for ease in turning the soul around, away from becoming and towards truth and being' (7.525c). These disciplines prepare would-be philosophers not for craft-based careers in the sensible world, where they might be bakers or cobblers or doctors (although it will prepare them to be generals, as they are the city's guardians), but rather for citizenship in the intelligible world. They will learn to think abstractly, grasping essences and integrating Forms, which is presumably why studying geometry 'tends to make it easier to see the Form of the good' (7.526d). As the way out of the Cave, these subjects are 'merely preludes to [...] the song that dialectic sings' (7.531d–32a), and that is a tune that is sung only in the intellectual sunlight of the intelligible world outside of the Cave.

In stage four, the prisoner is not just freed from their fetters but has made it out of the Cave into the intelligible world above, which corresponds to the top half of the Divided Line (segments c and d). Looking at the fire in the cave hurt their eyes, and they find emerging into the sunlight painful, just as a mid-afternoon moviegoer who leaves a dark theater is pained by the bright parking lot outside. At first, they will only be able to look at shadows of the objects in the world above, here cast by the light of the sun rather than the fire, or their reflections in water, or look at the objects at night. Just as the shadows on the cave wall were mere copies of the artifacts held before the fire, those artifacts are mere copies of the Forms, which are 'the things themselves' (7.516a). Although Socrates does not say, we can assume that there is one Form for each of the many particular objects in the cave. Whether there is one tree—the Form of treeness itself—or one oak tree, one maple tree, one white pine, one yellow pine, etc. is an interesting question to ponder, but it is not one we need to answer to understand the Cave Allegory or the *Republic* as a whole.

At stage five, the former cave dweller is able to look directly at the sun, 'not images of it in water or some alien place, but the sun itself, in its own place, and be able to study it' (7.516b). Presumably not everyone who makes it out of the Cave is able to do this. Mathematicians and scientists study the Forms relevant to their disciplines, but they do not see other Forms or how the Forms they contemplate are related to these other Forms, and they certainly do not see the Form of the good—that vision is reserved for genuine philosophers, and there are *very* few of them. So presumably the fourth stage in the Cave Allegory corresponds to Thought on the Divided Line, while the fifth stage is where Understanding operates.

In stage six, the sun-contemplating philosopher first thinks back on his life in the cave, and reflecting on 'what passed for wisdom there' (7.516c), smiles ruefully and feels pity for the others still trapped in their ignorance, who 'know' only the shadows on the wall or the artifacts casting them. What would happen if the enlightened philosopher descended into the cave? They will not be greeted as a returning, liberating hero, Socrates thinks. The denizens of the dark world below will first think the returning philosopher a fool: until their eyes, used to the bright light of the intelligible world, have adjusted to the darkness of the cave, they will be unable to recognize the shadows or the puppets. Like the ship owner who thinks the true captain is a useless stargazer (6.489c), the cave dwellers will think the enlightened philosopher a fool who has ruined their eyesight (not to mention his economic prospects) by looking too long at the sun. But if they persist and try to free the prisoners and turn them toward the firelight or drag those who are able out of the cave, they will think their 'liberator' is worse than useless: they will think them dangerous, and 'if they could somehow get their hands on him [...] they [would] kill him' (7.517a).

Plato does his readers a good turn by having Socrates explicitly connect the Sun and Cave metaphors (7.5157bc), but he leaves the task of fitting together the Divided Line and Cave to us. Fortunately, connecting them is fairly straightforward, as we have already seen. The shadows on the Cave's wall correspond to the images seen at the Divided Line's lowest section (segment a), the realm of *Imaging*. The shadow-casting puppets held before the fire correspond to 'the originals of [the Line's] images' (6.510a), in segment b. Just as the shadows are copies of the originating artifacts, these artifacts, which are at home in the Visible World, are in turn copies of the Forms, which of course reside in the Intelligible World (section c). Plato is not suggesting that the images, shadows, and reflections are not real, but rather that they are *less* real than the originals they are images of. This has a lot of intuitive appeal: I can create a shadow of my hand by interposing it between my desk and lamp, but the shadow cast seems less real than my hand in at least a couple of ways. First, while my hand is a three-dimensional object, the shadow is only two-dimensional, lacking the dimension of depth. Second, the shadow depends for its existence on the presence of my hand (and on the presence of the 'third thing' that features in the Sun Analogy: light). My hand still exists when I turn off my desk lamp or move it out of the lamp's range, but the shadow no longer exists. Shadows, reflections in mirrors and water, etc.—the stuff of segment a of the Line—are ephemeral. They are not unreal— my seeing the shadow is not an optical illusion: there is something there, just something whose existence is thinner and flimsier than the objects at the Line's second section (segment b). Now—and here's the metaphysically important point—just as the shadows and reflections are copies of what seem to be independently existing objects, these objects themselves are copies of the Forms they instantiate. The bed the carpenter makes, Socrates argues in Book X, is 'something which is like that which is' (10.597a). The second 'is' is the 'is' of existence: the built bed is like what is real, what fully exists. Its resembling the Form of bedness is what makes it a bed and not a table, but, just as Van Gogh's paintings of his bed at Arles are copies of the bed he slept in, so too is that bed a copy of the Form. Thus Plato's metaphysical point can be put as a ratio, image: original :: original: Form.

There is much that Plato leaves unsaid about the Cave. Who first frees the prisoner? Who drags them up and out of the cave? Who are the puppeteers? What, if any, benefit do they derive from keeping the prisoners occupied with shadows? Glaucon says toward the outset that these are 'strange prisoners', to which Socrates replies, 'they are like us' (7.515a), so with a bit of imagination we can fill in some of these blank spots.

Trouble in Paradise: The Powers Argument Casts a Shadow on the Cave Allegory

There is a problem lurking in the background of the Cave Allegory that should be brought to the forefront and addressed. Indeed, all three of the key analogies—the Sun, the Divided Line, and the Cave—are analogical or metaphorical accounts of two distinct worlds or realms: the intelligible world, where the Forms reside, and the visible world, home to spatiotemporal particulars. The Powers Argument was supposed to provide some reason for believing in Plato's two-worlds metaphysics and indeed for taking the Metaphysical Elevator to the fourth floor, where the Forms are not just real but are *more* real than the particulars that instantiate them. But we have seen that that the Powers Argument is logically invalid, since its conclusions could be false even if its premises are true, and even if its logical problems could be fixed, it would still not provide a good reason to accept Plato's two-worlds metaphysics, given the implausibility of belief and knowledge having distinct objects. Presumably what Socrates says about agreed-to hypotheses that prove to be false goes for arguments, as well: 'that if it should ever be shown to be incorrect, all the consequences we have drawn from it will also be lost' (4.437a). Since the Sun, Divided Line, and Cave Analogies all require the distinction between the Visible and the Intelligible Worlds, they are infected, perhaps fatally, by the failure of the Powers Argument.

Of course, Plato's two-world metaphysics could still be correct, since the conclusion of an unsound argument can still be true. But unsound arguments do not justify belief in their conclusions. What should we make of the major analogies of Books VI and VII in light of the failure of the Powers Argument? One option is to proceed in a hypothetical or conditional way: *if* these are the two worlds, then here is how they differ.

Given the hypothetical nature of Socrates' procedure in the *Republic*, this is not a bad way to go. Another option is to interpret the two worlds non-literally but metaphorically, which fits well with the prevalence of metaphor in the *Republic*. On this view, the two worlds are ways of thinking about or conceptualizing reality rather than assertions about the nature of reality itself. And perhaps this is how the two-worlds metaphysics should be interpreted even if the Powers Argument were sound: think of the Forms populating the intelligible realm (and that realm itself) as useful fictions. This metaphysically more cautious view would appeal to fans of Ockham's Razor.

A problem with the metaphorical interpretation, however, is that Plato himself seems to take the two worlds literally: 'there are these two things [i.e., the Form of the good and the sun], one sovereign of the intelligible kind and place, the other of the visible' (6.509d). Plato thinks of these as *places,* which suggests their reality. Although the word being translated as 'place' (τόπος [*topos*], whence the English word 'topographical') could mean *realm* in a non-physical sense, it is difficult to think that Plato intends his talk of the Forms and the intelligible realm to be taken only metaphorically. Still, for readers bothered by the failure of the Powers Argument, this may be the best interpretation, even if it is not Plato's. After all, we can still distinguish Understanding from Thought, the two kinds of cognition at work in the intelligible realm, without being realists about the Forms. Even if we take Plato's Metaphysical Elevator only to the second floor, we can still distinguish people who grasp the essence of a perhaps narrow range of things from people who do not merely grasp more essences but also *see connections* between them. Integrative thinking is one of the hallmarks of dialectic, and one can prize that capacity while at the same time denying that the Forms existent mind-independently. Even Socrates himself is agnostic— in the literal sense of not knowing—about the metaphysical status of the Forms and the intelligible realm: 'Whether it's true or not, only the god knows' (7.517b). He seems to *believe* that the Forms are real, but perhaps this remark is Plato's way of indicating that he is aware of the Powers Argument's shortcomings: Socrates himself does not think he has proven the argument's conclusion. Early in Book X he recounts his 'usual procedure', which is to 'hypothesize a single form in connection with each of the many things to which we apply the same name' (10.596a).

So he seems aware of the hypothetical, mathematician-like nature of his investigation. If Socrates can live with this sort of uncertainty, perhaps readers can as well.

Food for thought. But it is now time to turn to another worry about the Cave Allegory, the enlightened philosopher's return to the world below.

Going Back Down into the Cave (7.519b–520b)

Having been fully liberated from the dark, smoky world of the Cave, the enlightened philosophers are in no hurry to return. Readers will remember that the problem Socrates faces in responding to the Third Wave—and it is worth remembering that the Sun, Divided Line, and Cave analogies are all part of that response—is that in the actual world, 'political power and philosophy' are separated, with philosophers as uninterested in participating in the messy world of politics and government as those in power are in studying metaphysics and epistemology. The solution, both to the ideal city's real possibility and to individual and communal happiness, is that these philosophers and political leaders be 'forcibly prevented' from pursuing their own interests exclusively. Somehow, 'political power and philosophy [must be made to] entirely coincide' (5.473cd). The philosophers would prefer to remain in the sunlit world above, contemplating the Forms. But possessing knowledge of the good, they and they alone are capable of governing. They have been compelled to ascend to the sunlit, intelligible world above; is it fair to compel them to go back down to the dark, smoky cave, the visible world below?

There is a substantive philosophical problem for Socrates' view that the just life is happier than the unjust life, an issue that Plato does not notice or at least does not remark upon. But before investigating that, we should attend briefly to one of the *Republic*'s most gratifying literary delights. The issue before us is compelling the enlightened philosophers to go back down into the cave to govern it. The Greek word at issue is καταβαίνειν (*katabainein*), to go down. If you turn to the *Republic*'s first page, you will see that Socrates' first words, the very first words of the *Republic*, are 'I went down' (1.327a). The Greek there is κατέβην (*katebên*), the first-person singular form of καταβαίνειν in the aorist (past) tense. The implication is that we are all cave-dwellers and that Socrates' going down to the Piraeus is like the enlightened philosopher's going back down into the cave, where we muck about in the dark as we look for justice. It is no wonder that, having discovered the other three political virtues (wisdom, courage, moderation), Socrates finds justice hard to locate at first: 'the place seems to be impenetrable and full of shadows [...] dark and hard to search' (4.432c). The conversation that is the *Republic*, then, takes place in the Cave, where 'we contend about the shadows of justice or the statues of which they are the shadows' (7.517d). Although Plato could have had Socrates just say this simply and directly, it is more powerful and more aesthetically pleasing for readers to see this for themselves. Although some readers will yawn, others will be delighted at Plato's literary artistry, and perhaps will be able to understand more fully why some people devote their lives to understanding and appreciating his philosophical thought and literary craft and the way he integrates them.

Now on to the substantive philosophical question of the enlightened philosopher's return to the cave. An important point to grasp is that the liberated philosopher is not on a mission of liberation, at least not complete liberation, since on Plato's view not everyone is capable of making it out of the cave. As we have noted several times already, he thinks that 'the majority cannot be philosophic' (6.494a). The returning enlightened philosopher will free whom he can, dragging those who are able to follow 'up the rough, steep path' (7.515e), but their main task is to govern in the Cave—'to guard and care for the others' (7.520a). We know they will not be received well, but if through 'some chance event' or divine intervention (6.499b) they are able to take charge of the cave, they will govern well, since they have the virtue needed to do so: political wisdom. Even so, the philosophers do *not* want to return to the Cave, and interestingly enough, Plato takes this as a plus: 'A city whose prospective rulers are least eager to rule must of necessity be most free from civil war, whereas a city with the opposite kind of rulers is governed in the opposite way' (7.520d). Since 'it is those who are not lovers of ruling who must rule' (7.521b), the returning philosophers' reluctance counts in favor of their doing so.

So why do the philosophers descend into the cave and do what they do not really want to do? Just as they were compelled to ascend out of the cave, they are compelled to descend into it, but the compulsion in the two cases is different. They were physically dragged up, at least metaphorically speaking, but they are not physically dragged back down. It is no accident that their being compelled upward would be metaphorically physical, since our particular individual bodies belong in the visible realm of particulars, while our souls, by contrast, are not physical, so there is nothing to drag. Their being compelled downward is mental or psychic, but it is not the irrational or non-rational compulsion that consists in brainwashing or advertising by people who seek to *cause* us to pursue ends they have chosen for us. Instead, the enlightened philosopher is compelled to return by rational persuasion. If one recognizes that an argument is sound—that its conclusion must be true if its premises are true *and* that its premises are in fact true—one is rationally compelled to accept the conclusion. This is not as a matter of internal or external causation, but rather of rational compulsion: the force of rational persuasion. So what is the argument that the enlightened philosophers should find so compelling?

As I hinted earlier, Socrates does not argue that any enlightened philosopher has a duty to descend to the cave and govern. Instead, only those whose enlightenment results from the city's having educated them have that duty. 'What grows of its own accord and owes no debt for its upbringing', he argues, 'has justice on its side when it is not keen to pay anyone for that upbringing' (7.520b), where the currency of repayment is governing. It might be noble of an accidentally- or divinely-self-enlightened philosopher to do what they do not really want to do and descend into the cave, but this is not a requirement of justice: they would not act wrongly were they to remain above, pursuing their philosophical interests. But a philosopher educated by the city has a duty of reciprocity and gratitude to descend and govern.

We should note that Plato here shows that he is not a consequentialist about morality. We can assume that the consequences of the philosopher's descending would be better, all things considered, than the consequences of their remaining in the intelligible world above. If we take the good they would do by governing, which is presumably substantial, since there can be no real happiness for the citizens if philosophers do not rule (5.473e), and subtract from it the personal cost to them of sacrificing their own preferences for the good of the group, the net consequences of descending would still be overall better than those of not descending.

But this fact alone is not sufficient to generate a duty for the enlightened philosopher to descend and govern. Were they to go down into the cave, they would be going beyond the call of duty—going down would be supererogatory, as philosophers say. Supererogatory actions are praiseworthy to perform, but not blameworthy to omit. Donating a kidney to a stranger is, other things being equal, praiseworthy, but my not doing this is not blameworthy: I do not act unjustly if I keep both of my kidneys. (Of course, if I have promised to donate the kidney and the stranger has relied on my promise, then 'other things' are not equal, and the moral situation has changed considerably.) Actions required by justice are different: failure to perform them *is* blameworthy, and, other things being equal, performing them is not praiseworthy. Special circumstances are required for refraining from violence to be praiseworthy, as envisioned in a *Sopranos* episode when Tony, a violence-prone mafioso, forgoes killing his daughter's sexually predatory soccer coach and lets the police deal with it. 'I didn't hurt nobody today', Tony drunkenly tells his wife, and for him, this is suitably praiseworthy.[1] For the rest of us, not killing people who bother us or whom we regard as moral reprobates is what is minimally expected, and there is no praise for doing what we ought to be doing.

So not just any enlightened philosopher, but only the enlightened philosopher who owes their enlightenment to the education that the city has provided for them, has a duty to go down into the cave and govern. Here is the argument Socrates gives them:

> We have made you kings in our city and leaders of the swarm, as it were, both for yourselves and for the rest of the city. You are better and more completely educated than the others and are better able to share in both types of life. Therefore each of you must go down to live in the common dwelling place of the others and grow accustomed to seeing in the dark. When you are used to it, you'll see vastly better than the people there. And because you have seen the truth about fine, just, and good things, you'll know each image for what it is and also that of which it is the image. Thus, for you and for us, the city will be governed, not like the majority of cities nowadays, by people who fight over shadows and struggle against one another in order to rule [...] but by people who are awake rather than dreaming (7.520bc)

---

1   *The Sopranos*, Season 1, Episode 9, 'Boca', dir. by Andy Wolk (HBO, 1999).

This is an interesting argument, and it certainly has a lot of intuitive appeal. There is something compelling, after all, about obligations of gratitude: if you have gone out of your way to benefit me, I seem to incur a debt of gratitude. What it takes to repay that debt varies with the circumstances: often, a simple 'thank you!' is all that is required, but other times—as in the present case—more is required. Here, Socrates argues that, as a matter of justice, the enlightened philosophers must (temporarily, at least) give up the life they prefer—a philosophical life devoted to contemplating the Forms—for a life of political action. (These are the 'both types of life' referred to in the quotation above.)

Plausible though the argument is, there is something troubling about duties of gratitude, even when the benefit to be reciprocated was bestowed intentionally, for the sake of the beneficiary. The worry is that one can go around obligating others to do good turns for oneself by doing good turns for them. If I show up unbidden and start harvesting your wheat for you, does my supererogatory act really bind you to do the same for me? Many of us would *feel* obligated to reciprocate, but the issue is not the psychological one about our feelings but rather the philosophical, normative one about our duties. Consider how your views would change if the helpful harvester helped not primarily because he wanted to benefit you, but because he needed your help harvesting his large wheat field, and, knowing you to be a 'nice' person but not wanting to ask for your help, decided that the best way to get you to help him was to help you. I suspect you would feel a bit manipulated. And suppose that your neighbor harvested your wheat when you were away in town on Saturday, without asking if you needed or wanted their help. They would have imposed this benefit on you, without your consent. Your supposed duty to return the favor would look flimsier and flimsier.

The trouble with Socrates' argument is that the city's actions in educating the philosopher too closely resemble the 'helpful' neighbor harvesting your wheat. Remember that the would-be rulers are *compelled* to leave the cave: 'someone dragged him away from there by force, up the rough, steep path, and did not let him go until he had dragged him into the sunlight' (7.515e). The benefit has been bestowed and received non-voluntarily, which surely makes a difference to whether there is a duty of gratitude to reciprocate. In addition, Socrates misspeaks when he claims that the philosophers were educated 'both for [them]selves and for the rest of the city' (7.520b). Any benefit the philosophers personally receive is foreseen, but not intended. Given the strong communitarian thrust of the ideal city, it is clear that the education is not primarily intended for the philosopher's benefit but rather for the city's; any benefit the individual philosopher receives is a side effect or by-product.

But even if Socrates' argument for a duty to return is sound, there are disquieting implications for his view that the just life is happier than the unjust life, that justice benefits its possessor. Thrasymachus insisted that while justice benefits others it is always bad for its possessor: being just and acting justly makes one worse off in the long run. Thus Thrasymachus sees a wedge between *what is good* (or right) and *what is good for me*. Consider the situation of the enlightened philosopher. They would strongly prefer to remain in the Intelligible World, basking in its sunlight and contemplating the Forms. They will return because, being just, they will do what justice requires of them, even when they do not want to do it. But make no mistake about it, they do not want to return, and ruling is 'something compulsory' (7.520e), not enjoyable in itself as doing philosophy is. And notice that ruling does not really fit into any of the three categories of goodness that Glaucon articulates at the beginning of Book II. While ruling seems at first to belong to the category of goods that are 'onerous but beneficial' (2.357c), upon reflection we can see that it does not really fit there, since this mixed category contains goods that are 'onerous but beneficial *to us*' (my emphasis). Few people enjoy flossing their teeth, but those who do this regularly derive a benefit and presumably decide that on the whole flossing is worth it: but its value is extrinsic and instrumental, not intrinsic. But imagine if flossing benefited not the flosser but someone else. This seems to be the position of the enlightened philosopher. They return to the cave to govern, but they would rather not, since they would be personally better off ignoring the demands of justice. When Glaucon worries that justice is 'making them live a worse life when they could live a better one' (7.519d), Socrates does *not* reply that they *are* better off acting justly; instead, he reprises the response he made to Adeimantus at the beginning of Book IV: his concern is not 'to make any class [or particular citizens] in the city outstandingly happy but to contrive to spread happiness throughout the city' (7.519e; compare 4.419a and 5.466a), which concedes the assessment underlying Glaucon's question.

The philosopher's return benefits the cave's residents, since 'there can be no happiness, either public or private' in any city not governed by a philosopher-king or -queen (5.473e). But returning does not benefit them personally, and that is the real issue here. Socrates seems to be conceding that Thrasymachus is right after all: justice benefits someone else, not its possessor. Even if the overall consequences of the philosopher's returning were better than the consequences of their remaining above, their return would not benefit them. So it looks like justice does *not* benefit its possessor: leading a good life seems to come at the cost of having a good life.

Thus it seems that the philosopher's situation is analogous to the far-fetched scenario in which flossing does not benefit the flosser but somehow benefits others. It would be a mistake to think that even in this scenario I would have no self-interested reasons for flossing. If there is a community norm that everyone should floss, my flossing would help sustain and promote this norm (and thus indirectly contribute to the benefit adherence to the norm produces) and encourage others to do so as well. If this is the case, then my flossing would benefit me indirectly. In doing my part to uphold norms that benefit the community, the burden of compliance might be counter-balanced by the benefit received. The same might be said for the returning philosopher, who lives a better life in a well-governed city than they do in the poorly governed city of the Shelter from the Storm analogy, which we considered in the last chapter. Although they would rather not descend, perhaps the philosopher's doing so really does benefit them when we look at the big picture. So perhaps Socrates does not give away the game to Thrasymachus after all. Even though the philosopher's return seems altruistic—they return to 'labor in politics and rule for the city's sake' (7.540b) rather than their own, they might in fact benefit by their return. Though the city's good is the outcome they intend, they can perhaps foresee that they will benefit too.

A worry remains, though: in the imaginary scenario in which flossing benefits others, it seems unlikely that *my* not flossing will have bad consequences so long as enough of my fellow citizens floss regularly. Or, to take a less far-fetched example, I might reason that while I enjoy National Public Radio, I can still receive this benefit without bearing my share of the burden, since NPR's not receiving $100 from me will not cause them to close up shop. It seems to be in my self-interest to be a free-rider, benefiting from the good behavior of others while not burdening myself with doing my share. The ethics of Immanuel Kant rules out such free-riding behavior: if everyone's acting on the maxim or principle I plan to act on would make it impossible for me to act on it, then my acting on it is wrong. But Kant did not share Socrates' view that doing the right thing makes me better off all things considered: the demands of morality are frequently at odds with those of self-interest and happiness.

Now perhaps free-riding would not even tempt the fully just philosopher, who takes their turn at ruling without complaint. But the self-interested Thrasymachan, who is 'vicious but clever' (7.519a), is unlikely to be persuaded: the philosopher would clearly be better off if they missed a turn every once in a while, if they called in sick when they really wanted a day of metaphysical sun-bathing. And things look even worse for the view that the just life is happier if we bear in mind the lives Socrates is to compare to settle the question of which life is happier: a just person who appears unjust versus an unjust person who appears just. The philosopher who does not go back down to the cave would be unjust, but under the terms agreed to they would not appear to be so: their free-riding would have to go unnoticed and thus would not undermine the norms governing the small community of philosophers, so their not going back down to the cave to rule benefits them without the negative effect on norms of justice.

These are some of the issues readers will want to keep in mind as we explore Books VIII and IX, where Socrates resumes his investigation of the *Republic*'s second question. In Book VII, though, he does not seem to notice them—or if he does, he gives no explicit indication of this.

Some Suggestions for Further Reading

There is a large literature on Plato's Allegory of the Cave. Readers interested in the thought of Martin Heidegger will want to see *The Essence of Truth*, trans. by Ted Sadler (New York: Contiuum Books, 2002). For an account more in keeping with the style and concerns of contemporary Anglophone philosophy, readers might turn to Chapter 10 (Understanding the Good: Sun, Line, and Cave') of Julia Annas, *An Introduction to Plato's Republic* (New York: Oxford University Press, 1981), pp. 243–71, reprinted in *Plato's Republic: Critical Essays*, ed. by Richard Kraut (Lanham, MD: Rowman & Littlefield, 1997), pp. 143–68.

Readers with a taste for serious cinema and an interest in the Cave Allegory will certainly want to watch *The Conformist*, dir. by Bernardo Bertolucci (Paramount Pictures, 1970), about a young fascist tasked with assassinating his former philosophy professor. The film is rife with Platonic imagery as well as a cinematically brilliant discussion of the Cave.

Interested readers can find an animated version of the Cave Allegory on YouTube, narrated by the great Orson Welles, at https://www.youtube. com/watch?v=_jmJGBJRlUQ.

Readers interested in the enlightened philosopher's descent back into the Cave should see Richard Kraut, 'Return to the Cave: *Republic* 519–521', in *Plato 2: Ethics, Politics, Religion, and the Soul*, ed. by Gail Fine (New York: Oxford University Press, 1999), pp. 235–54.

Readers interested in gratitude as a basis for duties of justice might start with Chapter 7 of A. John Simmons, *Moral Principles and Political Obligations* (Princeton: Princeton University Press, 1979), pp. 156–90.

M. A. Barth, *Return of Peisistratus to Athens with the False Minerva* (1838). Photograph by Patna (2018), Wikimedia, Public Domain, https:// commons.wikimedia.org/wiki/File:Return_of_Peisistratus_to_Athens_ with_the_false_Minerva.jpg#/media/File:Return_of_Peisistratus_to_ Athens_with_the_false_Minerva.jpg

12. The Decline and Fall of the Ideal City-Soul

Books VIII–IX

Having addressed the Three Waves to the satisfaction of Glaucon and company, Socrates picks up where he left off at the end of Book IV, 'enquir[ing] whether it is more profitable to act justly, live in a fine way, and be just [...] or to act unjustly and be unjust' (4.444e–45a). To settle this question, he plans to trace the decay of the ideal, just city and soul into their unjust opposites. This is as we should expect, given the city-soul (*polis-psychê*) analogy that guides him in answering the *Republic*'s two main questions, *What is justice?* and *Is the just life happier than the unjust life?* There are five mirroring pairs here, with each city corresponding to a kind of soul, both organized and governed in the same way and having a distinctive good that it pursues. This is a story of decay, of psychic and political disease rather than mere change. Matters go from best to worst as the aristocratic soul and city—so called because the best (*ariston*) part of the city and the soul has power (*kratos*)—gives way to the honor-loving timocracy, which in turn degenerates into the money-loving oligarchy, and this to freedom-loving democracy until the worst psychic and political arrangement is reached: tyranny. Ultimately, Socrates will compare the aristocratic and the tyrannical souls as he answers the *Republic*'s second question.

There is a lot going on here, so our discussion will be selective. Of course we will want to attend to which part of the city or soul is in charge and what end or goal each pursues as good in itself. We will

 https://doi.org/10.11647/OBP.0229.12

also attend to the transvaluation of values—to the ways in which virtues become vices and vices virtues—in this long, dark night of the soul and city, noting both the internal and external causes of decay. A common thread throughout the discussion is the role played by changes to the educational program developed earlier in Books II and III.

The Aristocratic City and Soul (8.543a–547c)

Philosophers govern the aristocratic city and reason governs the aristocratic soul. The former is the paradigm of political justice, the latter of personal justice—which is what Plato most cares about in the *Republic*, a fact that is easy to forget, given the attention lavished on city-building. It is interesting that Socrates does not make explicit what the best and the worst cities and souls take the good to be—here by 'the good' he means not the Form of the good but rather '[the] single goal at which all their actions, public and private, inevitably aim' (7.519c). It is their *telos*, their end or overarching aim, the goal that organizes their thought and action. It is by reference to this good that their activities make sense. There are a few plausible candidates for the aristocratic city's and soul's good, and I suggest that we take *justice*, the outstanding virtue in the *Republic*, to be their good. With each part of the city or soul performing its role well, the city and soul will function well and flourish and thrive: it will be happy.

By this point we have a pretty good idea of what the aristocratic city and soul are like, given the care with which Socrates has described them. So what causes the decay of these ideals? Why does aristocracy decay into the second-best arrangement, timocracy? Socrates' answer is a bit of a downer. It is not that aristocracy *does* decay but rather that it *must*: 'everything that comes into being must decay' (8.546a). Perhaps this is a prescient nod to a moral analog of the law of entropy. Depressing though it is, it should come as no surprise, for if the ideal, aristocratic *polis* were ever realized, it would be realized in the visible, sensible world. This is the world of coming-to-be and passing-away, the world of becoming rather than the world of being, where the changeless Forms reside. Decay is inescapable in the sensible world of concrete particulars, which are ceaselessly coming to be and passing away.

The initial cause is somewhat surprising, though: the guardians, as wise and mathematically gifted as they are, miscalculate the 'perfect number' (8.546b) that should govern the reproductive schedule of the guardians. It is not their fault, really. They are bringing 'calculation (λογισμός [*logismos*])', the heart of the first subject of advanced study for would-be rulers, to bear upon 'sense perception' (8.546b), and one of the abiding lessons of the Third Wave is that while we can have beliefs, even true beliefs, about the objects that populate the visible world, 'there is no knowledge of such things' (7.529b). It is not a defect in the philosopher-rulers so much as a defect in the world: they lack knowledge of the correct number because such things are by their very natures not knowable: one can have beliefs about particulars, but not knowledge. Even if the philosopher-queens and -kings get it right most of the time (which we can assume they will), they will miss the mark often enough to make a difference: they will 'join brides and grooms at the wrong time, the children will be neither good natured nor fortunate' (8.546d). In short, non-gold children will be born to gold parents— but, like lawlessness and other evils, this will go unnoticed (4.424d). The problem posed by these defective natures is exacerbated by their being nurtured badly, as the program of education that was laid out in such detail in Books II and III begins to go awry: 'they will have less consideration for music and poetry than they ought' (8.546d). Thus the rulers will fail in their great duty, that they guard against 'the mixture of the metals in the souls of the next generation' (3.415b).

The rulers whose golden souls are infected with bronze and iron begin to see a gap between the city's good and their own. They question the prohibition on possessing private property, required by the city's foundational myth. They expect ruling to pay and so begin to drive a wedge into the ever-widening gap, hastening the aristocratic city toward the ruin prophesized at the end of Book III. The city is not unified— literally, it has dis-integrated—being no longer 'of one mind' (8.545d) about who should rule and what is best for the city. As false rulers pull the city toward money-making, the true rulers and auxiliaries, whose souls are still pure gold and silver, pull in the other direction, 'towards virtue and the old order' (8.547b). To end the strife, a deal is struck, settling on a middle way, between rational, aristocratic virtue and appetitive, oligarchic wealth: timocracy, in which the good is honor and in which spirit rules the soul and the auxiliaries rule the city.

The Timocratic City and Soul (8.547c–550c)

The timocratic city and soul do not exhibit justice. They cannot, as they are governed by the honor-loving spirited element, which is supposed to be reason's ally and helper (4.441a), not governor of soul and city. Only a soul and city in which each part performs its proper task can be just. Still, calling them *un*just seems too strong. People for whom honor is the good will regard shame as bad—perhaps as *the* bad, the thing most to be avoided—and thus will avoid conventionally unjust conduct. This love of honor is fueled by their 'valu[ing] physical training more than music and poetry' (8.548b), which also fuels a change for the worse in fundamental values. Justice, we know, 'is doing one's own work and not meddling with what is not one's own' (4.433a), but in a timocracy those 'who do their work are called fools and held to be of little account, while those who meddle in other people's affairs are honored and praised' (8.550a). Thus justice begins to be regarded as the kind of simple-minded foolishness that Thrasymachus mocked in Book I.

In accounting for the rise of the timocratic person, Socrates seems to give more evidence that he is not really a feminist, as he lays the blame for its rise at the feet of a carping, status-hungry wife who complains to her son about his father's shortcomings. The aristocratic father, who is reminiscent of Book VI's shelter-seeker who wants to 'lead a quiet life and do [his] own work' (6.496d), is not interested in ruling as his city degenerates, and this negatively affects his wife's status among the other wives. He is uninterested in money and 'does not fight back when he is insulted' (8.549c). In short, his wife complains to their son that his father is 'unmanly [and] too easy-going' (8.549d), since, presumably, he subscribes to Socrates' proto-Stoic view that 'human affairs are not worth taking very seriously' (10.604b) and thus is among those who are 'unwilling to occupy themselves in human affairs' (7.517c). At his mother's urging, their son wants 'to be more of a man than his father' (8.550a). It clear that Plato is criticizing a kind of masculinity that typifies and would be ascendant in an honor-driven, competitive culture. The timocratic son is not bad by nature, Socrates insists, but he is surrounded by people who value honor and victory more than virtue and truth, so it is no wonder, given how readily children absorb values from their culture, that he turns out as he does.

Honor is a fine thing, as it can lead one to have a soul that is *kalon,* fine and noble and beautiful, and thus *worthy of being honored.* Kant thought it a facsimile of virtue, as it provides a nobler motive than self-interest. Aristotle writes of a healthy competition in which people strive to emulate and even outdo each other in virtue.[1] But honor as an internal good can easily give way to the external good of *being honored,* especially in a competitive, victory-loving culture. Being honored should be merely a foreseeable consequence of acting well, but it becomes instead the intended outcome, the goal aimed at.

The Oligarchic City and Soul (8.550c–555b)

Changes to education and changes in value are again part of the story as timocracy degenerates into oligarchy. The most momentous change is wealth's replacing honor as the over-arching goal of city and soul, as the competition for honor that drove the timocratic person finds a new object. It is no accident that Plato twice appeals to the notion of emulation in explaining this transition (the Greek term is ζῆλος (*zêlos*), which is the root of the words 'zealous' and 'jealous'). Iron- and bronze-souled rulers see their fellows stretching and then disregarding the rules against private property; they emulate and compete with each other, which ultimately leads them to formally establish wealth as a qualification for ruling. Wealth is the criterion by which they choose the captain of the ship of state, 'refusing to entrust the ship to a poor person even if he was a better captain' (8.551c). As wealthy craftspeople govern the oligarchic city, appetite—in particular the desire to make money—governs the soul. Thus appetite and the craftspeople operate in areas beyond their expertise, 'meddling in other people's affairs' (8.551e)—the affairs of the guardians and auxiliaries.

Plato's psychology of the oligarchic person is subtle and fascinating. The oligarchic person subordinates reason to appetite, reducing reason to the merely instrumental role of determining the best means to the end

---

1   Aristotle, *Nicomachean Ethics*, IX.8 1169a6–10.

which appetite sets for him—and thus embodies the Humean picture on which 'Reason is and ought only be the slave of the passions, and can never pretend to any other office but than to serve and obey them'.[2] This is not to say that Hume endorses the oligarch's substantive goal: he does not think our primary aim is or should be the pursuit of wealth. Hume's point is structural, concerning the relation of reason and passion, not the substantive ends we pursue: passion, not reason, provides us with our goals and ends; reason's job is merely to determine the best means to achieve those ends. Although Plato regards wealth and virtue as polar opposites (8.550e), he implies that there is something about the desire for wealth that gives the oligarch's life order and discipline. The oligarch is unwilling to indulge what Socrates calls 'his dronish appetites' (8.554c) for sensual gratification but instead is 'a thrifty worker, who satisfies only his necessary appetites' (8.554a). Since reason does not govern his soul, he is not just, but he is not quite unjust—at least his conduct is not reliably unjust. His baser appetites are kept in check, not by reason, as they are in the just, aristocratic soul, nor by a healthy sense of shame, as they are in the spirit-governed timocratic soul, but instead by fear. The oligarch fears that indulging his other appetites will be financially too costly. The contest between force and persuasion, raised in the opening scene of the *Republic,* is decisively settled in favor of force by the time oligarchy arrives. The oligarch's dronish appetites are 'forcibly held in check by his carefulness' (8.554c) and thus 'his better desires are in control of his worse' (8.554d).

Carefulness is a fine quality; indeed, it is a trait the guardians must possess, given the importance of their task to the city's wellbeing (2.374e). Caution keeps the oligarchic person on the straight and narrow, more or less, but 'where they have ample opportunity to do justice with impunity' (8.554c), they will probably take it. After all, what is needed for success in business, they will reason, is a reputation for justice: not *being* just but merely *seeming* just. Despite the oligarch's devotion to financial gain, Socrates insists that 'the true virtue of a single-minded and harmonious soul far escapes him' (8.554e). This may seem an odd remark for Socrates to make, given the oligarch's focus on wealth, which certainly seems single-minded. But as is so often the case in the *Republic,*

---

2   Hume, *Treatise,* p. 415 (II.iii.3).

the way things *seem* is not the way they *are*. I take Socrates' point to be that while the oligarch's devotion to wealth is indeed single, it is not single-*minded:* it is not a product of rational reflection but rather of appetite. The tune his soul sings must be dissonant at times, since its parts are not playing their proper roles—reason should govern but here is subordinated to appetite—and the soul is ordered not by reason and persuasion but by force, and fear does not make for harmony. This lack of single-mindedness is also a feature of the timocratic city and soul, which, like the oligarchic city and soul, is in tension with itself.

Toward the beginning of Book IV, Socrates worried about the corruptive and corrosive powers of wealth, fearing their 'slipping into the city unnoticed' (4.421e). The changes all seem minor and inconsequential. What harm, for example, could allowing flutes and the Lydian mode do? But it is precisely their seeming innocuousness that makes changes to education and relaxing the Specialization Principle so dangerous. We can imagine the processes of rationalization at work as values such as justice and nobility are replaced by the drive for wealth. The oligarch is not someone who 'pays any attention to education' (8.554b), at least not education in music and poetry! What a waste of time, we can imagine the oligarchs complaining. Education—especially if it is publicly funded—should be practical, teaching marketable skills to people regarded primarily as consumers and only secondarily if at all as citizens. If we listen closely, we can almost hear Dickens' Mr Gradgrind weighing in: 'Teach these boys and girls nothing but Facts. Facts alone are wanted in life. Plant nothing else, and root out everything else'.[3] While the oligarch will perhaps embrace the pre-dialectic mathematical education spelled out in Book VII, they will re-purpose it in an anti-Socratic way, insisting that number be studied by 'tradesmen and retailers, for the sake of buying and selling' (7.525c), that its aim be practical, never theoretical.

The careful and hard-working oligarch 'has a good reputation and is thought to be just' (8.554c), but whatever his reputation, we know that his soul is not in fact just. He is the midpoint in the decay of the ideal city and soul. He is not good, but he is not thoroughly bad, either. He is someone like Cephalus, whom Socrates clearly respects. Cephalus is

---

3   Charles Dickens, *Hard Times* (London: Penguin Books, 1994), p. 10.

wealthy, and while he is fond of money, he is not *too fond* of it (1.330bc).
He does not use his considerable wealth to indulge his sensuous
appetites; instead, it has given him a moral cushion of sorts: because
he is (and was born) wealthy, he is not tempted to act unjustly in in the
pursuit of wealth. Cephalus has enough self-awareness to admit that his
moral decency is not a consequence of unshakable inner virtue but owes
a great deal to luck and external circumstance.

The oligarchic city is really two cities, rich and poor, at war with each
other, and it is relatively stable, but as its stability is born of fear and
power rather than justice, it is not a stability that can last. And it does not
last, Socrates thinks: it inevitably decays into democracy.

The Democratic City and Soul (8.555b–562a)

Etymologically, 'democracy' means rule (*-cracy*) of the *demes*—the
people. Readers are often taken aback at the dim view Plato has of
democracy, but it really should not be a surprise. Plato thinks that 'the
majority cannot be philosophic' (6.494a), so most people are incapable
of possessing wisdom, knowledge of what is best for the city as a
whole, which is the virtue required to govern well. I trust that we can
understand why he takes this view, even if we disagree with him.

The good in a democracy is freedom, which for Plato is not
unambiguously good. He quickly associates it with 'license to do what
[one] wants' and to 'arrange [one's] own life in whatever manner pleases
him' (8.557b). License carries with it a hint of arrogance, and perhaps
immaturity, reminiscent of the 'silly, adolescent idea of happiness'
(5.466b) condemned earlier. One way to think about Plato's discomfort
with this sort of freedom is that it is ungrounded in any rational principle
and that it underwrites choices based on whim. The Specialization
Principle has long since given way to the impulse of the moment. 'There
is neither order nor necessity in his life' (8.561d), Socrates says of the
democratic person. He is unfocused, with the attention span of a golden
retriever. Today he gives himself over to drinking and debauchery; next
week he drinks only water and becomes an exercise addict; he tries
business, he then dabbles in philosophy, etc. He lacks the discipline his
oligarchic father had, and indeed his lifestyle is a reaction to parental
frugality and austerity.

Following the late Isaiah Berlin, philosophers often distinguish between positive and negative freedom. Freedom conceived negatively is the absence of constraint. The freedom of speech guaranteed in the First Amendment of the US Constitution, for example, is a guarantee against state interference with expressing one's views. But conceived positively, freedom is genuine autonomy and self-direction. As Berlin puts it, 'I wish my life and decisions to depend on myself, not on external forces [...] I wish to be a subject, not an object; to be moved by reasons, by conscious purposes, which are my own, not by causes which affect me, as it were, from outside'.[4] The democratic person's freedom is largely negative; they are not prevented from doing as they like (subject, of course, to various reasonable constraints, e.g., that their conduct does not harm others). But the democrat seems too impulsive and reactive, too susceptible to external influences to count as positively free. They do not scrutinize their values or plans or adopt only those endorsed after a period of reflection, as the positively free person does. There is a deep sense in which the democrat's reasons and purposes are not really their own. At the very least, they are ephemeral and shifting, and do not reflect the presence of a well-thought-out life-plan.

So, we know what the democratic city and soul take the good to be. And in place of oligarchy's wealth requirement, in the democratic city all citizens—or, at least, all *male* citizens—have political rights: the city is ruled not by the wealthy craftspeople but by all the craftspeople. The political classes of the aristocratic city are a thing of the past, and the army comprises citizen-soldiers, rather than the professionals that Plato envisioned. But what governs the democratic soul? There are *five* kinds of constitutional arrangement, Socrates insists, but only *three* parts of the soul—so by the time we arrive at democracy, we seem to have run out of parts. So what governs?

---

4   Isaiah Berlin, 'Two Concepts of Liberty', in Berlin, *Liberty: Four Essays on Liberty*, ed. by Henry Hardy (New York: Oxford University Press, 2002), https://doi.org/10.10 93/019924989x.001.0001, p. 178.

Interlude: Necessary versus Unnecessary Appetites

Appetite governs the democratic soul, as it does in the oligarchic soul, but here Socrates makes a philosophically interesting distinction between *kinds* of appetites or desires. The democratic soul is governed by *unnecessary* desires, the sort the oligarch steadfastly and cautiously refused to indulge, while necessary desires govern the oligarchic soul. Socrates alluded to the distinction (without explaining it) when describing the oligarch, whom he called 'a thrifty worker who satisfies only his necessary appetites' (8.554a). And indeed, the distinction between necessary and unnecessary desires is implicit in the difference between the rustic and the luxurious ideal cities. The latter comes about because the citizens have 'overstepped the limit of their necessities' (2.373d), which suggests that in the rustic city, which Socrates regards as 'the true city [...] the healthy one' (2.372e), the citizens satisfy only their necessary appetites, whereas satisfying the unnecessary appetites fuels the luxurious city. So how do necessary and unnecessary desires differ?

Plato gives a two-pronged definition of necessary desires: 'those we cannot desist from and those whose satisfaction benefits us [are] rightly called necessary for we are by nature compelled to satisfy them' (8.558e). This 'and' should be an 'or', however, since a desire that meets either criterion will count as necessary. Consider bread. As a basic element in the Greek diet, we can think of it as proxy for food generally. A desire for bread is necessary on both counts: first, we cannot desist from it—we cannot not want it, as a desire for food comes with our animal nature. Someone without this desire—e.g., someone suffering from anorexia, which etymologically is the absence (the privative *an-*) of desire (*orexis*)—would be very badly off and in an unnatural, unhealthy state. Second, satisfying a desire for bread is good for us, and indeed we enjoy it. While bread makes life possible, good bread makes life enjoyable. So, too, do the delicacies we put on the bread make life more enjoyable, but we can learn to do without them. Remember that it was the absence of delicacies that Glaucon decried in the first, rustic ideal city back in Book II (2.372c), claiming the city was fit only for pigs. So a desire for delicacies will also count as a necessary desire, since it is *natural* for us to desire something to put on the bread. Only an appetite that fails both counts will be unnecessary. Though Socrates does not say so, presumably this will vary from person to person: you may be able to enjoy a cocktail before and a glass or two of wine with dinner, but for an alcoholic, even a couple of drinks starts them on the road to self-destructive drunkenness. So wine—also a Greek staple—is necessary for some of us but unnecessary for others.

Though the distinction between necessary and unnecessary desires is needed for Socrates to distinguish between the oligarchic and democratic souls, the democratic person rejects it, taking all desires to be equally worthy of pursuit: the democrat 'puts all his pleasures on an equal footing' (8.561b). The democratic person does not deny the distinction in a conceptual way, holding it to be incoherent or non-existent. Instead, they deny that the distinction is a suitable basis for action and choice, 'declar[ing] that all pleasures are equal and must be valued equally' (8.561c). They do not think that necessary desires are *better* than unnecessary desires or that there is any reason to blush at pursuing what those frugal oligarchs regard as 'unnecessary [desires] that aim at frivolity and display' (9.572c). Where their fathers pursued only necessary desires, the young democrats reject this frugal austerity (and thus the order and discipline their focus on necessary desires gave rise to) and seek to indulge the desires that characterize the ne'er-do-well drones.

Although the democrat seems uninterested in thinking philosophically about Plato's way of distinguishing necessary and unnecessary desires, *we* might find it worthwhile to do so, to see if there are independent reasons to reject it or at least to reformulate it, as it seems awkward to regard a desire for delicacies as necessary, since, as Socrates himself points out, we can learn to give them up. So we do not get too far afield, let us consider briefly the taxonomy of desires Epicurus (BCE 341–270) proposed. First, a word of warning: though the word 'epicurean' has some resonance with ancient Epicureanism (which took pleasure alone to be good in itself, the view we identified in an earlier chapter as hedonism), Epicurus actually took the absence of pain and disturbance to be what pleasure truly is. For him, the pleasure that constitutes the good is not a full belly but a tranquil mind.

Where Plato fuses necessary and natural desires, calling some desires necessary because they are natural, Epicurus distinguishes between what is natural and what is necessary. For Epicurus, a necessary desire is one whose non-satisfaction causes physical pain. When we do not eat, we experience the pangs of hunger. Thus a desire for food—for bread, as Socrates put it—counts as necessary. While every necessary desire is natural, for Epicurus, not all natural desires are necessary. The desire for bread is both natural and necessary. But desires for relishes, while natural, are not necessary. Think of a favorite dish. I love the *Pha Ram Long Song* at Ruam Mit Thai in downtown St Paul; its deliciousness makes my life better, but I can clearly live without it: it is a natural but unnecessary desire. If I show up only to find that the restaurant is no longer open on Sundays, I should react with mild disappointment: 'Oh, dang it! I was really looking forward to that. Oh well.' I will ask my companions where we should go instead. If, on the other hand, I am not disappointed but really angry that the restaurant is closed and am still muttering 'I cannot fricking believe it!' hours later, sulking and ruining dinner for everyone because I did not get what I wanted, then my desire is not only unnecessary, it is also unnatural. Excessive psychological distress at a desire's not being satisfied is not natural: there is something wrong with me. So the difference between *natural but unnecessary* desires and *unnatural and unnecessary* desires is not a difference in objects desired but rather in the desirer themself. *I* should be able to eliminate my desire for *x* when *x* is difficult to obtain—or if *x* is bad for me. Epicurus thinks that the source is usually 'a groundless opinion'—some false belief that I cannot be happy unless I have *this* particular Thai dish or *that* flavor of ice cream or that I get a promotion, etc. In fact, for Epicurus eliminating such desires is one of the keys to happiness. No gourmand himself, Epicurus thought that

> Plain fare gives as much pleasure as a costly diet, when once the pain of want has been removed, while bread and water confer the highest possible pleasure when they are brought to hungry lips. To habituate oneself, therefore, to simple and inexpensive diet supplies all that is needful for health, and enables a man to meet the necessary requirements of life without shrinking, and it places us in a better condition when we approach at intervals a costly fare and renders us fearless of fortune.[5]

---

5   Epicurus, 'Letter to Menoeceus', in *The Art of Happiness*, ed. by George Strodach (New York: Penguin Books, 2012), p. 159 [DL 10.130–31].

Epicurus' taxonomy of desire seems an improvement on Plato's largely because he separates naturalness and necessity, which Plato conflates. Plato's way of distinguishing necessary and unnecessary seems awkward and even mistaken—but if so, it is not a fatal mistake but rather one that is easily repairable.

Democracy, Continued

Equality comes a close second to freedom as democracy's defining good. Not only are all pleasures and desires equal, but so too are men and women (8.563b) (which is yet another point against the view that Socrates is a feminist, given the disdain he has for democracy), slave and owner, citizen and non-citizen (8.562e), and even humans and non-human animals (8.563c). Where the oligarchic father 'satisfies only his necessary appetites [...] and enslaves his other desires as vain' (8.554a), his democratic son celebrates 'the liberation and release of useless and unnecessary pleasures' (8.561a).

Plato stresses how attractive the democratic polity appears: it is 'multicolored' (8.559d, 561e) and 'embroidered with every kind of character type' (8.557c). But it is a specious beauty. The democratic children of oligarchic parents seem to suffer from what is sometimes called *affluenza*: they are 'fond of luxury, incapable of effort either mental or physical, too soft to stand up to pleasures or pains, and idle besides' (8.556b). Their teachers, perhaps afraid of low scores on student surveys, fear and flatter them (8.563a), and their parents want most of all to be their friends. It is a prescription for disaster, Plato thinks. Despite its obvious shortcomings, taking the good to be wealth has its benefits, because it is a value with content and moreover one that imposes discipline and order. Freedom, on the other hand, is formal rather than contentful, and indeed it is perhaps *too* formal and too open-textured to guide one's life. Aristotle wrote that 'not to have one's life organized in view of some end is a mark of much folly'.[6] Plato surely agrees; he seems to be arguing that freedom is ill suited to play the role the democrat has cast it in. *Do whatever you want* is, technically, a life-guiding principle, but so long as there are few or no restrictions on what

---

6   Aristotle, *Eudemian Ethics*, I.2 1214b10.

one should want or desire, it is going to lead to chaos. So what we have is not so much democracy as anarchy—ἀναρχία (*anarchia*): the absence of a leader or leading principle (8.562e).

We see this most clearly in the way the correct, aristocratic scheme of values is turned on its head in the democratic city and soul. Reverence, the proper sense of respect and shame that proper stories about the gods were meant to cultivate, is thought of as foolishness. The cardinal virtue of moderation is regarded as the cardinal vice of cowardice, and the vice of shamelessness is now become courage. Insolence—literally, ὕβρις (*hubris*)—is regarded as good breeding and anarchy is freedom. They mistake prodigality or wastefulness as the public-spirited virtue of magnificence (private spending for public goods such as producing a tragedy, outfitting a trireme, etc.). Where the oligarchic father was not willing to spend on such matters, the democratic son goes wrong in the other direction, spending wildly. It is an upside-down world, but of course the democratic person thinks it is the best of all worlds, free of stuffy conventions and old-fashioned thinking.

The Tyrannical City and Soul (8.562a–9.576b)

Plato's explanation of the transformation from democracy to oligarchy has the elegance of Newton's third law of motion, which states that for every action, there is an equal and opposite reaction. For Plato, 'excessive action in one direction usually sets up a reaction in the opposite direction' (8.563e), so the extreme freedom found in democracies leads inexorably to the total lack of freedom found in tyrannies. Plato thinks his proto-Newtonian principle is not merely political—it explains changes in seasons, plants, and bodies, too—but alas we do not have space to pursue this fascinating line of thought.

It is no accident that Plato appeals to a principle of physics here. Nor should it be a surprise; after all, it is something like entropy that explains why the ideal state begins to decay in the first place. In addition to physical explanations of political events and changes—and it is helpful to keep in mind that our word 'physics' derives from the ancient Greek word φύσις [*phusis*], which means nature more broadly— he also appeals to economic factors. Consider first the change from oligarchy to democracy. Having exploited existing sources of wealth, the oligarchs need new sources, new markets, so they hit upon one with great contemporary relevance: they find young people to be a potentially lucrative market to lend money to. More interested in profit than people, 'they are unwilling to enact laws to prevent young people who have had no discipline from spending and wasting their wealth, so that by making loans to them, secured by the young people's property, and then calling those loans in, they themselves become ever richer and more honored' (8.555c).

Although the details differ, something similar is afoot in the US, where student loan debt now tops one trillion dollars, exceeding even credit card debt. Though the cause is massive state disinvestment in higher education rather than predatory lending, the results seem the same: indebted young people. While indebtedness in the US seems to push us away from democracy and toward oligarchy, in Plato's world things go in the opposite direction: as the rich become fewer but richer and the poor become poorer but grow in number, an actual and not merely metaphorical civil war breaks out and the people are victorious.

In true Thrasymachan fashion, the holders of political power pass laws that benefit themselves rather than the citizenry at large or the state as a whole. They resist suggestions that 'the majority of voluntary contracts be entered into at the lender's own risk' (8.556b), much as contemporary bankers resist calls to eliminate the moral hazards of a system that privatizes profit but socializes loss by having the citizenry bail out the 'too big to fail' banks and investment firms that crashed the world economy in 2008. The transition to tyranny is fueled by the would-be tyrant's 'making all sorts of promises both in public and private, freeing the people from debt [and] redistributing the land to them' (8.566e). Thus economic factors are at work here, as well. Many readers will note eerie similarities with today's global political climate, which seems to feature the emergence of the 'strongman' whom 'the people' have set up 'as their special champion' (8.565c). I will leave it to more economically and politically sophisticated readers to pursue this for themselves; there is plenty of food for thought here, where—as elsewhere—the *Republic* is surprisingly contemporarily relevant.

Interlude: Lawless versus Lawful Desires

Earlier it seemed that Socrates had run out of parts of the soul, there being five kinds of souls (and cities) but only three parts in the soul. To distinguish oligarch and democrat he distinguished between necessary and unnecessary desires. Here a similar problem arises: what governs the tyrannical soul? And so, at the beginning of Book IX Socrates makes a distinction between kinds of unnecessary desires: some are lawless, and some are law-abiding or at least law-amenable. In an account that rings some Freudian bells, Plato indicates that the lawless, unnecessary appetites are most apparent in our dreams, for it is there that our 'beastly and savage part' (8.571c) emerges—as anyone who has had not just a weird but a genuinely creepy dream can attest. There is nothing that is off-limits for the lawless, unnecessary desires; in their grip a person 'does not shrink from trying to have sex with a mother [...] or with anyone else at all, whether man, god, or beast. It will commit any foul murder, and there is no food it refuses to eat' (9.572d). Whom one has sex with, whom one kills, and what one eats form an unholy trinity indeed. The role played here and elsewhere in the *Republic* is intriguing; it was pivotal in the rejection of the first ideal city and in understanding the lawless unnecessary desires which define the tyrant. (It may be helpful to note that the Greek word translated as 'lawless' is παράνομος [*paranomos*], which connotes not the absence of law so much as going beyond it.)

It is not that only the tyrant has lawless unnecessary appetites; they are present in almost everyone, Plato thinks, but they *govern* the tyrannical soul. In most of us they are kept at bay by constraints internal (reason, in the best of us; shame or fear, in the rest of us) or external (the law). Indeed, Plato's account of psychic and political degeneration is an account of how these constraints change. In the aristocratic, philosophical soul, it is reason—rational persuasion— that keeps the beastly desires at bay. They are tamed by arguments (8.554d) and by the meditative practice Plato counsels undertaking before one goes to bed at night (9.571e–2a). The spirit-governed timocrat, more responsive to honor than to reason, is motivated by a healthy sense of shame, honor's opposite. Remember that much of the point of musical-poetic education is cultivating 'the right distastes' (3.401e)—of being properly disgusted. The timocrat should be disgusted at the thought of ignoble or dishonorable thoughts and deeds and presumably would not even be tempted to embezzle from or cheat a widow or orphan, though the oligarch probably is. For the oligarch's dronish, unnecessary desires are not held in check by reason or shame but rather by fear; and if the oligarch believes they can 'do injustice with impunity' (8.554c), they probably will, just as Gyges did back in Book II (2.360c). The democratic person wavers between fear and shame, being too unsettled to have a constant, characteristic motivation: sometimes their disordered soul is ordered by 'a kind of shame' (8.560a), which overcomes some of their base appetites and expels others. But at other times they 'feel neither shame nor fear in front of [their] parents' (8.562e), thinking themself their parents' equal and taking shamelessness to be a form of courage (8.560e). The tyrannical soul is 'free of all control by shame or reason' (9.571c). As the tyrannical city long ago abandoned proper education in music and poetry, the main bulwark against lawlessness (4.424d), this should come as no surprise.

Tyranny, Continued

Although Plato is less explicit about the tyrannical soul's good than he is with the defining goods of the timocratic, oligarchic, and democratic souls, it seems that the tyrant's good is erotic love and desire: ἔρως [*erôs*]. But this is not really erotic love, as opposed to familial or friendly love. It is mad, addictive, erotic desire for *everything*. Plato told us back in Book III that the right kind of erotic love—ὁ ὀρθὸς ἔρως: the *orthos erôs*— is 'the love of order and beauty that has been moderated by education in music and poetry [... which] has nothing mad or licentious about it' (3.403a). The tyrant's erotic love, by contrast, is a kind of 'madness (μανία [*mania*])' (9.573b) that leads not merely to house-breaking, purse-snatching, temple-robbing and the like (9.575b), a cluster of unjust acts that pop up elsewhere in the *Republic* (1.344a, 4.443a, 8.552d), but to 'complete anarchy and lawlessness' (9.575a). It is outdoing—*pleonxia*—gone mad.

Thus the tyrant when awake is what most of us are when we sleep and have dark dreams of fulfilling lawless unnecessary desires (9.574e).

The tyrant is the inversion of the philosopher, who, in contrast to lovers of opinion and the cave-dwellers, is awake (5.476d, 7.520c). The tyrant's 'waking life is like the nightmare we described earlier' (9.576b). Their desires are not merely many but are insatiable, for they are 'like a vessel full of holes' (9.586b): no sooner has one appetite or lust been satisfied than another makes its demands. Always wanting more, nothing is ever enough. Epicurus seems to have diagnosed him exactly: 'Nothing is enough for the man for whom enough is too little'.[7]

The portrait of the tyrant is interesting, but some readers may feel that it misses the mark. It does not seem to fit tyrants most of us are familiar with—for example, Hitler and Stalin, neither of whom seemed to be a bubbling cauldron of lust, unable to control himself. Plato seems to have captured the essence of an addict running wild, manic and disordered and undisciplined. But he seems not to have captured the cold, calculating tyrant that Thrasymachus praises. The tyrant, after all, is supposed to be like a wolf (8.566a), preying upon the flock that the guardian-shepherds try to protect with the help of the sheepdog-auxiliaries, to bring the metaphor full circle. While the wolf as portrayed by Plato poses a threat to the flock, it is hard to see how this undisciplined, manic, deeply disturbed person can *appear* a paragon of justice, as the argument of the *Republic* requires. Someone more ordered and calculating seems needed, someone possessing the oligarch's singular focus and discipline, someone whose soul is as ordered and reason-governed as the just person's—but someone who possesses cleverness rather than wisdom: that is, someone who knows what best serves *their* interests rather than the city's. In short, the tyrant should be a 'wise villain' (3.409c).

No doubt there are people with dark secret lives who manage to convey an ordered, mild façade. But it is difficult to imagine how someone whose inner life is as deranged and insane as Plato's tyrant is could manage to appear completely respectable. Readers might wish that Adeimantus would push back here, as he has done elsewhere in the *Republic*. It is a shame that Adeimantus does not resist Glaucon's 'taking over the argument' (9.576b) at the conclusion of the account of the tyrant and raise some of these objections to Socrates. Because

---

7   Epicurus, 'Vatican Sayings' #68, in *The Art of Happiness*, p. 183.

he does not, we will want to keep them in mind as we look at the arguments that the just life is happier than the unjust life, to which we now turn.

Some Suggestions for Further Reading

Readers interested in the philosophical thought of Epicurus will find his extant writings along with a helpful introductory essay in *The Art of Happiness*, trans. by George Strodach (New York: Penguin Classics, 2012). Epicurus' thought is expressed vividly in one of the great poems of world literature, Lucretius, *The Nature of Things*, trans. by Alicia Stallings (New York: Penguin Books, 2007). The story of the fifteenth-century rediscovery of it is the subject of Stephen Greenblatt, *The Swerve: How the World Became Modern* (New York: W.W. Norton & Company, 2012), which won both the Pulitzer Prize and the National Book Award. In presenting Epicurus' taxonomy of desire, I draw on an excellent essay, Raphael Woolf, 'Pleasure and Desire', in *The Cambridge Companion to Epicureanism*, ed. by James Warren (New York: Cambridge University Press, 2009), https://doi.org/10.1017/ccol9780521873475, pp. 158–78.

Readers interested in an accessible, erudite discussion of the decay of the city and soul will profit from G.R.F. Ferrari, *City and Soul in Plato's Republic* (Chicago: University of Chicago Press, 2005).

As many readers will have noticed for themselves, there has been a revival of popular interest in Plato's conception of tyranny in light of recent electoral events in America. There are many interesting opinion pieces online. For a scholarly take, interested readers might see the essays collected in *Trump and Political Philosophy: Patriotism, Cosmopolitanism, and Civic Virtue*, ed. by Marc Benjamin Sable and Angel Jaramillo Torres (London: Palgrave Macmillan, 2018), https://doi.org/10.1007/978–3–319–74427–8, or in *Trump and Political Philosophy: Leadership, Statesmanship, and Tyranny*, ed. by Angel Jaramillo Torres and Marc Benjamin Sable (London: Palgrave Macmillan, 2018), https://doi.org/10.1007/978–3–319–74445–2.

Readers interested in a brief, wise, and oddly hopeful look at tyranny from one of the world's leading historians of modern Europe will certainly want to read Timothy Snyder, *On Tyranny: Twenty Lessons from the Twentieth Century* (New York: Tim Duggan Books, 2017).

LE TENNIS CHEZ LES ANCIENS. — Socrate, Platon, Criton, etc., sur l'Agoras.

Unidentified artist, 'Image satirique du tennis chez les Anciens', *La revue athlétique*, 3 (1890), 169. Photograph by Skblzz1 (2018), Wikimedia, Public Domain, https://commons.wikimedia.org/wiki/File:Image_satirique_du_tennis_chez_les_Anciens_(1890).jpg

13. The *Republic*'s Second Question Answered

Three and a Half Arguments that the Just Life is Happier

Book IX

At long last, in Book IX Socrates is ready to address the *Republic*'s second question, *Is a just life happier than an unjust life?* There is a lot at stake here, as 'the argument concerns no ordinary topic but the way we ought to live' (1.352d). It is important to bear in mind that the 'ought' here is not necessarily a moral ought. Indeed, it seems trivially true that one morally ought to live a morally good life. Socrates is asking a question that does not presuppose a moral answer.[1] He is asking what is the best sort of life for a human being: is it a life of acting justly, or am I personally better off acting unjustly when it pays to do so, all things considered? If I cannot be happy without being just, then I have a good, self-regarding reason to live justly. Socrates initially thought that he had answered this question with Book I's Function Argument, but he quickly realized that he jumped the gun in concluding that the just life is happier before determining what justice itself *is*. But now, having determined what

---

1 This is a point driven home forcefully in the opening chapter ('Socrates' Question') of Bernard Williams, *Ethics and the Limits of Philosophy* (Cambridge, MA: Harvard University Press, 1986), esp. pp. 5–6.

    https://doi.org/10.11647/OBP.0229.13

justice is to the satisfaction of Glaucon and Adeimantus and the rest, Socrates is ready to deliver.

Argument #1: Comparing Characters (9.576b–580c)

'It is clear to everyone', Socrates says, 'that there is no city more wretched than one ruled by a tyrant and none more happy than one ruled by kings' (9.576e). So much for political happiness. As for personal happiness, settling the question requires us to compare the just and unjust lives—the lives of the aristocratic philosopher and the tyrant, respectively. Actually, it does not require *us* to do this; it requires someone 'who is competent to judge' (9.577a) to do so. Their verdict will decide the case. So, 'who is fit to judge'? (9.576e) The person, Socrates answers, who 'in thought can go down into a person's character and examine it thoroughly, someone who does not judge from outside' (9.577a). After my making so much of the enlightened philosopher's *going down* into the Cave, readers might be deflated at learning that a different verb, ἐνδύειν [*enduein*] is being translated 'go down'. Its primary meaning is 'to try on', as clothes; it can also mean 'to go into'. Though it lacks literary razzle-dazzle, the crucial point is that this is something that the fit judge can do *in thought*: they need not actually (i.e., in body) become a drug addict to assess the addict's life, for example; they can understand this life without having lived it because a philosopher grasps the relevant Form and its relation to the Form of the good. This squares with Socrates' earlier observation that a good judge is aware of injustice 'not as something at home in his own soul, but as something present in others [... he] recognize[s] injustice as bad by nature, not from his own experience of it, but through knowledge' (3.409b).

Another crucial point, related to the first, is that the fit judge does not judge from the outside; they are not 'dazzled by the façade that tyrants adopt [...] but [are] able to see through that sort of thing' (9.577a). This echoes and indeed answers Adeimantus' earlier complaint that the way justice is praised in Athenian culture leads young people to cynically conclude that they 'should create a façade of illusory virtue around [them] to deceive those who come near' (2.365c). The Greek being translated 'a façade of illusory virtue' (σκιαγραφίαν ἀρετῆς [*skiagraphian arêtes*]) should remind us of the shadow-filled world of the Cave, as it literally means 'a shadow-painting of virtue.' What the competent judge finds is that the tyrannical soul is 'full of disorder and regret' and indeed is 'least likely to do what it wants' (9.577e). The tyrannical soul lacks self-control (9.579c) and its desires are not merely unsustainable but are unfulfillable: the tyrannical addict always wants more.

One especially striking feature is the tyrant's friendlessness: 'someone with a tyrannical nature lives his whole life without being friends with anyone, always a master to one man or a slave to another and never getting a taste of either freedom or true friendship' (9.576a). For most readers, friendship is an important component of a happy life, and Plato would agree. His student Aristotle regarded friendship as one of life's greatest goods, one we cannot lack and still flourish. It seems a general—but not exceptionless—truth that friendship is necessary for happiness. It is not too difficult to see why the tyrant is incapable of friendship. First, friendship is typically a relationship between equals, which the contemporary philosopher Laurence Thomas takes to mean that neither party is under the authority of the other or entitled to the deference of the other.[2] One friend might be wiser and the other might frequently heed their advice, but the other friend is not obligated to do so: a friend can make suggestions but not issue commands. This is one reason that workplace friendships can be problematic: there may come a time when my friend has to switch roles, from friend to boss, which puts us in a relationship of inequality—and to that extent, at that moment, our friendship recedes into the background. 'I thought you were my friend', I pout. 'I am', she replies. But I am also your supervisor, and you need to clean up that spill in aisle six *right now* or we're going to have a real problem'. The tyrannical soul is bent on outdoing everyone; life is a constant competition in which one dominates or is dominated, and that does not leave much room for friendship, as the tyrant cannot abide anyone being their equal, let alone their superior.

A second reason that friendship is unavailable to the tyrant is that friendship requires—and indeed is a kind of—love. Even if we think Plato's conception of love is overly cognitive and insufficiently affective, we can agree with him that love involves a commitment to the other's

---

2   Laurence Thomas, 'Friendship and Other Loves', *Synthese*, 72.2 (1987), 217–36 (pp. 217, 221–23).

wellbeing, for the other's own sake. This seems like an impossibility for the tyrant, who always seeks to further their own interests and sees others merely as a means to their own ends. The tyrant might cultivate what *seem* to be friendships, but insofar as they seek their own and not their would-be friend's wellbeing, they are cultivating an ally, not a friend. So when it is in the tyrant's interest to turn on the ally—or the ally's interest to turn on the tyrant—they will do just that. It is no accident that *The Godfather, Part Two* ends with Michael Corleone alone and brooding, isolated and friendless.

Argument #2: The Soul's Distinct Pleasures (9.580d–583a)

The second argument subtly shifts the terms of the argument from *happiness* to *pleasure*. Despite Socrates' earlier rejection of hedonism, there is nothing problematic about the shift to talk of pleasure here. Indeed, it makes perfect sense for Socrates to do so, given that he is trying to show that everyone has good reasons to live justly rather than unjustly. Thus it makes sense to focus on happiness in terms of pleasure, since how pleasant or enjoyable a life is takes up the individual's own perspective, as the argument requires.

Each of the soul's three parts has its own distinctive pleasure, so the question becomes which part's pleasures are most pleasant—the pleasures of the rational part or the spirited part or the appetitive part? In other words, is the just life, in which reason governs, more first-personally pleasant than the life in which appetite rules? There is a wrinkle in Socrates' approach here: he insists that 'there are three primary kinds of people: philosophic, victory-loving, and profit-loving' (9.581c). Offering three possibilities may be an improvement upon thinking that 'there are two kinds of people in this world', but even here readers may rightly object that this division is far from exhaustive, as it omits people who are peace-loving or family-loving. Indeed, Socrates himself earlier suggested another option toward the end of Book V: lovers of beautiful things. Such people (and many others) do not seem to fit any of Socrates' three types, so we might rightly resist Socrates' attempt at shoehorning here. But the wrinkle becomes difficult to iron out if we recall that Socrates has just finished a detailed account of *five* kinds of people. His distinction between three kinds of people accounts for the aristocratic, timocratic, and oligarchic souls, but what about the democratic and tyrannical? It is puzzling, especially since he is supposed to show that the really just but apparently unjust person is happier than the really unjust but apparently just person, which requires that he compare the aristocrat and the tyrant. Socrates might respond that the third, appetitive kind of life includes the democrat and tyrant as well as the oligarch, but given the way the oligarch's desire for wealth tempered their other desires and bestowed order in their soul, this seems less than satisfactory. This might be a significant problem if this were the only argument given by Socrates that the just life is happier, but as the argument that will follow is 'the greatest and most decisive' (9.583b), all is not lost. Still, though, this is another place where the reader might wish Glaucon or Adeimantus or someone might notice the issue and speak up.

Now, if we ask each representative of the kinds of life which is the happiest, each will insist that their own is. We have no reason to doubt the sincerity of their testimony: each believes their life is more pleasant than the others. It is crucial here to appreciate Socrates' caveat: the dispute is 'not about which way of living is finer or more shameful or better or worse, but about which is more pleasant and less painful' (9.581e). That is, the dispute is not a moral or normative one: the philosopher is *not* arguing that while the money-lover's life is more pleasant the philosopher's own pleasures are better, higher quality pleasures (as John Stuart Mill suggests in *Utilitarianism*); the philosopher asserts the descriptive, quantitative claim that the pleasures of reason are *more* pleasant than those of spirit or appetite.

A relativist or subjectivist will suggest that the dispute cannot be settled, shrugging and rhetorically asking, 'Who's to say?' Socrates, though, does not think that the relativist's question is rhetorical and offers an answer: the competent judge is to say. While it is true that each of the three offers testimony that their life is most pleasant, only the philosopher offers *expert* testimony, so to speak, since only the philosopher is really competent to judge the issue. Judging competently and indeed judging well is a matter of 'experience, reason, and argument' (9.582a), Socrates tells us. The philosopher clearly has the advantage as regards reason, since reason governs their soul. And they clearly have the edge as regards argument: argument is the instrument by which we judge, and 'argument is a philosopher's instrument most of all' (9.582d). As for experience, Socrates argues that the philosopher alone has experienced all three kinds of pleasure: the philosopher has enjoyed the pleasures that come with having one's desires and appetites satisfied and with being honored, but neither the honor-lover nor the appetitive money-lover has any experience of the pleasure of knowing the Forms. Thus, Socrates argues, since the philosopher alone is a competent judge, we should accept their verdict: the philosophical, aristocratic life, which is the just life, is the happiest of the three.

Many readers will be less confident about this than Socrates seems to be. First, some will doubt that grasping the Forms exhausts the possibilities for intellectual pleasure. It is not as though investment bankers and plumbers do not find their work intellectually challenging and rewarding. While they no doubt enjoy being well compensated, many also enjoy the challenges of putting together complex financial instruments and solving construction problems. Although one would hope that intellectual snobbery is not at work here, one might well fear that it is, leading Plato to downgrade not only the manual arts but also intellectual arts not aimed at abstract knowing.

A second concern focuses on that claim that the philosopher has experienced the pleasure of being honored and thus is a better judge than the honor-lover. This is difficult to square with the attitudes towards philosophy that Socrates dealt with in Book VI, where he conceded that people who think that philosophers are vicious or useless 'seem [...] to speak the truth' (6.487d). It turned out, of course, that the public mistakenly takes sophists to be philosophers and thus that the 'slander [against] philosophy is unjust' (6.497a). But even so, in the very act of defending philosophy against this slander Socrates gives evidence that slander is afoot and thus that philosophers know very little of being honored. Remember that Glaucon imagined the idea of philosopher-kings would be met not with relief but with people 'snatch[ing] any available weapon, and mak[ing] a determined rush at you, ready to do terrible things' (5.474a), so it is not difficult to doubt Socrates' claim that philosophers are well acquainted with being honored. Nor does his claim that 'honor comes to each of them, provided that he accomplishes his aim' (9.582c) encourage confidence. In the last chapter we discussed the difference between the external good of being honored and the internal good of being honorable or worthy of honor. Indeed, in defending philosophy against slander, Socrates argues that philosophers—the genuine philosophers he tries to distinguish from the frauds in Books V, VI, and VII—are honorable, but he does not (and seemingly cannot) show that they have in fact been honored. He needs to establish the latter, descriptive claim that philosophers are actually regarded, not the former, normative claim about what sort of treatment they deserve or are entitled to.

So there is reason to doubt the cogency of the second argument. As usual, we might agree with its conclusion—that the just life is happier and preferable—but regard this argument as failing to justify it. That is the bad news. The good news is that, as noted above, Socrates regards the next argument as 'the greatest and most decisive' (9.583b) of the three. Let us see what it has to offer.

Argument #3: The Metaphysics of Pleasure (9.583b–588a)

The third argument, which I call 'the Metaphysics of Pleasure Argument', is the philosophically most interesting of the three, arguing that the pleasures of reason are more pleasant than the pleasures of spirit or appetite because they are more real; the latter seem the result of 'shadow-painting (ἐσκιαγραφημένη [*eskiagraphêmenê*])' (9.583b) by comparison, the sorts of things we expect to encounter on the wall of the Cave. It is also the philosophically most precarious, since it presumes the reality of the Platonic Forms. I will go a little out of order in presenting the argument and make the existential sense of the verb 'to be' more apparent. Here is the heart of the argument, as Socrates makes it (with a little help from Glaucon):

> And isn't that which is more [real], and is filled with things that are more [real], really more filled than that which is less [real], and is filled with things that are less [real]?
>
> Of course.

Therefore, if being filled with what is appropriate to our nature is pleasure, that which is more filled with things that are more [real] enjoys more really and truly a more true pleasure, while that which partakes of things that are less [real] is less truly and surely filled and partakes of a less trustworthy and less true pleasure.

That is absolutely inevitable. (9.585d-e)

At the heart of the argument is an understanding of pleasure as the result of being appropriately filled. Think of the pleasure a good, simple meal affords when you are hungry, or the pleasure of enjoying—i.e., being filled with—good music. Too much filling, be it too much food or music that is too loud, does not yield pleasure, since pleasure requires *appropriate* filling. Since what is more real is more filling and what is more filling is more pleasant, it follows that what is more real is more pleasant. But since the Forms are more real than any particulars, they are more filling, and thus the pleasure of knowing the Forms—which is the distinctive pleasure of the reason-governed, just person—is greater than the pleasures of being honored or having one's appetites satisfied. Stated in premise-conclusion form, the argument looks like this:

P1   What is more real is more filling.

P2   What is more filling is more pleasant.

P3   The objects of the rational pleasures are more real than the objects of the spirited pleasures and the appetitive pleasures.

C1   Therefore, rational pleasures are more filling than spirited and appetitive pleasures. (From P1, P3)

C2   Therefore, rational pleasures are more pleasant than spirited and appetitive pleasures. (From P2, C1)

P4   Each kind of life has a distinctive pleasure, determined by which part of the soul rules: the just person's pleasures are rational pleasures; the unjust person's pleasures are appetitive pleasures.

C3   Therefore, the just life is more pleasant than the unjust life. (From C2, P4)

C4   Therefore, the just life is happier than the unjust life. (From C3)

As with the previous argument, it is important to bear in mind Socrates' caveat that the argument concerns quantity, not quality: it is not an argument 'about which way of living is finer [...] or better [...] but about which is more pleasant' (9.581e). The argument concerns which life contains the most pleasure, not a ranking of the pleasures in terms of quality, where, for example, intellectual pleasures are superior to appetitive pleasures. It would not be unreasonable for Socrates to insist that the just person's pleasures, being pleasures of the best part of the soul, are better, higher quality pleasures, but to concede that rational pleasures are not as pleasant as appetitive pleasures. But Socrates does *not* make this argument. Instead, he argues that rational pleasures are more pleasant than appetitive pleasures. So the Metaphysics of Pleasure Argument implies that the pleasures of doing philosophy or solving a calculus problem are more pleasant than the pleasure of sex. And that is going to strike many readers as preposterous.

I think Plato is fully aware of how preposterous this seems, and he has a response ready. This response actually comes *before* the argument as I have stated it, hence the 'going out of order' I mentioned above. Plato's response is that while it *seems* that appetitive pleasures are more pleasant than rational pleasures, this is an illusion and not how things really are.

Contrary versus Contradictory Opposites

This is the point, I think, of the analogy he draws between pleasure and space. There is an up, a down, and a middle in space (Plato seems to be thinking of *space* as *place*, as a large container or room). If I am down and start ascending, I might mistakenly think I am at *up* when in fact I am merely at *middle*. Someone who is at *up* and then descends might think they are at *down* when they are at *middle*. If we meet, we might disagree about where we are, neither of us realizing that we at *middle*. Just as there is an up, a down, and a middle in space, Socrates suggests that there is pleasure, pain, and a neutral state of calm. And we regularly, wrongly take up/down and pleasure/pain to be contradictory opposites when in fact they are contrary opposites. A pair of opposites is contradictory when at least and at most one of them must be true or apply in a given situation; a pair is contrary when at most one must be true, but it might be that neither is true or applies. Consider *hot* and *cold*. They are clearly opposites, but they are contrary opposites: while at most one of them applies to a given object, it may be that neither does. The place where you are reading this book might be hot or it might be cold, but it might be neither: it might be cool, warm, tepid, chilly, balmy—even room temperature. (Here we should remember the Opposition Principle from Book IV: if both of a pair of opposites applies, this suggests that the thing they apply to has parts. If I am both hot and cold, part of me is hot and part is cold, or I am hot now and then cold in an instant, etc.) While hot and cold are contrary opposites, cold and not-cold are contradictory opposites: everything is either cold or not-cold. Tucson in July? Not cold. Eau Claire in January? Cold. The number twelve? Not cold: numbers have no temperature, so they go in the not-cold column. On a well-written true-false question, 'true' and 'false' are contradictory opposites: at least and at most one of them is correct. But, other things being equal, 'true' and 'false' are contrary opposites: many things are neither true nor false. Questions are neither true nor false (although the answers to them might be true or false); exclamations ('dang!') are neither true nor false; and of course non-linguistic items—picnic tables, peanut butter, pencils, etc.—are neither true nor false, since they make no assertions (though of course they can be what assertions are about).

Many of us make mistakes when it comes to opposites. We think that 'helping' and 'harming' are contradictory opposites when in fact they are contrary: action can make a thing better off (helping) or worse off (harming) or leave it neutral. The good-hearted but dim-witted Ricky Bobby of *Talladega Nights* lives his life mistakenly thinking that *first* and *last* are contradictory opposites: 'If you ain't first, you're last!' he insists.[3] With the help of his father (his confusion's source), Ricky later comes to see the folly of this "wisdom". Plato's suggestion, I think, is that most of us take pleasure and pain to be contradictory opposites when in fact they are contraries. After a week in bed with the flu, the first day of feeling normal again *seems* pleasant, but it is really only not painful: I am mistaking the neutral state of calm for pleasure. After an exhilarating, inspiring vacation a return to normal is a real downer, but

---

3   *Talladega Nights: The Ballad of Ricky Bobby,* dir. by Adam McKay (Sony Pictures, 2006).

I am probably just mistaking the neutral state of calm for pain, having been experiencing so much pleasure.

Optical and Hedonic Illusions

A person who is 'inexperienced in what is really and truly up, down, and in the middle' (9.584e) will regularly make mistakes about where they are since they will mistake up and down to be contradictory opposites. And similarly, 'those who are inexperienced in the truth [and] have unsound opinions' (9.584e) will regularly make mistakes about what they are experiencing. Here's the catch: becoming experienced in the truth and having sound opinions will not ensure that we are no longer subject to illusions about where we are or what we are feeling: it still feels like I am at up when I am only at middle, and this still feels like pleasure when in fact it is only non-pain. But being experienced in the truth and having sound opinions I can now know that things are not as they appear to me. Consider the famous Müller-Lyer illusion, below in Fig. 4:

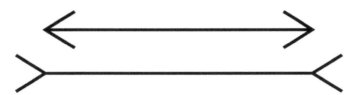

Fig. 4. Müller-Lyer illusion. Photograph by Fibonacci (2007), Wikimedia, CC BY-SA 3.0, https://commons.wikimedia.org/w/index. php?curid=1792612)

It seems to be psychologically impossible to see the line segments as the same length: try as we might, the lower one just looks longer. If we measure the lines, as in Fig. 5, we can see that they are the same length:

Fig. 5. Müller-Lyer illusion. Photograph by Fibonacci (2007), Wikimedia, CC BY-SA 3.0, https://commons.wikimedia.org/w/index. php?curid=1792612)

Even so, when I look back at Fig. 4, I cannot see them as being the same length—I assume readers have the same experience. Our senses deceive us: what *seems* to be the case is not what *is* the case: This deception is persistent and not correctable by reasoning and measurement in that we see the lines as having different lengths even when we know that they are the same length. That is what makes it an optical illusion.

The philosopher Jessica Moss argues that Plato is suggesting that just as we are prone to optical illusions, we are also prey to *hedonic* illusions: illusions about pleasure.[4] Of course sexual pleasure *seems* more pleasant than rational pleasure, just as the bottom line *seems* longer than the top line: there is no way to perceive the comparative lengths of the lines accurately, just as there is no way to perceive the comparative amounts of the pleasures accurately. Measuring the lines tells us that our visual perception tricks us, just as rational argument tells us that our hedonic perception tricks us. 'Calculating, measuring, and weighting are the work of the rational part of the soul' (10.602d), Socrates will tell us in Book X. And of course, 'argument is a philosopher's instrument most of all' (9.582d), since it is the rational instrument *par excellence.* Reason cannot alter our visual experience of the lines, making us see them as having the same length—but it can remind us that our perception is faulty and that they are in fact the same length. And similarly, reason cannot make us experience rational pleasures as more pleasant than appetitive pleasures, it can tell us that they are. Reason cannot make us experientially immune to optical or hedonic illusions: we will continue to experience them. But it can render us rationally immune to them:

4   Jessica Moss, 'Pleasure and Illusion in Plato', *Philosophy and Phenomenological Research*, 72 (2006), 503–35, https://doi.org/10.1111/j.1933–1592.2006.tb00582.x

we can know that they are systematically misleading and that the way things *appear* is not the way things really *are*.

The upshot of all this is that, appearances to the contrary notwithstanding, the just person's life is happier than the unjust person's—in fact, it is 729 times happier, if Socrates' geometric 'proof' is to be believed. The tyrant, he reasons, is, counting himself, 'three times removed' from the oligarch: tyrant–democrat–oligarch. And the oligarch is three times removed from the aristocrat. Three times three is nine, which cubed—that is, three-dimensionalized—makes the aristocrat 729 times happier than the tyrant. As with the 'perfect number' at the start of Book VIII, I am not sure that Plato intends this to be taken seriously; I am inclined to take it as a joke, and, like most philosophical jokes it is not especially funny. I suggest that we think of it as Plato's way of suggesting that the contest between the just and unjust lives is not even close: the just life is *way* happier than the unjust life.

The Metaphysical Elevator and the Metaphysics of Pleasure

As many readers will expect, there is a major worry about the Metaphysics of Pleasure Argument. It is not a *logical* worry, since the Metaphysics of Pleasure Argument is valid: its conclusion must be true if its premises are true. But its soundness—that is, the question of whether its premises are actually true, given that it is valid—is another matter. P3, that the objects of the rational pleasures—the Forms—are more real than the objects of the spirited pleasures and the appetitive pleasures—concrete particulars—is not obviously true, and indeed for many readers it is obviously not true. P3 is true only if Plato's Metaphysical Elevator goes all the way to Level Four, where the Forms are not only mind-independently real but are *more real* than the many particular things that are instances of them. Even going to Level Three, where the Forms are mind-independently real, is not enough to make P3 true, and many readers will balk at going even to this level. More readers, I suspect, will get off the Elevator at the second floor, insisting that the Forms are human constructs and that the concrete particular things are more real than the Forms so conceived, since the Forms so conceived are mind-dependent entities while the particulars are not. For these readers, P3 should be replaced with:

P3*   The objects of the appetitive pleasures are more real than the objects of the spirited pleasures and the rational pleasures.

This yields these conclusions:

C1*   Therefore, appetitive pleasures are more filling than spirited and rational pleasures.   (From P1, P3*)

C2*   Therefore, appetitive pleasures are more pleasant than spirited and rational pleasures.   (From P2, C1*)

This better fits with the commonsensical views that eating a donut is more pleasurable, because more filling, than grasping the Form of the donut and thus understanding the essence of donut-ness, and that sexual pleasure is more pleasant than philosophical pleasure. Perhaps Socrates was wrong to focus on quantity rather than quality. Many readers might concede that while appetitive pleasures are *more pleasant* than rational pleasures, rational pleasures are *better, higher quality* pleasures than appetitive pleasures, as they appeal to our higher nature as rational creatures. But this is expressly *not* what Socrates is arguing.

Even readers inclined to think that Plato's theory of the Forms is right and thus to take the Metaphysical Elevator all the way to the fourth floor should concede that, at least in the *Republic*, Plato has not provided good reasons to believe in the Forms. The argument that supports his two-worlds metaphysics, the Powers Argument, is logically invalid, and even if this invalidity can be fixed, we have good reason to doubt that knowledge and belief have different objects. This casts a long, dark shadow across the *Republic*.

Socrates regards the Metaphysics of Pleasure Argument as 'the greatest and most decisive' (9.583b) in answering the *Republic*'s second question, but it depends for its soundness on the problematic Powers Argument. So even if we agree with Socrates that the just life is happier—perhaps even 729 times happier—than the unjust life, we will have to concede that he has not really given Glaucon and Adeimantus what they asked of him, a justification for this belief.

Argument #3½: 'an image of the soul in words' (9.588b–590e)

Given the dependence of the Metaphysics of Pleasure Argument on the Powers Argument, things look bleak for Socrates' view that the just life is happier than the unjust life. But Plato follows up the philosophically abstract Metaphysics of Pleasure Argument with an intuitive metaphor that he does not officially count as an argument—hence the '½'—but which seems more powerful than the supposedly 'decisive' argument he just gave, and not merely because it does not depend in any way on the contentious metaphysics of the Forms. To argue against the view that the unjust but seemingly just life is happier, Socrates offers 'an image of the soul in words' (9.588b). Perhaps this is Plato's way of indicating that he understands that the Metaphysics of Pleasure Argument will not persuade skeptics unconvinced of the reality of the Forms. Or perhaps it is a subtle way of reminding us that we are in the Cave, where images and shadows are the cognitive coin of the realm.

Imagine first a 'multicolored beast' (9.588c) with many heads, some the heads of gentle animals, others more savage. 'Multicolored' translates ποικίλος [*poikilos*], a nod to the multicolored garment that is worn by the defective democratic *polis* in Book VIII. Then imagine a lion, smaller than the beast, and last a human being, smallest of the three. Then join these three so that they 'grow together naturally' (9.588d): the resulting creature is not mere artifice, a jumble of separate parts having nothing to do with each other, but something that functions as an integrated organism. Finally, cloak them in a human exterior, so anyone aware only of the exterior will think the creature a human being.

The analogy is fairly straightforward: the multiform beast represents the appetites, the lion represents the spirited part of the soul, and the inner human being represents reason. Now, Socrates argues, when someone who maintains that injustice is more profitable, better for you than justice, what they are telling you, is that you are better off feeding the beast, starving the human, and getting the lion to do the beast's bidding. But no one would think that is prudent. To claim that the unjust life is happier implies something false—namely, that you are better off feeding the voracious, multiform beast and starving reason—so it follows that the unjust life is *not* happier than the just life.

It is perhaps surprising that Socrates argues that one should not starve the beast, but earlier he indicated that the philosopher 'neither starves nor feasts his appetites' (9.571e) in his nighttime ritual to keep his dreams free of lawless, unnecessary appetites. Nor should we let the beast's different parts attack and kill each other. Though Plato would likely agree with Immanuel Kant's view that 'it must be [...] the universal wish of every rational being to be altogether free of them'[5] our appetites are not going anywhere, at least not as long as we inhabit a body. The beast is part of us. So we should bring our parts into harmony with each other, as much as possible, 'accustoming them to each other and making them friendly' (9.589a). In living a just life we tend the beast as a farmer cares for their animals, domesticating some and separating and containing the feral ones.

It is a compelling picture in many ways, but Socrates takes it even further. Someone who lives unjustly is enslaving the best part of himself, reason, to feed the worst, appetite. When the financial rewards are great enough, that might seem a bargain worth striking. But no one, Socrates argues, would enslave his children to 'savage and evil men' (9.589d); there is no amount of money that would make *that* a good deal: 'it would not profit him, no matter how much gold he got' (9.589e). Why, then, are we willing to treat ourselves so poorly, in ways we cannot imagine treating those we love? It is a fascinating insight. What philosophers sometimes call 'self-other asymmetry' usually involves our problematically treating ourselves *better* than we treat others. Virtues and moral reasons are often correctives to this egoistic tendency to think our interests count for more than the interests of others. While some advocate altruism, the view that our interests count for *less* than the interests of others, correcting egoism requires only the egalitarian view that everyone's interests have the same weight—that self and other are symmetric. What is so interesting about Plato's point here is the suggestion that the self-other asymmetry at work when we are trying 'to determine which whole way of life would make living most worthwhile for each of us' (1.344e) is one in which we give our interests, at least our true interests, *less* weight than we should.

I suspect that this will resonate with many readers. If I have promised a friend to meet for an early morning bike ride, it is extremely unlikely

---

5   Immanuel Kant, *Groundwork of the Metaphysics of Morals*, p. 40 [*Ak*. 4:428].

that I will roll over and go back to sleep when the alarm wakes me. But if it is a promise I have made only to myself, well, if it is a cold and dark morning there is a decent chance that I will turn the alarm off and stay in bed. If I would never casually blow off a commitment made to a friend, why would I do so when it is one I have made to myself? If reason fully governed my soul, my appetites for sloth and comfort would have been tamed by reason and its ally, spirit. Readers tempted to judge themselves harshly on this issue should take some comfort from the fact that Marcus Aurelius, the great Stoic and indeed the Emperor of Rome, often wanted to stay in bed, too, and tried to have arguments at the ready to rouse himself (*Meditations* 5.1).

One great advantage of Socrates' analogy is that it does not presuppose the problematic theory of the Forms. It is simple and intuitive, as the best analogies are. It is not without objection, however. As mentioned much earlier, the great eighteenth-century Scottish philosopher David Hume thought that philosophers regularly overstated the claims of reason; Hume thought that reason was but the slave of the passions, so he would be skeptical of the ideal person Plato has sketched here. So too would Epicurus, whose taxonomy of desire we explored in the last chapter. Neither of these philosophers advocated egoism and injustice, but neither had the lofty view of reason that one finds in Plato in particular and in the Western philosophical tradition in general. It is worth noting that much contemporary psychology sides with Hume and Epicurus against Plato and most of the Western philosophical tradition. Reason, the eminent social psychologist Jonathan Haidt argues, is like someone riding an elephant; only a fool could think they are in charge of the elephant. But they can learn the elephant's ways, learn that there is wisdom in the emotions, and use their rationality to guide the elephant toward the goals it naturally has.

So even if we are skeptical of the role Plato assigns to reason, we might find a modified version of this analogical argument plausible, one in which the inner human being is constituted not by pure reason but by emotions such as compassion, care, and love. And we might well wonder, too, if what Hume called a sensible knave—someone who generally acts justly but cheats when they can do so without detection—would be persuaded, and indeed if *we* should be persuaded, that the just person's life is more pleasant than the sensible knave's. Socrates' argument seems plausible against the tyrant but perhaps this is only because a reason-governed philosopher-king will always fare better than the manic basket of addictions, neuroses, and psychoses that is the tyrant. But how a philosopher-king would fare against someone who is decent but cuts corners (perhaps when the harm he does is not significant and the gain to him vastly outweighs it) is another matter. Socrates insists that the unjust person's injustice can remain undiscovered only for so long, and while we can think of examples confirming this claim—off the top of my head, I offer Lance Armstrong, Bernie Madoff, and any number of politicians who are brought down by scandals—it is worth noting that this is spurious evidence for Socrates' claim. That we can list unjust people whose injustice has been discovered does not provide reasons for thinking that there cannot be unjust people whose injustice remains undiscovered. It may well be that the just person and the sensible knave have incompatible conceptions of happiness.

Paternalism (9.590d)

So the just life, which for Plato is the life in which reason governs the soul, is significantly happier than the unjust life. It may not always be the happiest possible life, since, as we have seen, living in an unjust or a non-just *polis* precludes full happiness. So justice, while necessary for happiness, is not by itself sufficient for it (something Stoicism, which began around 300 BCE and which is currently enjoying a renaissance in our troubled age, disagrees with, taking virtue to be sufficient for happiness).

We have noted on several occasions Plato's insistence that 'the majority cannot be philosophic' (6.494a). Most of us are not capable of grasping the Form of the good, Plato thinks, so most of us are not capable of acquiring the personal virtue of wisdom. We may have true beliefs about what is best for our souls, but by our natures we lack the capacity for *knowledge* in this area. But if that is the case, how can the non-philosophers among us be happy? It seems that most of us are doomed to live unhappy lives. Is there any way to escape this pessimistic conclusion?

There is, Plato thinks—though his solution is unlikely to be attractive to most readers. Since most of us cannot be ruled by our own power of reason, it is best that we be ruled by the philosopher-king's (and -queen's) reason:

> Therefore, to insure that someone like that is ruled by something similar to what rules the best person, we say that he ought to be the slave of that best person who has a divine ruler within himself. It is not to harm the slave that we say he must be ruled [...] but because it is better for everyone to be ruled by divine reason, preferably within himself and his own, otherwise imposed from without, so that as far as possible all will be alike and friends, governed by the same thing. (9.590c–d)

Even if Plato means 'slave' (δοῦλος [*doulos*]) only metaphorically, many if not most readers will reject this out of hand. Most readers, I suspect, are liberals—not in the contemporary American political sense of voting Democratic instead of Republican, but in the philosophical sense of valuing liberty over wellbeing. Paternalists prioritize wellbeing over liberty where the two conflict, holding that interfering with another person's liberty or autonomy is justified if the interference benefits the person being interfered with. Philosophical liberals, by contrast, typically hold that the only justification for interfering with someone's liberty is to prevent harm to another person; if my conduct harms only me or is harmless but regarded as immoral, the liberal argues, neither the state nor another person is justified in interfering. Of course, if I am not in my right mind or if I am lacking vital information, most liberals will countenance temporary interference. If I do not know that the bridge ahead is out, the liberal might try to stop me from bicycling across it— but only to make sure that I am aware of this materially relevant fact or that my judgment is not impaired. If I know that the bridge is out— for me, the whole point is to try to jump across the missing span—the liberal will not think interfering is justified.

It is not surprising that Plato endorses paternalism. But most Americans, I think, take liberalism (in the philosophical sense) for granted, at least to a significant degree. Most of us, I suspect, share John Stuart Mill's view that 'the only purpose for which power can rightfully be exercised over any member of a civilized community, against his will, is to prevent harm to others'.[6] One of Mill's arguments

---

6   John Stuart Mill, *On Liberty*, ed. by Elizabeth Rappaport (Indianapolis: Hackett Publishing, 1978), p. 9.

for this view is that paternalism does not work: given the centrality of autonomy and spontaneity to the conception of happiness many of us share, outside interference for our own good will likely backfire, since the resentment we feel at being interfered with will outweigh the good that the interference does. We can probably think of cases where Mill is mistaken, especially where the benefit done is significant and the interference is minimal, as in seatbelt laws. Many readers will think Mill's argument is beside the point, holding that interfering with a competent adult for that adult's benefit is wrong in itself, regardless of any beneficial consequences, since paternalism manifests a failure of respect. We interfere with our and even others' children when doing so is required to protect the children from themselves. But adults are another matter entirely.

We will not adjudicate this dispute between liberalism and paternalism here; I raise it largely to give readers a framework and vocabulary with which to agree or disagree with Plato. To justify the belief that, fundamentally, liberty trumps wellbeing, may prove more difficult than even die-hard liberals imagine. And it may be that our shared ideology shapes our views on questions like this in a non-rational way. Many readers are familiar with Patrick Henry's saying 'Give me liberty or give me death!', and many of us know that New Hampshire's license plate reads 'Live Free or Die' (which, admittedly, makes Wisconsin's motto, 'America's Dairyland', sound pretty tame). But, like Glaucon and Adeimantus, our task as rational creatures is to think through these core values and to try to find good reasons to justify what we already believe. Of course, we may fail, or we may change our minds, perhaps thinking that the liberal, individualistic conception of happiness that grounds our objections to Plato's paternalism is, if not 'a silly, adolescent idea of happiness' (5.466b), one we no longer fully endorse after reflection.

Plato's paternalism is fueled by, among other things, his anti-egalitarian belief that most people are incapable of wisdom as well as his highly demanding conception of what counts as knowledge. Some readers will be skeptical that we can ever *know* what is best, in Plato's sense, insisting that the best we can do is to have justified beliefs about how to live, and that views very much at odds with each other might be justified. Such readers may insist that the intellectual virtues of humility and open-mindedness are crucial to thinking about how to live well, and that while Plato has challenged them to think through some of their fundamental values and presuppositions, he has not succeeded in convincing them that those values are mistaken and those presuppositions are false.

At best, Plato's arguments seem to provide a reason for those who already find themselves in agreement with their conclusion—but that does not render wrestling with the *Republic* a worthless, circular enterprise. Even if one's reasons for living justly will not convince the Thrasymachuses of the world, it is valuable to ensure that our beliefs form as consistent a set as possible. Most of us, I suspect, are more like Glaucon and Adeimantus than we are like Thrasymachus (though we probably all have a bit of him in us), who want Socrates to show them that their belief that the just life is happier is justified or at the very least not foolish, wishful thinking. It would be nice if egoists found these reasons persuasive, but that may be asking too much of philosophy. Plato and Socrates thought philosophy could do this, but we have seen over and over that their arguments fall well short of the mark and that only people who share their fundamental assumptions (e.g., about the Forms) will find their arguments persuasive.

Even so, those of us who do not share those fundamental assumptions can find their arguments intriguing and worthy of the time and attention of reflective people who take seriously the question of how to live their lives.

Some Suggestions for Further Reading

Readers interested in exploring the philosophy of friendship will find no better place to start than with Books 8 and 9 of Aristotle's *Nicomachean Ethics,* which they will find, along with other excellent readings, in *Other Selves: Philosophers on Friendship,* ed. by Michael Pakaluk (Indianapolis: Hackett Publishing, 1991). Readers will find Laurence Thomas' excellent essay, 'Friendship and Other Loves' and others in *Friendship: A Philosophical Reader,* ed. by Neera Badhwar (Ithaca: Cornell University Press, 1993).

Readers interested in Mill's distinction between higher and lower pleasures will find it discussed in Chapter Two of John Stuart Mill,

Utilitarianism, 2nd ed., ed. by George Sher (Indianapolis: Hackett Publishing, 2002), pp. 8–11.

Matthew Crawford, *Shop Class as Soulcraft* (New York: Penguin Books, 2010) is an excellent discussion of, among other things, the role reason plays in the 'manual arts', offering a powerful antidote to Plato's views from a Ph.D. philosopher who repairs vintage motorcycles for a living.

Readers interested in a leading psychologist's take on the role reason plays in a happy life should start with Jonathan Haidt, *The Happiness Hypothesis: Finding Modern Truth in Ancient Wisdom* (New York: Basic Books, 2006).

Readers interested in philosophical or legal liberalism would do well to start with John Stuart Mill, *On Liberty*, ed. by Elizabeth Rappaport (Indianapolis: Hackett Publishing, 1978). For an interesting collection of essays on paternalism, readers might have a look at *Paternalism*, ed. by Rolf Sartorius (Minneapolis: University of Minnesota Press, 1984).

Readers interested in a brief musical exploration of the multicolored beast who dwells within should listen to Nick Lowe, 'The Beast in Me', on *Quiet Please... The New Best of Nick Lowe* (Yep Roc Records, 2009).

Muse tuning two kitharai. Detail of the interior from an Attic
white-ground cup (c. 470–460 BCE). Photograph by Jastrow (2006),
Wikimedia, Public Domain, https://commons.wikimedia.org/wiki/
File:Muse_lyre_Louvre_CA482.jpg#/media/File:Muse_lyre_Louvre_
CA482.jpg

14. Are We There Yet?
Tying up Loose Ends in Book X

Book IX ends with Socrates telling Glaucon that if the *polis* one lives in is far from ideal, even if the ideal *polis* exists only in theory but not in reality, one can still 'make himself its citizen' (9.592b), and thus learn to live justly in an unjust or a non-just world. It would be a fine place to end the *Republic,* but Plato has other ideas. Three of them, in fact.

The 'Ancient Quarrel' between Poetry and Philosophy (10.595a–608b)

The first of these is tying up a loose end regarding poetry in the ideal *polis.* Since the restrictions on poetic form and content developed in Books II and III preceded the division of the soul in Book IV, Socrates thinks it would now be fruitful to revisit the status of poetry, armed with an account (*logos*) of the soul (*psuché*)—a psychology—he lacked earlier. He argues that the three-part soul further confirms the earlier conclusion that 'imitative [...] poetry should be altogether excluded' (10.595a) from the ideal *polis.*

Readers who think they have misremembered the earlier discussion should feel free to indulge in an 'it's not me, it's you' moment, for it is *Socrates* whose memory seems faulty. Earlier, Socrates allowed imitations of 'the words or actions of a good man' (3.396c) and of 'someone engaged in peaceful, unforced, voluntary action [...] acting with moderation and self-control' (3.399ab), not to mention modes and rhythms 'that would suitably imitate the tone and rhythm of a courageous person who is

   https://doi.org/10.11647/OBP.0229.14

active in battle' (3.399a). A lot has happened in the *Republic* since Book III, so perhaps we can forgive Socrates' misremembering his earlier view. It may be that Plato is poking a little fun at Socrates here, for at least half a dozen times in Book VI we are told one must possess the intellectual virtue of having a good memory to be a true philosopher.

Socrates' target is narrower than is frequently claimed. He is not arguing against poetry (or, even more broadly, art) in general but rather against imitative poetry—and indeed it is even narrower than this: he wants to exclude 'poetry that aims at pleasure and imitation' (10.607c) from the ideal *polis,* which would leave room for imitative poetry that aims not at pleasure but at moral improvement. The ideal city *can,* then, 'employ a more austere and less pleasure-giving poet and storyteller, one who would imitate the speech of a decent person' (3.398a). In arguing that would-be guardians should not be imitative (μιμητικός [*mimêtikos*]) (3.394e), Socrates is really arguing that guardians should not be *imitatively promiscuous*: they should not be able, willing, or disposed to imitate any and every type of character, since this would prevent them from cultivating the sense of shame and disgust at dishonorable action that is the basis of good character. Since 'imitations practiced from youth become part of [one's] nature and settle into habits of gesture, voice, and thought' (3.395d), Socrates is very leery of imitative promiscuity.

That all poetry inspired by 'the pleasure-seeking Muse' (10.607a) must be excluded from the ideal *polis* is a conclusion that Socrates comes to reluctantly. He loves poetry, especially Homer, and is loath to live without it. There is no Homer or Hesiod, no Aeschylus or Sophocles or Euripides in the ideal *polis.* Instead, 'hymns to the gods and eulogies to good people are the only poetry we can admit into our city' (10.607a)— which, interestingly, is the only kind of poetry one encounters in the first, rustic city (2.372b). It is as though Socrates looks longingly at a copy of the *Iliad,* weepily confessing, 'I can't quit you'. But quit it he must, for his commitment to philosophy is a commitment to going 'whatever direction the argument blows us' (3.394d), even when we do not like the destination or find the winds too strong. We might expect Glaucon, who objected to life in the rustic first city because the food was too simple, to object to the absence of a key cultural and aesthetic staple, but he finds Socrates' arguments so compelling that he makes no objections to the restricted poetic diet Socrates prescribes.

Our task as readers is to determine if we find Socrates' arguments as compelling as he and his audience do. Since the arguments are overlapping and interrelated, separating them into distinct arguments is somewhat artificial, but doing so aids in clarity, so I will divide the arguments into three.

The Metaphysical Argument: Art Merely Makes Copies of Copies, and Thus is not Worth Taking Seriously

I have dubbed the first argument 'metaphysical' since the Forms play a significant role in it. Perhaps surprisingly for an argument meant to support a conclusion about imitative poetry, Socrates focuses on painting more than poetry in the metaphysical argument. But we will see that painting more clearly makes the point he wants to establish against poetry.

All beds, Socrates argues, have in common the Form of the bed itself: that essence that makes them beds rather than chairs or knives or sheep. Any particular bed that one might sleep in is a spatio-temporal copy of this Form, just as the shadows on the Cave wall are copies of the artifacts held before the fire, and just as those artifacts are ultimately themselves copies of the Forms that inhabit the sunlit intelligible world above. So someone who paints a bed is making a copy of something that is itself a copy. The painter is imitating the appearance of a bed, and indeed how it appears from a particular vantage point, not the reality or being of the bed: 'painting [...] is an imitation of appearances [...] [not] of truth' (10.598b).

Where the painter represents objects, the poet represents actions, but the argument is the same for both: paintings and poems are too metaphysically thin, too much like the shadows and reflections one sees on the wall of the Cave. 'Imitation is a kind of game', Socrates says, 'and not something to be taken seriously' (10.602b). There is no hint here of the danger lurking in the games we play, as there is elsewhere in the *Republic* (e.g., 4.424d, 7.539b, 8.558b). His point is that anyone who could construct a bed would spend his or her time on these metaphysically more substantial objects; and anyone who could philosophically understand the Form of bedness would spend their time on this metaphysically more substantial task. Only someone insufficiently skilled in either would waste their time on something so trivial as making art.

Two recurring themes in Socrates' animadversions against imitative art are worth bringing out here. The first is that he shows little if any interest in artistic skill. On the one hand, this makes sense, given his metaphysical views. But on the other, he simply ignores the skill required to make copies of copies. Whatever one's metaphysics, *trompe l'oeil* paintings and modern photo-realism are impressive in and of themselves; they need not be written off as 'trickery' (10.602d) and bogus magic. A second, related theme is his lack of interest in the joy of artistic creation. This is perhaps a particular instance of a more general disregard for the importance of play in a well-lived and happy life. It is ironic, given the artistic care and skill with which Plato constructed the *Republic*, that its protagonist would be so uninterested in artistic creation. Earlier we criticized Socrates' narrowness in asserting that there are three primary kinds of people ('philosophic, victory-loving, and profit-loving' (9.581c)), and here we can see yet another type to add to the list: artists, who devote their lives to artistic creation. Perhaps some of this emanates from a contempt for 'those who work with their own hands' (8.565a), itself an odd thought from someone who is himself a stonemason. But this may be Plato's upper-class snobbery more than anything. Artistic readers who have made it this far in the *Republic* often get righteously—and rightfully—indignant or shake their heads in pity at this foolishness. It is not just that Socrates is not interested in and does not revere the *products* of artistic creation, but that he is not interested in the *process* of artistic creation and indeed denigrates it by likening it to walking around with a mirror (10.596d). Thus it is no surprise that he dismisses most painting and poetry as trivial wastes of time. One need not fully agree with Schiller's dictum that one is fully human only in play to think Plato is missing something important here.[1] Play's value is thoroughly instrumental for Plato, useful as a means of moral education, but in itself possessing no intrinsic value. Schiller—and many readers, I suspect—would disagree.

---

1   Friedrich Schiller, *On the Aesthetic Education of Man*, trans. by Keith Tribe, ed. by Alexander Schmidt (New York: Penguin Books, 2016), p. 45 [Letter 15].

The Epistemological Argument: Artists Literally Do Not Know What They Are Talking and Painting about

Given the way metaphysics and epistemology are fused in the *Republic,* it should be no surprise that the next argument is intertwined with the metaphysical argument. Here, the worry is epistemological: that artists do not need knowledge of what they are imitating in order to imitate it. While it is true that the imitator needs to know how to imitate that appearance, such *know-how* is rather trivial, Socrates thinks, given the metaphysical thinness of what it results in.

To make his epistemological point, Socrates contrasts the user, the maker, and the imitator of a flute. An expert flute-player knows what a good flute should sound like and what makes it play well. (Here, Socrates uses 'know' in an ordinary sense, not the technical sense he established in Book V and developed in Books VI and VII.) The flute-maker, who has a correct belief about what a good flute is (having just had this explained to them by the expert flutist), sets about making a good flute. Socrates does not say, but presumably the flute-maker possesses knowledge about the effects of different kinds of wood, different drying times, etc. They know *how* to make a good flute; the flutist knows *what* a good flute is—and this conceptual knowledge is always superior to practical know-how, for Socrates. 'An imitator', by contrast, 'has neither knowledge nor right opinion' (10.602a) about good flutes. Knowledge and correct belief about what makes a flute good is not needed to paint a flute; what the artist has—ignorance—will suffice for their purposes, which is imitating how flutes appear, not what they are.

Given how important epistemology is to Plato, we can see why he is down on artists. But the epistemological argument is even more serious than this, as we see when we shift focus from painting to poetry. Just as one can paint a flute without knowing what a good flute is or what makes good flutes good, one can 'imitate images of virtue [...] and [yet] have no grasp of the truth' (10.600e). People look to Homer for moral guidance, but they should not, Socrates argues, since Homer does not know what courage, for example, *is;* he only knows how to create an image of it in poetic song. 'If Homer had really been able to educate people and make them better' (10.600c), Socrates reasons, 'if Homer had been able to benefit people and make them more virtuous, his companions would [not] have allowed either him or Hesiod to wander around as rhapsodes' (10.600d). Instead, they would have insisted that Homer and Hesiod stay put and teach them about virtue, or they would have followed them in a caravan of moral education. And Homer, had he actually possessed such knowledge, would have surely obliged. But Homer and Hesiod were allowed to wander, so Socrates concludes that they did not possess genuine moral knowledge.

While poets and painters might have good ears and eyes for what a culture takes virtue and the virtues to be, one of the lessons of the First Wave back in Book V was that we should not take our culture's norms at face value: 'it is foolish to take seriously any standard of what is fine and beautiful other than the good' (5.452e). Socrates, of course, is not a relativist about norms, but neither is he a conservative, at least of the sort that gives great weight to tradition as a source of moral wisdom. That one's culture has long approved of certain values carries little or no epistemic weight for Socrates. One of philosophy's tasks is to subject these values to rational scrutiny. We saw earlier that the ridiculousness of women wrestling naked and governing 'faded way in the face of what argument (λόγος [*logos*]) showed to be the best' (5.452d). A perhaps unexpected upshot of the 'image of the soul in words' in Book IX is an objective test of one's culture's 'conventions about what is fine and what is shameful. Fine things', Socrates says, referring to things that are *kalon*, 'are those that subordinate the beastlike parts of our nature to the human [...] shameful ones are those that enslave the gentle to the savage' (9.589d).

Someone friendly to the arts might concede that many artists lack philosophical knowledge of the nature of goodness and the virtues but they might also insist that many of these artists possess true beliefs about these topics and are not ignorant, as Socrates claims. But Socrates might reply that this leaves an essential problem untouched—namely, the epistemic authority his (and our) culture accords to artists. If they lack knowledge, why care what they have to say? Distracted by their 'multicolored' (10.604e, 10.605a) productions, we think they can teach us how to live—an assumption that may seem odd in our age of entertainment—but they lack the knowledge required to do so. But if we are fools to follow them, the problem seems to be with *us* rather than *them*.

Even readers who are not persuaded by Socrates' argument might concede that it points to something important, something perhaps more important in our day than in Socrates': the supposed authority of celebrities to pronounce upon issues of the day, especially political issues. Many of us—too many of us—fall for the *argumentam ab celebritas,* as we might call it. While we can revere them as actors, why should we take seriously the political pronouncements of Meryl Streep or Robert De Niro? They can teach us a great deal about the craft of acting, but is there any reason to think that they have a great deal to teach us about public policy? They might; but if they do, it is not because they are great actors—that is, highly skilled at imitation.

Many readers will not share Socrates' expectation that artists teach us how to live; but readers of a serious, aesthetic bent will think that some novelists, poets, filmmakers, musicians, composers, etc. *do* aim for more than entertainment. Indeed, there is good reason to think of some artists as creating philosophical art: art that wrestles with some of the same moral, metaphysical, and epistemological problems that occupy philosophers. I suspect that many readers have a more expansive view of what constitutes philosophy and argument than Socrates does, and so are willing to take these artists' views seriously. But even so we would do well to maintain a healthy dose of Socratic skepticism about the moral and epistemological authority many of us see them as having. We are all prone to confirmation bias, of thinking certain bits of evidence are *good* evidence because they confirm what we already believe. Holding our favorite artists' feet to the philosophical fire and querying the views and arguments they offer is a show of respect for them as thinkers that is consistent with respecting them as creative artists.

The upshot of the epistemological argument is that, even though one might really enjoy reading (or, more likely in the Greek world, listening to a performance of) Homer, one would be foolish to 'arrange one's whole life in accordance with his teachings' (10.606e), since there is no good reason to think that poetic skill overlaps with philosophical insight. Thus we should not, as Polemarchus does in Book I, quote poets like Simonides as moral authorities on the nature of justice, for example. Instead, we should critically examine their sayings and adopt them as guides for living only if they pass rational muster.

The Moral Argument: Art Corrupts Even the Best of Us

Some readers will have noticed a pattern in the *Republic:* Plato tends to list items in increasing order of importance; the third of three items is almost always the most important. The Third Wave is 'the biggest and most difficult one' (5.472a) and the third argument that the just life is happier is 'the greatest and most decisive' (9.583b). We see that pattern again here: the moral argument against art, to which we now turn, is 'the most serious charge against imitation' (10.605c).

In the first two arguments, the key notion of imitation (μίμησις *mimêsis*]) seems roughly synonymous with representation: an object or action is re-presented by the painter or poet. But in this final argument we should keep in mind the more precise sense Socrates had in mind when he distinguished the *content* of poems and stories or *what* they say from *how* they say it—i.e., their style. Imitation is a matter of 'mak[ing] oneself like someone else in voice or appearance' (3.393c) and thus the poet or performer impersonates a character, speaking from that character's point of view, as that character would speak and act—as actors do onstage. Imitation in this sense is contrasted with pure narration, in which the author or speaker describes but not does enact actions and events, telling the audience that a character said such-and-such but not directly quoting a character's speech (or if doing so, not attempting to imitate the speaker's voice and mannerisms). Unlike the imitative poet, the purely narrative poet 'never hid[es] himself' (3.393d) behind characters: the narrative poet is always present, never impersonating another and never being anything but themselves. Socrates' example is a non-poetic summary of the opening scene of the *Iliad,* a summary of events as one might find in a high school 'book report' or in Cliff or Spark Notes. But narration is also the style of the hymns to the god of wine and fertility, Dionysus, known as dithyrambs, which were typically sung in the Phrygian mode, one of the two musical modes Socrates allows in the ideal *polis* (3.399a). So presumably dithyrambs are among the 'hymns to the gods' that are allowed in the ideal city—indeed, the city's poets will 'compose appropriate hymns' (5.459e) to celebrate and consecrate the eugenic marriages discussed in Book V. A third kind of style is a mix of narration and imitation, which is the form epic poetry takes: a narrator tells the audience about certain events and not merely quotes but enacts other events by imitating or impersonating some of the characters.

In Book III Socrates focused on the moral danger imitation in the strict poses to performers, and presumably the creators of such poetry would also face moral danger as well. The title character in J. M. Coetzee's *Elizabeth Costello* wrestles with something like this latter problem. Her concern is not with the perils of imitation but with the dangers that come with writing about profound evil. To do so well, one must confront evil deeply and indeed sympathetically, imaginatively entering into the consciousness of Himmler and Hitler and their ilk (which suggests a disagreement with the conclusion of Socrates' epistemological argument). And 'she is not sure that writers who venture into the darker territories of the soul always return unscathed'.[2] In Book X Socrates shifts his attention away from the moral dangers that imitative poetry poses to its performers and toward the dangers it poses to the audience, who identify with the characters the performers impersonate.

Where the epistemological argument focused on poetry's incapacity to make us better, the moral argument focuses on its power to make us worse: 'with a few rare exceptions it is able to corrupt even decent people' (10.605c). We take seriously the sufferings of the protagonist and not only enjoy watching or listening but actually 'give ourselves up to following it' (10.605d). Instead of being properly disgusted at the hero's lamentations (an earlier focus of censorship, for example at 3.387d), we enjoy and even praise them (10.605e). But, Socrates argues, enjoying other people's sufferings is 'necessarily transferred to our own' (10.606b), and thus we nurture 'the pitying part' of our soul, which, nourished by tragedy, 'destroys the rational [part]' (10.605b). The problem is not merely that in taking our own sufferings seriously we forget that 'human affairs are not worth taking very seriously' (10.604c), but rather that we dethrone reason from its rightful place and live lives guided by emotion when we 'hug the hurt part' (10.604c)—which prevents us from being just, and thus happy. Socrates' arguments against comic poetry run parallel to his arguments against tragedy: instead of being overcome by grief, we are overcome by hilarity. Both involve a dethroning of reason

---

2 J. M. Coetzee, *Elizabeth Costello* (New York: Viking, 2003), p. 160.

which we think is temporary but which, Socrates thinks, is anything but. Whether we are giving ourselves over to laughter or lamentation, we are nourishing and nurturing the appetitive and spirited parts of our souls, which house the emotions, and we are unlikely to be able to contain this beast within when we leave the theater.

It is telling that Socrates is especially concerned with imitative poetry's power to make us act, feel, and think differently in private than we do in public. He seems suspicious of and often hostile to privacy, which is unsurprising given the priority of the community over the individual that animates his thought. Socrates' animus toward privacy pops up in various places. For example, that the guardians and auxiliaries have little to no privacy, living and eating communally and having no private property, fuels Adeimantus' doubts about whether they can be happy. So Socrates' concern about what we might call emotional privacy should not surprise us. A good person who has lost a child, for example, will be 'measured in his response to [his] pain [...] and put up more resistance to it when his equals can see him [than] when he is alone by himself in solitude [...] [where] he will venture to say and do lots of things that he'd be ashamed to be heard saying or seen doing' (10.603e–4a).

Socrates seems concerned that imitative poetry will encourage a kind of hypocrisy: in public, we will follow reason, which bids us to quietly bear misfortune, tempering our feelings of grief with proto-stoic thoughts that 'human affairs are not worth taking very seriously' (10.604e), that what now seems like a tragedy might ultimately be for the best, etc.; but in private we will indulge and give vent to feelings of grief. It is no accident that the English word 'hypocrite' derives from the Greek word for actor, ὑποκριτής (*hupokritês*), since hypocrisy involves *pretense* (and not mere inconsistency): hypocrites pretend to believe what in fact they do not, since *appearing* to believe certain things and acting in certain ways is in their self-interest.

Socrates' worry about the way imitative poetry works its dark magic in private is perhaps motivated more by simplicity and the unity of the soul as ideals of character than by a concern to avoid hypocrisy. 'A just man', we are told, 'is simple and noble and [...] does not want to be believed to be good but to be so' (2.361b). Although Thrasymachus thinks that Socrates' just person is a sap exhibiting 'high-minded simplicity' (1.348c), Socrates thinks of simplicity as integrity and purity, in contrast with Thrasymachan duplicity and the specious 'multicolored' attractions of the democratic constitution and character. The person who scorns imitations of excessive grief while at the theater but who indulges their grief at home, or who keeps a stiff upper lip in front of the children or the troops and then indulges their grief while in private, will not be 'of one mind' (10.603c). Socrates insists that such a person is 'at war with himself' (10.603c), his soul beset by 'civil war' (10.603d)— which of course has been a major concern throughout the *Republic*.

But must a person whose emotional responses vary by context fail to achieve the virtue of one-mindedness? Socrates treats a person's expressing grief differently in different circumstances as cases of changing one's mind, but perhaps we should think of them instead as appropriately varying their responses to the differing demands of different situations. That Socrates wants more than a situation-specific, context-sensitive ethics was clear almost immediately in the *Republic*: since it is wrong to return the weapon to the deranged friend, returning what one has borrowed cannot be what justice is. But as we noted earlier, one may think that there are no universal ethical truths of the sort Socrates is after; perhaps the best we get are general principles or rules-of-thumb that give limited guidance and which must always be supplemented with situation-specific insight. (Something like this seems to have been Aristotle's view.)

We have already remarked on Socrates' love for poetry, but it bears repeating. He loves poetry, but he thinks that it is a love for a dangerous object, one best avoided: 'we will behave like people who have fallen in love with someone but force themselves to stay away from him because they realize that their passion is not beneficial' (10.607e). But since he lives in the actual world and not in his ideal *polis*, Socrates will keep his arguments against poetry ready to be chanted 'like an incantation' when he encounters it (10.608a), like 'a drug to counteract it' (10.595b). Up to this point, 'useful falsehoods' (2.382c, 3.389b) have been the most prominent drugs in the *Republic*, prescribed by the guardian-rulers most famously in the foundational myth of origin known as the Noble Falsehood (3.415b). Here the drug (φάρμακον [*pharmakon*], from which English words like 'pharmacy' and 'pharmaceutical' derive) is knowledge—truth, rather than falsehood—and it is self-prescribed. It is as if Socrates recognizes an addiction to something that *seems* so attractive and benign, but which is in fact insidiously harmful. It is a kind of self-help that seems to be available only to philosopher-kings and -queens; for the rest of us, the 'drug' that the rational part of our souls can concoct is not strong enough, or, the soul's rational part has been subordinated to the appetitive part—'the part of the soul [...] that hungers for the satisfaction of weeping and wailing' (10.606a).

In his *Poetics*, Aristotle famously disagrees with Plato's assessment of tragic poetry, arguing that tragedy is actually good for us, achieving a catharsis (κάθαρσις [*katharsis*]) of pity and fear, the tragic emotions par excellence: 'A tragedy, then, is the imitation of an action that is serious [...] in dramatic, not a narrative form, with incidents arousing pity and fear, wherewith to accomplish its catharsis of such emotions'.[3] Pity and fear, Aristotle argues in the last chapter of his *Politics*, 'exist very strongly in some souls, and have more or less influence over all',[4] so we are benefitted when our souls are purged of pity and fear. Aristotle says surprisingly little about catharsis, given how frequently it takes center stage in discussions of his *Poetics*, and while this is not the place to explore it in any depth, a word or two is in order. 'Catharsis' means cleansing or purification. Understood medically, catharsis is purgation, a process by which we are purged of harmful substances. But Aristotle, unlike Plato, does not think that emotions are in themselves harmful states that get in the way of virtue and are thus to be purged. For Aristotle, 'moral excellence [i.e., virtue] [...] is concerned with passions and actions',[5] and while reason governs a well-ordered soul, he thinks that many emotions and desires can be brought into harmony with reason, rather than being forever recalcitrant and in need of subjugation. Thus catharsis need not be exclusively a matter of purification by purgation; it can also be clarification by education. Consider the tragic emotion of pity, which is essentially directed at another's unmerited distress. While Plato thinks that identifying with the tragic hero's distress via pity will displace reason and thus lead to an unjust (or at least non-just) soul, Aristotle seems to think that it can lead us to appreciate our own vulnerability to the slings and arrows of outrageous fortune and to cultivate appropriate fellow-feeling and compassion.

---

3   Aristotle, *Poetics*, 6 1149b24–7.
4   Aristotle, *Politics*, VIII.6 1342a6–7.
5   Aristotle, *Nicomachean Ethics*, II.6 1106b16.

As the eminent contemporary philosopher Martha Nussbaum puts it, 'tragedy contributes to human self-understanding precisely through its exploration of the pitiable and the fearful'.[6] Far from being something to be purged from an ideal city, good tragedy should be welcomed, not because it is good entertainment or because good art enriches our lives, but because it contributes to the moral development and improvement of the citizens—much as reading good literature might make us more empathic and more sensitive to moral nuance.

It seems that Plato and Aristotle disagree about the value tragedy because they disagree about the value of our emotions, and indeed the value of our bodies. Socrates does not fear death, because his death means that his soul will at least be freed from 'the contamination of the body's folly',[7] which prevents the soul from encountering the pure reality of the Forms. Readers who share something like Aristotle's attitude toward the emotions—which shows that one need not be a full-blown romantic, giving absolute priority to emotion over reason, to value emotions positively—will have good reason to be skeptical about Plato's attitude toward imitative poetry.

A Four-Part Soul?

There is an additional problem with Socrates' treatment of poetry that we ought to deal with. It is a problem that at first might seem hardly worth noticing, but which is potentially devastating to the project of the *Republic*. In dismissing imitation as a silly waste of time, Socrates focuses on the metaphysically thin nature of its objects: they are shadows on the cave wall, not to be taken seriously. This critique requires his two-worlds metaphysics, and we have already dwelled on the inadequacy of the support Socrates provides for this distinctive and bold metaphysical theory. But after attending to the shadowy nature of the products of imitative art, Socrates briefly turns his attention to the activity of perceiving these objects. He does not, as we might expect, refer back to the Divided Line, the lowest portion of which has artistic creations

---

6   Martha Nussbaum, *The Fragility of Goodness: Luck and Ethics in Greek Tragedy and Philosophy* (Cambridge, University of Cambridge Press, 1986), p. 390.

7   *Phaedo*, in *Plato: Five Dialogues*, trans. by G. M. A. Grube (Indianapolis: Hackett Publishing, 1981), p. 103 [67a].

as its objects. Instead, he asks, 'on which of a person's parts does [imitation] exert its power?' (10.602c) Both *trompe l'oeil* painting and ordinary optical illusions can lead us to false judgments about reality. My canoe paddle *appears* bent or fractured when it is submerged, but it is not; the lines of the Müller-Lyer illusion, discussed earlier, *seem* not to be the same length, but they are. Only measuring them reveals this, and measuring, like calculating and weighing, are rational activities, the work of the rational part of the soul (10.602d).

So where do these potentially erroneous perceptions and perceptual beliefs come from? Since 'the part of the soul that forms a belief contrary to the measurements could not be the same as the part that believes in accord with them' (10.603a), they cannot come from the rational part of the soul, given the Opposition Principle (4.436b). Nor does the spirited part of the soul provide a plausible home for perception. Perhaps perception is a function of the appetitive part. In another dialogue, the *Theaetetus,* Plato suggests this possibility and casts the net of perception widely, counting 'desires and fears' as perceptions, along with more obvious examples like 'sight, hearing, smelling, feeling cold and feeling hot' (156b). Not only do both perception and belief work with appetite—my desire for ice cream and my seeing (and believing) that there is some in the freezer together explain my reaching in to get some—but they have the same objects: I see the ice cream, I want the ice cream, etc. Still, it is not clear how perception can be a function of the appetitive part of the soul. Perceptions, like desires, are representations, pictures of the world, if you will. But they are pictures having different *directions of fit,* as philosophers sometimes say. Beliefs and perceptions are mental representations of the world that are supposed to match the way the world is; thus they have a mind-to-world direction of fit: the mind's picture is supposed to match the world, and when they do not match, I need new beliefs and perceptions—I need a different picture. Appetites and desires, by contrast, have a world-to-mind direction of fit: they are representations not of how the world is but of how it ought to be or I would like it to be. So when the world does not fit my picture, I change the world to make it match—as if desires are skippered by Captain Picard of *Star Trek: The Next Generation*, with a 'make it so' built into their very nature. Wanting more ice cream but seeing my bowl is empty, I go to the freezer and get some, so my picture of reality (me eating ice cream) matches reality. (Of course, if one is inclined to Stoicism or Buddhism, one often tries to give up the unfulfilled desire, since it is the source of one's discontentment.)

Thus it seems that there must be another part of the soul, one that forms (potentially erroneous) perceptual beliefs—a fourth part of the soul, distinct from reason, spirit, and appetite. Okay, so there is another, fourth part of the soul. So what? What is the big deal? Well, the big deal is that the *Republic* turns on the analogy between the city and the soul: Socrates theorizes the ideal city not for its own sake but as a means to investigate the *Republic*'s two main questions. Back in Book IV all 'agreed that the same number and same kinds of classes as are in the city are also in the soul of each individual' (4.441c), but the argument against imitative art now suggests that that agreement was a bad one, and that there is an important *dis*analogy between city and soul. Thus what followed from that agreement—the answers to the *Republic*'s two main questions about the nature and value of justice—are now called into question.

Alas, neither Glaucon nor anyone else present objects to Socrates' seeming to introduce a new part of the soul and to the problems this raises for the *Republic*'s central analogy. Perhaps this is another one of those places in which Plato is hoping his readers see a philosophical problem that eludes his characters. And perhaps he is making a point about the nature of philosophical inquiry: Socrates now has two views that seem to be in conflict with each other, and he needs to do more philosophical work to determine which view is more reasonable to retain. Readers will be forgiven for thinking that Socrates should have left well enough alone and ended things in Book IX.

The Immortality of the Soul (10.608c–614b)

Having excluded almost all poetry from the ideal city, Socrates continues to tie up loose ends. Since the genuinely just but seemingly unjust life has been shown, he thinks, to be happier than the genuinely unjust but seemingly just life, we can now consider the consequences and rewards of justice. Adeimantus was especially adamant about excluding consideration of the reputational benefits of being thought of as just; too much of Athenian culture praised the rewards of being thought just, ignoring justice itself. But now those rewards can be considered, and of course they incline in favor of the just life.

But the philosophically most interesting part of the discussion concerns the benefits of being just that extend beyond this mortal coil—and thus the claim that our souls are immortal. Earlier we emphasized that the concept of the soul at work in the *Republic* lacked the religious dimensions of the modern notion of the soul. But here is a place where they seem more similar than different. I imagine that many readers will agree with Socrates' claim that each of us has a soul that will survive our bodily death. We will see in the final section of this chapter that Socrates' account of the soul's life after the death of the body differs significantly from religious conceptions involving eternal reward or damnation, this feature of its nature—immortality—is common to both.

That the soul is immortal comes as news to Glaucon; more surprising still is Socrates' claim that arguing for it 'is not difficult' (10.608d). The argument is fairly straightforward and interestingly enough employs an inversion of the familiar Specialization Principle. Everything, Socrates argues, has a 'natural' evil or badness that is 'proper' or 'peculiar' to it. Rot is the natural evil proper to wood, as blight is for grain and rust is for iron (10.608e). While we usually think of 'proper' as a normative term with a positive valence, here it functions descriptively. If a thing is not destroyed by its proper evil, it cannot be destroyed by anything. Injustice, or vice more generally, is the soul's proper evil, just as its proper good is justice; but while the soul is worsened by injustice, it is not destroyed by it. Therefore, the soul cannot be destroyed, and so it is immortal. Here is the argument, spelled out in premise-conclusion form:

P1   Everything has a natural evil which worsens and corrupts it. (608e)

P2   If something is worsened but not destroyed by its natural evil, then nothing else will destroy it. (609a)

P3   Vice is the soul's natural evil. (609b)

P4   Vice worsens but does not destroy the soul. (609c–d)

C1   Therefore, the soul cannot be destroyed.

P5   If something cannot be destroyed then it must always exist. (610e)

P6   If something must always exist then it is immortal. (611a)

C2   Therefore, the soul must always exist.

C3   Therefore, the soul is immortal.

It is an interesting argument in many ways. The picture of the soul that emerges is of a thing that despite having parts is simple; the soul is *not* 'multicolored (ποικιλίας [*poikilias*])' (10.611b), which, we learned in the discussion of democracy, is a bad thing to be. Plato and Socrates value simplicity and unity over complexity and variety, which should come as no surprise by this point in the *Republic*. Nor, given the role reason plays in Plato's thoughts, should we be surprised at the suggestion that 'the soul [...] is maimed by its association with the body' (10.611c). A soul is what you and I most fundamentally are, for Plato; we are not primarily bodies or body-soul unities.

While the argument is logically valid, it is far from clear that it is sound, since P2 is not obviously true, and indeed seems obviously not true. Consider some of the examples Socrates employs to illustrate the idea of a proper evil: wood's proper evil is rot; iron's is rust. But clearly wood and iron can be destroyed by things other than rot and rust— fire comes quickly to mind. So even if the soul cannot be destroyed by injustice, it is possible that it can be destroyed by an evil not proper to it. We might also question P4, the claim that injustice worsens but does not destroy the soul. The tyrannical person starves his rational part and not only takes no steps to domesticate the savage elements of his inner beast, but actually cultivates them and delights in their wildness. It is not at all implausible that such a paradigmatically unjust soul can destroy itself, 'consumed with that which it was nourished by', as Shakespeare says in Sonnet 73.[8]

It is not clear how seriously Plato intends this argument, especially given its rather obvious shortcomings. Its purpose may well be more strategic in a literary sense: it gets us thinking about life after death, which is the subject of the *Republic*'s finale, the Myth of Er. Rather than wring our hands or arch our eyebrows over the argument, let us turn to the

---

8   *Shakespeare's Sonnets*, ed. by Katherine Duncan-Jones, The Arden Shakespeare, revised edition (London: Bloomsbury Publishing, 2010), p. 257.

Myth of Er, which is fascinating in itself, and a fascinating way for the *Republic* to end.

The Myth of Er (10.614a–21c)

Why Plato ends the *Republic* not with an argument or an exhortation to the reader but with a myth is a question well worth pondering. Plato caps off the creation of the ideal *polis* with the Noble Falsehood, which suggests how important shared myths and stories are to political unity. His ending the *Republic* with a myth, especially after the many and various analogies and metaphors that populate the *Republic*, suggests the importance of myth and narrative to human self-understanding. Although philosopher-queens and -kings can subsist on an intellectual diet of 'theoretical argument', Adeimantus and the rest of us require that this diet be supplemented with the relish that stories provide.

The myth concerns a man named Er, who recounts his after-death experiences 'as a messenger (ἄγγελον [*angelon*, whence our word 'angel']) to human beings' (10.614d). Er's tale recounts what happens to our souls after they are separated from our bodies in death—hence the importance of the argument for the soul's immortality. There are three distinct stages in the myth. In the first, Er finds himself in a beautiful meadow, near two pairs of openings, one pair to and from what lies below the earth; the other to and from the heavens. The souls of those who have acted unjustly are sent to the world below, incurring a tenfold penalty for each injustice. The souls of those who have acted justly go to the world above. The openings are busy with punished and rewarded souls ascending from the world below and descending from the world above, and souls of the recently deceased receiving their reward and punishment and thus ascending or descending.

In the myth's second stage, the returned souls travel to the place where the individuals' fates are spun. I will not replicate Plato's descriptions of the Fates, the Spindle of Necessity, and the entire scene, as I could not do them justice. The heart of this stage of the myth is a choice: each soul, whether it is returned from heavenly reward or heavenly punishment, chooses the life it will inhabit in its return to the world. Only for 'incurably wicked people' (10.615e) is punishment eternal; and presumably—though Plato is mum on the topic—there is eternal reward for the very best. But for everyone else, life after death is a matter of having a new bodily life. Although this part of the myth concerns the spinning of one's fate, it is crucial that each soul *chooses* its fate. When one chooses is determined by lot, so there is an element of randomness in the procedure, but each person will 'choose a life to which he will then be bound by necessity' (10.617e). It is an interesting kind of necessity or determinism, very different from the causal determinism that contemporary philosophers concerned with free will tend to worry over. Rather, it is what we might call *type* determinism: a person's choices are determined by the type of person they are and will determine the type of person they will be—and thus the kind of life they will lead. Hence the importance of choosing well. And here, Socrates tells Glaucon, is 'the greatest danger' (10.618b), given that the soul's choice of a life determines to a great extent how happy or unhappy that life will be. Thus we see the importance of the *Republic's* second question: a person's answer to this question determines the kind of life they will lead. We need to choose carefully, and not be dazzled by exteriors, which may prove to be false façades.

The first person to choose 'chose [his life] without adequate examination' (10.619b); dazzled by wealth and pomp, he chose the life of a great tyrant, not realizing until after the choice was made that he was fated to eat his own children—a fate that might well be worse than death. His reaction is instructive: 'he blamed chance [...] and everything else [...] but himself' (10.619c). Blaming others for the results of our own poor choices is a profoundly human reaction, it seems to me. In *Genesis,* Adam blames Eve for suggesting they eat the apple, and Eve blames the serpent. The irony here is that this chooser had returned from a life in heaven, his reward for having lived a virtuous life, though he had been virtuous 'through habit and without philosophy' (10.619d). That is, he was conventionally good but unreflective, which, Socrates argues, left him vulnerable to poor choices. His goodness, like Cephalus', was more a matter of luck and circumstance than of a firm inner state of his soul, and ironically it is the cause of his undoing.

The account of the various lives chosen is fascinating, with many people choosing to live an animal's life, and with almost everyone's 'choice depend[ing] upon the character of their former life' (10.620a). The most instructive choice is probably Odysseus'. He was among the last to choose, though there remained many kinds of lives to choose from. He scoured the possibilities for 'the life of a private individual who did his own work' (10.620c), insisting that he would have chosen this same life had he been first to choose. What Odysseus has chosen is, of course, a just life. That it was 'lying off somewhere neglected by the others' (10.620c) is no surprise; since most of us are easily dazzled by 'multicolored' exteriors and do not have a good grasp of the essence of justice and its necessity for a happy life, it is no wonder that it is not the one most of us choose.

In the myth's last stage, the souls, whose fates are now spun irreversibly, are brought to the Plain of Forgetfulness and the River of Unheeding, where they forget their choice and then re-enter the world.

Like most myths, the Myth of Er is best not taken literally. Its point, I take it, is that while we each have a natural bent, which is then developed in various ways by the kind of nurturing we receive from our educations, our cultures, and the constitutions we live under, whether we are happy or not depends to a great extent on the choices we make. Most of our choices are not as dramatic or as momentous as the one-off choices depicted in the Myth of Er. Instead, they are daily choices, some large, some small, which shape our characters. In an anticipation of Aristotle's doctrine of the mean, according to which every virtue is a mean between two vices (so courage is a mean between cowardice and recklessness, for example), Socrates suggests that a good choice is one in which we 'choose the mean [... and] avoid either of the extremes' (10.619a). We should make our choices carefully, after due deliberation. Indeed, we should make *choices*, not act on impulse like the fickle democrat discussed earlier. A wise person 'chooses [a life] rationally and lives it seriously' (10.619b).

There are fascinating issues here, which we can do no more than touch on. Given that our nature and nurture largely determine which options will seem sensible and be appealing to us, even though each individual makes life-shaping choices, it is not clear how free those choices are. And if indeed they are not free (or not sufficiently free)— as they seem not to be if *type* determinism is true—then readers may well wonder to what extent it makes sense to hold each other morally responsible for the choices we make and the actions we undertake. The great twentieth-century philosopher Peter Strawson famously argued that holding ourselves and others accountable is so central to being human, there is little chance that we could give it up, even if we believe determinism to be true. Or, one might argue that although we are not fully responsible for the choices we make, perhaps we are responsible enough to warrant holding each other accountable. This issue, though Aristotle briefly considers it in his *Nicomachean Ethics,* seems more a modern than an ancient concern, so we should not fault Plato for not addressing it. Still, it is something that interested, philosophically inclined readers will want to explore further.

Perhaps the most fascinating thing about the Myth of Er is that Plato chooses to end the *Republic* with it. Readers will notice the abruptness with which the *Republic* ends. The *Republic* begins with Socrates' narration: on his way back to town with Glaucon, he meets Polemarchus; he tells someone—whom he is speaking to is never made clear—about the long philosophical discussion that took place at the house of Polemarchus' father, Cephalus, a discussion which concludes with the Myth of Er. Plato reminds us of this by having Socrates address Glaucon directly in the *Republic*'s concluding paragraph. But conspicuous by its absence is something that would close the book, so to speak, on the book that is the *Republic.* There is no 'and then, exhausted, I went home' or 'and then we had a sumptuous meal' or anything that closes the narrative.

I suspect that this is Plato's taking his last opportunity to make a philosophical point with a literary device that is analogous to a sudden cut to black, as in the much-discussed final episode of *The Sopranos.* Earlier we observed how the opening of Book V echoes the opening of Book I; I suggested that this is Plato's way of making a substantive philosophical point—that philosophy is always returning to its beginnings, always starting over and reexamining its foundations. Here, I suspect, the point is similar, but about endings and conclusions rather than premises and beginnings. In not having a conclusive ending to the *Republic,* Plato seems to be telling us that philosophy never ends, that the conversation Socrates had at Cephalus' house does not end, but continues every time a reader engages with the *Republic,* as we have done here.

Some Suggestions for Further Reading

There is a large literature on Plato's attitude toward poetry. G. R. F. Ferrari, 'Plato and Poetry', in *The Cambridge History of Literary Criticism*, vol. 1, ed. by George A. Kennedy (New York: Cambridge University Press, 1989), pp. 92–148 is especially insightful and helpful.

Readers who enjoy historical fiction may want to read Mary Renault, *The Praise Singer* (New York: Vintage, 2003), an excellent and moving novel about Simonides, the lyric poet Polemarchus quotes in Book I.

Eric Brown, 'A Defense of Plato's Argument for the Immortality of the Soul at *Republic* X 608c–611a', *Apeiron*, 30 (1997), 211–38, is a sympathetic reconstruction and defense of the argument for the soul's immortality discussed in this chapter.

Readers interested in the Myth of Er will find an extended discussion in Stephen Halliwell, 'The Life-and-Death Journey of the Soul: Interpreting the Myth of Er', in *The Cambridge Companion to Plato's 'Republic'*, ed. by G. R. F. Ferrari (New York: Cambridge University Press, 2007), https://doi.org/10.1017/ccol0521839637, pp. 444–73.

Readers interested in a contemporary discussion of free will and determinism will find Robert Kane, *A Contemporary Introduction to Free Will* (New York: Oxford University Press, 2005) an excellent place to begin.

Readers interested in the idea of *direction-of-fit* might start with its source: G. E. M. Anscombe, *Intention*, 2nd ed. (Cambridge, MA: Harvard University Press, 2000), esp. pp. 56–7 (§ 32).

Head of Platon, Roman copy. Photograph by Bibi Saint-Pol (2007),
Wikimedia, Public Domain, https://commons.wikimedia.org/wiki/
File:Head_Platon_Glyptothek_Munich_548.jpg#/media/File:Head_
Platon_Glyptothek_Munich_548.jpg

Afterword

Having travelled so great a distance together, a few words about our journey seem in order. Few readers, I suspect, will want to live in Plato's ideal *polis*—and they will be in good company, if a recent biography of Socrates is to be believed: 'We can be in absolutely no doubt that Socrates would have disliked and disapproved of the republic Plato wanted to bring into being'.[1] Whatever its virtues, it is too lacking in individual liberty to suit most of us. Most of us will side with John Stuart Mill over Plato, and regard 'the free development of individuality [as] one of the leading essentials of wellbeing'.[2] Plato's utopia is far too much on the communitarian side of the spectrum for our comfort. We can set to one side the historical unlikelihood of the sort of aristocracy that Plato imagines; we are all familiar—though thankfully, for most of us, not in a first-hand way—with the evils of totalitarianism. The issue is more philosophical than that. Although romantics will demur at enthroning reason, many readers will agree that 'it is better for everyone to be ruled by divine reason, preferably within himself and his own' (9.590e), but many of these will insist that 'preferably [...] his own' is too weak and will deny to their dying breaths that this reason may permissibly be 'imposed from without'. Most readers will prefer a life in which they make their own choices to one in which their choices are made for them—even when they acknowledge that their own choices are often poor. Mill argues that the evils of paternalism—of interference with the choices of others *for their own good*—far outweigh its benefits. But one need not appeal to the consequences to be committed to the priority

---

1   Paul Johnson, *Socrates: A Man for Our Times* (New York: Penguin Books, 2011), p. 93.
2   Mill, *On Liberty*, p. 69.

          https://doi.org/10.11647/OBP.0229.15

of liberty and autonomy over wellbeing. One might, like Kant, take it to be a matter of respect for human dignity, which is grounded in our capacity to make choices, to deliberate and decide and then to act. We are justified in interfering, says the anti-paternalistic individualist, only where our choices harm others.

But even for such individualistically inclined readers, the *Republic* can offer salutary lessons. For while the pendulum swings too far to the communitarian end of the line in the ideal *polis*, one might concede that it swings too far to the individualistic side in, say, contemporary American culture. Perhaps we would do better to be more mindful of the good of the whole, to see our politics not as a means for advancing narrow individual and special interests but rather as a way to 'promote the general welfare'. Plato's anti-individualistic and anti-democratic animus is often expressed in his disdain for diversity and variety and complication—with things that are 'multicolored' (ποικίλος [*poikilos*]), as he often puts it. Too much variety in poetic meter is frowned upon (3.399e), as is medical treatment that is too complicated (4.426a). And of course, democracy's multicolored constitution is the source of its specious beauty (8.557c), as are its 'multicolored pleasures' (8.559d) and the cast of characters that are its citizens, 'characters fine and multicolored' (8.561e). And let us not forget about the 'multicolored beast' (9.588c) that embodies our emotions and desires. While we need not value diversity for diversity's sake, taking diversity as an intrinsic good when its goodness is more properly instrumental, we need not think of it as an intrinsic bad, as Plato seems to do. A community can celebrate its diversity while at the same time celebrating and nurturing its unity. It can be one from many—*e pluribus unum*, as it says somewhere or other. What is required for this is an attitude toward community and individuality that is more complex than Plato offers in the *Republic*. We can celebrate individuality and liberty while at the same time enabling individuals to be good team members, good cast members, etc. So while most of us do not accept Plato's full embrace of the good of the community over that of the individual, we can incorporate more communitarian thinking into our lives and politics. Simply put, to think this is a matter of individualism *versus* communitarianism is to commit the all too common (and all too human) fallacy of the false dilemma.

Similar considerations can apply to other aspects of Plato's thought where we recognize an important insight or truth that we do not feel comfortable taking fully on board. Consider justice as each person doing their own part and not meddling in the affairs of others. As we saw in Chapter Five, Confucius is in broad agreement with this, and one finds similar sentiments in the *Bhagavad Gita*: 'It is better to strive in one's own dharma than to succeed in the dharma of another. Nothing is ever lost in following one's own dharma, but competition in another's dharma breeds fear and insecurity'.[3]

Many readers will find that their peace and serenity and indeed their personal happiness increase as they strive to cultivate their own gardens, as Voltaire puts it toward the end of *Candide*, even though many of these readers will lament the political acquiescence they see in this idea. The trick, it seems, is to find the proper balance—to find when it is appropriate to mind one's own business, as it were, and when it is appropriate to demand and work for change. This, I think, is the task of practical wisdom, which functions not by applying abstract rules and principles but which, with principles operating in the background, assesses particular situations to see what each demands.

There are many other instances of such topics in the *Republic*, and I hope to have brought enough of them to the surface for readers to do their own thinking about them. But there is one last big-picture consideration I must address before we end. The *Republic* is one of the great books of philosophy, but as we have seen, sometimes in perhaps excruciating detail, there are stretches where it is far from great philosophy. Its central argument, the Powers Argument of Book V, is fatally flawed, yet it is the only argument Plato gives us in the *Republic* in support of his distinctive, two-worlds metaphysics. While the Allegory of the Cave can survive at least in part without its support, the Sun and Divided Line analogies sink or swim with it, as their central point is to make sense of the distinction between the intelligible world of the Forms, where knowledge lives, and the visible world of particulars, the realm of belief. Moreover, 'the greatest and most decisive' argument for the view that the just life is happier than the unjust life, the Metaphysics of Pleasure Argument, also depends on the Powers Argument. Socrates

---

3   *Bhagavad Gita*, trans. by Eknath Easwaran, 2nd ed. (Tomales, CA: Nilgiri Press, 2007), p. 108 [Chapter 3, verse 35].

may be correct in giving the palm to the just life, but he has not adequately argued for this conclusion, so his belief in it would seem to be unjustified. Socrates recognized in Book I that he jumped the gun in thinking he had shown that the just life is happier than the unjust life when he had not yet determined what justice is. But having determined the nature of justice to his and his interlocutors' satisfaction, he seems oblivious to the ways in which the Metaphysics of Pleasure Argument is fruit of the poisoned tree that is the Powers Argument. What gives?

There is a tendency, to which I am prone, to think that this must be intentional on Plato's part, that so smart a philosopher could not have unknowingly offered so poor an argument for so important a conclusion. Perhaps Plato took himself to be accurately reporting Socrates' own argument rather than giving his own. Perhaps he recognized the argument's shortcomings and left uncovering them to his readers, in hope that they—that we—would notice them and become better philosophers as we tried to work them out. It is hard to know.

The eminent philosopher and historian of early modern philosophy Jonathan Bennett, that rare bird who was as excellent a teacher as he was a philosopher, wrote in the preface to his first book on Kant's *Critique of Pure Reason:* 'Like all great pioneering works in philosophy, the *Critique* is full of mistakes and confusions. It is a misunderstanding to think that a supreme philosopher cannot have erred badly and often: the *Critique* still has much to teach us, but it is wrong on nearly every page'.[4]

Much the same could be said of Plato's *Republic*. It might be scant comfort to some readers, but it seems to me to offer a powerful lesson on the point of doing and reading philosophy, which always requires doing it for oneself. Though Socratic wisdom consists in knowing that one does not know, it does not require giving up those beliefs one cannot justify. The key to being ethically justified in retaining these epistemically unjustified beliefs, it seems to me, is humility: we recognize them *as* not justified, perhaps as a result of our intellectual shortcomings, and continue to reflect upon them. There is a lot of cognitive space between nihilism and dogmatism. That so great a philosopher as Plato is frequently wrong is a testament to how hard it is to do philosophy well.

---

4   Jonathan Bennett, *Kant's Analytic* (Cambridge: Cambridge University Press, 1966), p. viii.

That Plato fails to embody philosophical perfection is not a reason to give up on him or on ourselves.

Some Suggestions for Further Reading

Readers intrigued by Plato's thought will want to read Rebecca Goldstein, *Plato at the Googleplex: Why Philosophy Will Not Go Away* (New York: Vintage, 2015), a brilliant, wise, and funny book which imagines Plato on a contemporary book tour.

Readers interested in a brief, compelling account of the life of Socrates by an eminent biographer should see Paul Johnson, *Socrates: A Man for Our Times* (New York: Penguin Books, 2011).

Readers interested in exploring more of Plato's philosophical thought will find it all here: *Plato: Complete Works,* ed. by John Cooper (Indianapolis: Hackett Publishing, 1997).

For a canonical philosopher whose thinking is very much at odds with Plato's, interested readers might try both David Hume, *An Enquiry Concerning Human Understanding* (Indianapolis: Hackett Publishing, 1993) and Hume, *An Enquiry Concerning the Principles of Morals* (Indianapolis: Hackett Publishing, 1983).

List of Illustrations

Introduction

Chapter 1

Chapter 2

Chapter 3

Chapter 4

Chapter 5

Chapter 6

Chapter 7

Chapter 8

Chapter 9

Chapter 10

Chapter 11

Chapter 12

Chapter 13

Chapter 14

Afterword

Bibliography

Barnes, Jonathan, ed., *The Complete Works of Aristotle* (*Revised Oxford Translation*), 2 vols (Princeton: Princeton University Press, 1984), https://doi.org/10.1515/9781400835843 (vol. 1), https://doi.org/10.1515/9781400835850 (vol. 2).

Bennett, Jonathan, *Kant's Analytic* (Cambridge: Cambridge University Press, 1966), https://doi.org/10.1017/cbo9781316492901

Berlin, Isaiah, 'Two Concepts of Liberty' in Berlin, *Liberty: Four Essays on Liberty*, ed. by Henry Hardy (New York: Oxford University Press, 2002), https://doi.org/10.1093/019924989x.001.0001

Bhagavad Gita, trans. by Eknath Easwaran, 2nd ed. (Tomales, CA: Nilgiri Press, 2007).

Burnyeat, Myles, 'Culture and Society in Plato's "Republic"', in *The Tanner Lectures on Human Values,* vol. 20 (Salt Lake City: University of Utah Press, 1999).

Camus, Albert, *The Myth of Sisyphus,* trans. by Justin O'Brien (New York: Vintage International, 2018).

Coetzee, J. M., *Elizabeth Costello* (New York: Viking, 2003).

David Hume: A Treatise on Human Nature, ed. by L. A. Selby-Bigge, 2nd ed., rev. by P. H. Nidditch (Oxford: Clarendon Press, 1987).

Demos, Raphael, 'A Fallacy in Plato's *Republic?*', *Philosophical Review,* 73 (1964), 395–98, https://doi.org/10.2307/2183665

Dickens, Charles, *Hard Times* (London: Penguin Books, 1994).

Emerson, Ralph Waldo, *Essays* (New York: Harper Perennial, 1995).

Epicurus: *The Art of Happiness,* trans. by George Strodach (New York: Penguin Books, 2012).

Fitzgerald, F. Scott, *The Crack-Up* (New York: New Directions Publishing, 2009).

Frederick Douglass: Autobiographies: Narrative of the Life of Frederick Douglass, an American Slave/ My Bondage and My Freedom/ Life and Times of Frederick Douglass, ed. by Henry Louis Gates (New York: Library of America, 1994).

Johnson, Paul, *Socrates: A Man for Our Times* (New York: Penguin Books, 2011).

Kant: Groundwork of the Metaphysics of Morals, trans. and ed. by Mary K. Gregor (New York: Cambridge University Press, 1998), https://doi.org/10.1017/CBO9780511809590

McCarthy, Cormac, *No Country for Old Men* (New York: Vintage Books, 2006).

McEwan, Ian, *Enduring Love* (New York: Anchor Books, 1998).

Mill, John Stuart, *On Liberty,* ed. by Elizabeth Rappaport (Indianapolis: Hackett Publishing, 1978 [orig. pub. 1859]).

Murphy, Jeffrie, 'Forgiveness and Resentment' in Jeffrie Murphy and Jean Hampton, *Forgiveness and Mercy* (New York: Cambridge University Press, 1988). https://doi.org/10.1017/cbo9780511625121.003

Nails, Debra, 'The Dramatic Date of Plato's Republic', *The Classical Journal,* 93.4 (1998), 383–96.

Nussbaum, Martha, *The Fragility of Goodness: Luck and Ethics in Greek Tragedy and Philosophy* (Cambridge, University of Cambridge Press, 1986).

Nyhan, Brendan and Jason Reifler, 'When Corrections Fail: The Persistence of political Misperceptions', *Political Behavior,* 32 (2010), 303–30. https://doi.org/10.1007/s11109–010–9112–2

Plato: Five Dialogues: Euthyphro, Apology, Crito, Meno, Phaedo, trans. by G. M. A. Grube (Indianapolis: Hackett Publishing, 1981).

Plato: Republic, trans. by G. M. A. Grube, rev. by C. D. C. Reeve (Indianapolis: Hackett Publishing, 1992).

Plato: Theaetetus, tr. by M. J. Levett, rev. by Myles Burnyeat, ed. by Bernard Williams (Indianapolis: Hackett Publishing, 1992).

Rosch, Eleanor, 'Natural categories, *Cognitive Psychology,* 4 (1973), 328–50. https://doi.org/10.1016/0010–0285(73)90017–0

Russell, Bertrand, *Introduction to Mathematical Philosophy* (New York: MacMillan, 1919).

Sachs, David, 'A Fallacy in Plato's *Republic',* *Philosophical Review,* 72 (1963), 141–58. https://doi.org/10.2307/2183101

Schiller, Friedrich, *On the Aesthetic Education of Man,* trans. by Keith Tribe, ed. by Alexander Schmidt (New York: Penguin Books, 2016 [orig. pub. 1795]).

Thomas, Laurence, 'Friendship and Other Loves', *Synthese,* 72.2 (1987), 217–36.

Thompson, Hunter S., *The Great Shark Hunt: Strange Tales from a Strange Time* (New York: Simon & Schuster, 1979).

Thomson, Judith Jarvis, 'A Defense of Abortion', *Philosophy & Public Affairs*, 1 (1971), 47–66.

Williams, Bernard, *Ethics and the Limits of Philosophy* (Cambridge: Harvard University Press, 1986).

Wittgenstein, Ludwig, *Philosophical Investigations*, 3rd ed., trans. by G. E. M. Anscombe (Oxford: Basil Blackwell, 1973).

Wood, Gordon S., *Empire of Liberty: A History of the Early Republic, 1789–1815* (New York: Oxford University Press, 2011).

Zhuangzi: The Complete Writings, trans. by Brook Ziporyn (Indianapolis: Hackett Publishing, 2020).

Index

About the Team

Alessandra Tosi was the managing editor for this book.

Melissa Pukiss performed the copy-editing and proofreading.

Anna Gatti designed the cover using InDesign. The cover was produced in InDesign using Fontin (titles) and Calibri (text body) fonts.

Melissa Purkiss typeset the book in InDesign and produced the paperback and hardback editions. The text font is Tex Gyre Pagella; the heading font is Californian FB.

Luca Baffa produced the EPUB, MOBI, PDF, HTML, and XML editions — the conversion is performed with open source software freely available on our GitHub page (https://github.com/OpenBookPublishers).

This book need not end here...

Share

All our books — including the one you have just read — are free to access online so that students, researchers and members of the public who can't afford a printed edition will have access to the same ideas. This title will be accessed online by hundreds of readers each month across the globe: why not share the link so that someone you know is one of them?

This book and additional content is available at:

https://doi.org/10.11647/OBP.0229

Customise

Personalise your copy of this book or design new books using OBP and third-party material. Take chapters or whole books from our published list and make a special edition, a new anthology or an illuminating coursepack. Each customised edition will be produced as a paperback and a downloadable PDF.

Find out more at:

https://www.openbookpublishers.com/section/59/1

Like Open Book Publishers

Follow @OpenBookPublish

Read more at the Open Book Publishers BLOG

You may also be interested in:

Metaethics from a First Person Standpoint:
An Introduction to Moral Philosophy
Catherine Wilson

https://doi.org/10.11647/OBP.0087

Wellbeing, Freedom and Social Justice:
The Capability Approach Re-Examined
Ingrid Robeyns

https://doi.org/10.11647/OBP.0130

Ovid, *Metamorphoses*, **3.511-733.**
Ingo Gildenhard and Andrew Zissos

https://doi.org/10.11647/OBP.0073